STUDY GUIDE

Psychological Science

Mind, Brain, and Behavior

STUDY GUIDE

Psychological Science

Mind, Brain, and Behavior

Michael S. Gazzaniga • Todd F. Heatherton

Brett Beck

BLOOMSBURG UNIVERSITY

Jeffrey Henriques

UNIVERSITY OF WISCONSIN, MADISON

 W • W • NORTON & COMPANY • NEW YORK • LONDON

Printed in the United States of America

ISBN 0-393-97954-7 (pbk.)

W. W. Norton & Company, Inc., 500 Fifth Avenue, New York, NY 10110
  www.wwnorton.com

W. W. Norton & Company, Ltd., Castle House, 75/76 Wells Street, London W1T 3QT

1 2 3 4 5 6 7 8 9 0

CONTENTS

Psychological Science

Mind, Brain, and Behavior

CHAPTER 1 | Introduction to Psychological Science

GUIDE TO THE READING

The authors begin by laying out the major themes that they will explore throughout the text and by examining questions that have shaped the discipline. This is followed by a review of modern psychology that covers the different schools of thought that have emerged during psychology's history. Although some of these branches of psychology are more than 100 years old, you will see throughout the text that they still influence how we think about the mind, the brain, and behavior. The chapter ends with a review of the different disciplines within psychology and how psychology is used in a variety of fields.

What Are the Themes of Psychological Science?

There are four themes within psychological science that are identified in this section, starting with the idea that psychological science is cumulative. Over the last 125 years, our understanding of the mind, the brain, and behavior has evolved, and what we know now is built on the foundations of earlier work. Theories and principles have been revised and refined as psychological scientists have used more sophisticated techniques and ask more complicated research questions. The second major theme is the tremendous impact that the biological revolution has had on the field of psychology. Researchers now have the ability to examine the function of neurotransmitters in the brain, to decipher the human genome, and to observe the brain at work. The third theme within psychology is that the mind has evolved. The relatively new field of evolutionary psychology examines how the mind, the brain, and behavior have adapted and have been shaped by evolution. The final theme is that there are different levels of analysis at which psychological science operates. From the level of the gene all the way up to the level of the culture, psychological scientists work to understand behavior; throughout the text we examine these different levels of analysis to see how they explain the behavior or process under discussion.

What Are the Origins of Psychological Science?

One of the oldest questions facing the discipline is the extent to which biological versus environmental influences shape our behavior. This is the nature–nurture debate, and this question is one that continues to challenge psychological scientists. Another question that has long confronted psychologists is the mind–body connection. Can we separate the mind from the brain, or is the mind simply our experience of our brains? Descartes's theory of dualism was the first to propose that the mind and body were interconnected and that each affected the other. The final influence on psychology discussed in this section is the role of evolution and the idea that our behavior has been shaped by the process of natural selection.

How Did the Foundations of Psychological Science Develop?

This section broadly covers the history of psychological science and touches on some of the major psychological approaches that have shaped psychology. Modern psychology is generally held to have begun with the work of Wilhelm Wundt in the 1870s. Early psychology used the technique of introspection to study the structure and function of the mind. Other approaches were Gestalt theory, which focused on how the mind perceives the world, and Freud's theory of psychoanalysis, which focused on the role of the unconscious in determining human behavior. In the 1920s, there was a new school of psychology that concentrated on observable behavior rather than on the mind. Behaviorism was to be the dominant force in psychology for almost 50 years. In the 1960s, a cognitive revolution began as psychologists turned their attention to thinking, remembering, and language. Most of these approaches focus on the individual; however, social psychology, which emerged after World War II, explores how our behavior is affected by other individuals in our environment.

What Are the Professions of Psychological Science?

This section covers the various disciplines within psychological science today. The authors point out that these disciplines seek to understand behavior on different levels, a point that they return to throughout the text. The principles of psychology are used in fields outside of psychology, such as education and marketing, and we can all consider ourselves to be psychologists, in that we all attempt to understand and explain the behavior of ourselves and others around us.

FILL-IN-THE-BLANK QUESTIONS

1. _____ study of the mind, brain, and behavior

2. _____ observable actions

3. _____ chemical messengers that allow nerve cells to communicate

4. _____ neurochemical that plays an important role in reward

5. _____ new behaviors or skills that increase the chance of survival and reproduction

6. _____ process by which some inherited characteristics aid in survival and reproductive success and increase the likelihood that these traits will be present in the next generation

7. _____ theory arguing that to understand the mind and behavior, we must first understand how the brain has adapted over human history

8. _____ scientific discipline that studies the brain

9. _____ beliefs, values, rules, and customs that are shared by a group of people

10. _____ French philosopher who first suggested that the mind and body were interconnected

11. _____ theory that the mind is a separate entity from the body

12. _____ proposed that evolution occurred through the process of natural selection

13. _____ considered to have been the first psychologist

14. _____ research technique that involves the systematic observation of one's subjective mental experiences

15. _____ had as its goal the identification of the basic elements of consciousness

16. _____ approach to psychology that, in contrast to structuralism, focused on how the mind operates

17. _____ his approach to psychology was heavily influenced by the writings of Charles Darwin

18. _____ theory that focuses on the whole of an individual's experience rather than on the individual elements of experience

19. _____ founder of psychoanalytic thought

20. _____ theory that holds that our behavior is influenced by unconscious mental forces

21. _____ strategies that we use to guard against unacceptable thoughts and impulses

22. _____ psychoanalytic technique that encourages the patient talk about whatever comes to mind

23. _____ approach to psychology that focused on directly observable events

24. _____ psychologist that pioneered the branch of psychology known as behaviorism

25. _____ behavioral psychologist who focused on how the outcomes of a behavior influence the likelihood of the behavior being repeated

26. _____ area of psychology that focuses on mental processes such as how we think, feel, remember, and make decisions

27. _____ branch of cognitive psychology that conceptualizes the brain as a computer

28. _____ area of psychology that studies how behavior is influenced by the presence of others

29. _____ pioneered by Kurt Lewin, this theory emphasized the interaction between people and their environment in understanding behavior

30. _____ area of psychology that focuses on the study of the biological bases of behavior

31. _____ area of psychology that focuses on changes in psychological processes over the course of the life span

32. _____ area of psychology that studies differences among individuals

MULTIPLE-CHOICE QUESTIONS

1. Chemicals that nerve cells use for communication are known as
   a. hormones
   b. neurochemicals
   c. neurotransmitters
   d. regulatory substances

2. Over the course of human history, certain traits and behaviors helped our ancestors survive, and as a result, these behaviors were passed along to subsequent generations. This process is known as
   a. natural selection
   b. adaptation
   c. assimilation
   d. evolutionary progression

3. Psychology studies behavior at different levels of analysis. If you were interested in studying the thoughts of people who drink alcohol, you would be looking at the _____ level.
   a. brain systems
   b. perceptual and cognitive
   c. social and cultural
   d. behavioral

4. If you were interested in understanding why people differ in their achievement motivation, what level of analysis would you be looking at?
   a. social and cultural
   b. behavioral
   c. individual
   d. perceptual and cognitive

5. One of the major questions that psychological science has continued to grapple with is the extent to which our behavior is the result of our biology or our environment. This debate can be conceptualized as
   a. nature versus nurture
   b. internal versus external
   c. physiology versus psychology
   d. programmed versus learned

6. Dualism refers to the idea that
   a. our behavior is influenced by both our biology and our environment
   b. the mind and the brain are one and the same
   c. the mind is separate from the body
   d. the brain changes in response to changes in the environment

7. Who first suggested that the body could affect the mind, just as the mind could affect the body?
   a. Blakemore
   b. Da Vinci
   c. Darwin
   d. Descartes

8. Who is credited with being the founder of experimental psychology?
   a. Sigmund Freud
   b. William James
   c. Wilhelm Wundt
   d. John Watson

9. The early research technique of having individuals report on the contents of their conscious experience is known as
   a. introspection
   b. stream of consciousness
   c. meditation
   d. psychoanalysis

10. Which early branch of psychology was interested in identifying the basic elements of consciousness?
    a. functionalism
    b. Gestalt psychology
    c. psychoanalysis
    d. structuralism

11. Which early branch of psychology was influenced by Darwin's ideas of evolution?
    a. structuralism
    b. functionalism
    c. behaviorism
    d. constructivism

12. Which psychologist rejected the ideas of structuralism and instead focused on the function of the mind rather than its structure?
    a. Titchener
    b. Cattell
    c. Watson
    d. James

13. Functionalism argued that the mind was not static but ever changing, a continuous series of thoughts referred to as a
    a. flow of consciousness
    b. train of thought
    c. stream of consciousness
    d. thought stream

14. Which school of psychology was founded by Max Wertheimer and Wolfgang Kohler?
    a. psychoanalysis
    b. Gestalt
    c. behaviorism
    d. functionalism

15. Which branch of psychology held that the whole is greater than the sum of its parts?
    a. Gestalt
    b. functionalism
    c. behaviorism
    d. psychoanalysis

16. Psychoanalysis held that
    a. by studying the mind we could understand behavior
    b. the mind is separate from the body
    c. much of behavior is determined by unconscious motives
    d. all of the above

17. Sigmund Freud is associated with what branch of psychology?
    a. psychoanalysis
    b. Gestalt theory
    c. clinical psychology
    d. behaviorism

18. Which branch of psychology rejected introspection in favor of measuring observable psychological phenomena?
    a. constructivism
    b. structuralism
    c. functionalism
    d. behaviorism

19. John Watson argued that
    a. psychology should use the introspective method
    b. any behavior can be shaped and controlled
    c. psychology should study the function, rather than the structure, of consciousness
    d. psychologists should study the unconscious

20. In studying behavior, Watson focused on the _____ a behavior.
    a. stimuli that elicited
    b. consequences of
    c. time course of
    d. reinforcement and punishment of

21. In contrast to early behaviorists, B. F. Skinner took an approach to learning that focused on the _____ a behavior.
    a. stimuli that elicited
    b. time course of
    c. patterning of
    d. consequences of

22. The branch of psychology that studies thought, language, memory, and intelligence is known as _____.
    a. educational psychology
    b. clinical psychology
    c. cognitive psychology
    d. developmental psychology

23. Studying the brain as if it were a computer and viewing the mind as software that runs on the computer characterizes which cognitive theory?
    a. cognitive neuroscience
    b. biomechanics
    c. information processing
    d. neuromechanics

24. Field theory studies
    a. the interaction between people and their environment
    b. visual sensation and perception
    c. the dynamics of sports and athletes
    d. how information is organized in the brain

25. Psychologists that study, assess, and treat individuals with psychological disorders are known as _____ psychologists.
    a. applied
    b. rehabilitation
    c. experimental
    d. clinical

26. _____ psychology studies changes in behavior over the life span.
    a. Evolutionary
    b. Developmental
    c. Behavioral
    d. Cognitive

THOUGHT QUESTIONS

1. What are the four themes that the authors identify as shaping psychological science?

2. What are the similarities and differences between structuralism and functionalism?

3. What was behaviorism and who were the major theorists in this area?

ANSWER KEY

Fill-in-the-Blank Questions

1. psychological science
2. behaviors
3. neurotransmitters
4. dopamine
5. adaptations
6. natural selection
7. evolution
8. neuroscience
9. culture
10. Descartes
11. dualism
12. Darwin
13. Wundt
14. introspection
15. structuralism
16. functionalism
17. James
18. Gestalt
19. Freud
20. psychoanalysis
21. defense mechanisms
22. free association

23. behaviorism
24. Watson
25. Skinner
26. cognitive
27. information processing
28. social
29. field
30. physiological
31. developmental
32. personality

Multiple-Choice Questions

1. c Neurotransmitters are the chemicals that brain cells use to communicate.

2. a Natural selection is the evolutionary process whereby certain traits and behaviors confer an advantage to an individual's survival, leading to these behaviors being passed along to future generations.

3. b At the perceptual and cognitive level of analysis, we are interested in studying the thoughts and perceptions involved in behavior.

4. c We look for differences among people at the individual level of analysis.

5. a The nature versus nurture debate is a debate as old as psychology.

6. c Descartes proposed the idea of dualism, the idea that the mind and the body were separate.

7. d Renè Descartes made this radical proposal in his theory of dualism.

8. c Wilhelm Wundt is considered the father of modern psychology.

9. a Introspection was the technique used by both structuralists and functionalists.

10. d Structuralism used introspection to identify the basic elements of the mind.

11. b Functionalism focused on how the mind operates and was heavily influenced by Darwin's theories.

12. d William James was the founder of functionalism.

13. c William James coined the term stream of consciousness to describe the ever-changing nature of our thoughts.

14. b Wertheimer and Kohler founded Gestalt psychology in response to structuralism.

15. a Gestalt theory held that the whole of personal experience was greater than the sum of its component parts.

16. c Freud argued that the unconscious plays a large role in behavior.

17. a Freud founded the field of psychoanalysis.

18. d Behaviorism held that the mind was a black box that could not be studied, and as such, psychology should focus on observable behavior.

19. b Watson believed that any behavior could be shaped through learning.

20. a Watson studied the environmental triggers of behaviors.

21. d Skinner investigated how the outcomes of a behavior shape the learning of that behavior.

22. c Cognitive psychology is the study of thought, memory, intelligence, and language.

23. c Information processing theory views the brain as hardware and the mind as software.

24. a Kurt Lewin pioneered field theory, which examines the interplay between people and their social environment.

25. d Clinical psychologists are trained in assessing and treating individuals with psychopathology.

26. b Developmental psychology studies changes in the mind and behavior over the life course.

Thought Questions

1. The themes are (1) the principles of psychology are cumulative, (2) psychological science examines behavior across different levels of analysis, (3) the mind is adaptive and has been shaped by evolution, and (4) there has been a biological revolution in psychology as new tools allow researchers to examine brain function and genetic influences on behavior.

2. Both structuralism and functionalism used introspection to study the mind. Structuralism, as the name implies, was concerned with the structure of the mind (what the mind contains). Functionalism was influenced by Darwin's theories and focused on the function of the mind (how the mind operates).

3. Behaviorism emerged in opposition to psychological approaches that studied the mind. Because psychologists could not directly observe the mind, behaviorists argued that psychology should focus on behavior, which could be observed. Major figures in behaviorism were John Watson and B. F. Skinner. Watson was interested in stimuli that elicit behavior, and Skinner studied how the consequences of behavior influenced learning.

CHAPTER 2 | Research Methodology

In the previous chapter you learned that the principles of psychological science are cumulative—that good theories generate new questions, which can in turn be studied using the methods of science, and it is in this manner that scientific knowledge typically accumulates. In Chapter 2 you learn about the objective, systematic procedures that psychological scientists use to study behavior and mental activity. Here, the authors explain how research questions are formulated, describe the three basic types of studies (research designs) that scientists employ to test these questions, and discuss methods for collecting and analyzing data. Finally, they address some of the ethical issues involved in research and conclude by discussing how statistics allow us to summarize the data and draw conclusions.

What Is Scientific Inquiry?

In understanding behavior, psychological science has four goals: description, prediction, causal control, and explanation. As scientists, we must ask *empirical* questions if we are to achieve these goals. Science begins with a theory that represents our best guess for how and why something occurs. Theories give rise to hypotheses, specific predictions about what should occur if the theory is correct. It is the hypotheses, generated by theories, that psychological research sets out to test.

What Are the Type of Studies in Psychological Research?

There are three types of studies or research designs that can be used by the psychological researcher: experiments, correlational designs, and descriptive studies. It is important to be clear on what can and cannot be concluded from these different research designs. Experimentation is the only design that allows researchers to determine cause-and-effect relations. This is because the experimenter manipulates the *independent variable* while controlling other variables that might affect the outcome measure, also known as the *dependent variable.* Correlational designs allow us to identify relations between variables, but they do not allow us to determine causation. Correlation is not causation because the observation that two variables vary together does not provide information about the direction of the relationship between the variables, nor does it rule out the possibility that some third variable is responsible for the changes in the two correlated variables. The last type of research design covered is descriptive, or observational, studies in which the goal is simply to describe the behavior. This observation can be done from a distance, as in naturalistic observation, or the observations can be made while participating in the behavior being studied.

What Are the Data Collection Methods of Psychological Science?

The text outlines four basic methods for collecting data; you should be able to name examples of each of these and describe the relative benefits and limitations of each method in specific detail:

- *Observational techniques:* Involve the careful monitoring and coding of observed behaviors.
- *Asking-based methods:* Use surveys, questionnaires, self-reports, interviews, and case studies as a means of gathering data.
- *Response performance measures:* Quantify a perceptual or cognitive process by measuring individuals' reaction times, their response accuracy, or their ability to discriminate among stimuli.

- *Psychophysiological measures:* Collected via polygraphs, electrophysiology, brain imaging, etc.; allow for the direct measurement of bodily and brain function.

With all research designs, there are several ethical issues that must be considered, including issues of confidentiality and informed consent. You should be familiar with these issues—not just because you are reading this chapter but in the event that you someday participate in psychological research. Finally, the researchers also need to be aware of how their expectations and biases may subtly influence the way that they code behavior and affect how they interact with their research participants.

How Are Data Analyzed and Evaluated?

If the data that a researcher has collected are going to be of any use in testing a hypothesis, they must be *valid* (related to the question being studied), they must be *reliable* (consistent or stable), and they must be *accurate* (free from error). Descriptive statistics allow the researcher to summarize the data that have been collected. Measures of central tendency allow us to summarize the data into a single value. There are three measures of central tendency. The first is the *mean,* or the average of all of the scores. Sometimes a collection of data will have several extreme scores that will make the mean an inappropriate measure, in that case, the *median,* or middle score in the distribution, is a better measure of central tendency. The last measure of central tendency is the *mode,* or most common score in the collection of data. The mode is an appropriate measure when you have categorical data that cannot be averaged, such as gender or a diagnosis.

The next important piece of information to know about a collection of data is how the data vary around that measure of central tendency, and the standard deviation is the most commonly used measure of variability. Another descriptive statistic discussed in this chapter is the *correlation coefficient,* which describes the how two variables vary together. Correlations range from −1.00 to +1.00. The absolute value of the correlation describes the strength of the relationship, where 0 is no relationship, 1.00 is a perfect relationship, and the sign of the correlation indicates the nature of the relationship. A positive correlation means that as one variable increases the other variable also increases, and a negative correlation indicates that as one increases, the other decreases. Finally, in this section, the authors touch on inferential statistics. Inferential statistics enable a researcher to determine the likelihood that differences observed in a study occurred by chance. If the probability of such a chance difference is low, then the results are considered statistically significant.

FILL-IN-THE-BLANK QUESTIONS

1. _____ the objective examination of the world

2. _____ questions that can be answered by observing and measuring the world around us

3. _____ careful observations or numerical measurements

4. _____ to repeat a study and obtain results similar to those previously found

5. _____ framework for explaining various events or processes

6. _____ an assumption or a set of assumptions that can be tested to determine their accuracy

7. _____ the systematic and careful collection of data to test a hypothesis

8. _____ states that when two theories explain the same phenomenon, the simpler explanation is typically the preferred explanation

9. _____ some measurable aspect of a situation that can change or vary

10. _____ variable that is manipulated by the researcher

11. _____ variable that is measured by the researcher

12. _____ definition that quantifies variables to measure them

13. _____ research technique that establishes cause-and-effect relationships

14. _____ a variable that may unintentionally affect the dependent variable differently across experimental conditions

15. _____ steps taken by the researcher to eliminate the possibility that other variables may affect the results of a study

16. _____ measure that demonstrates how two variables are related to one another; it cannot demonstrate causation

17. _____ method by which each subject has an equal chance of being assigned to each of the experimental conditions

18. _____ occurs when there are differences between subjects assigned to different experimental conditions

19. _____ possibility that some other variable explains the relation between two variables in a correlational study

20. _____ studies in which behavior is simply observed and recorded

21. _____ observational study in which the researcher participates in the situation to describe it

22. _____ observational study in which the researcher does not attempt to alter or change the situation being observed and in which the researcher does not participate

23. _____ occurs when the act of observing a behavior changes that behavior

24. _____ systematic errors that occur as a result of the researcher's expectations

25. _____ results when subjects' behavior is affected by cues or signals from the researcher that lead them to respond in a particular manner

26. _____ methods such as surveys or questionnaires by which subjects record their own responses

27. _____ when a subset of the population is selected to be studied

28. _____ a sample in which every member of the population has the same likelihood of being included in the sample

29. _____ when subjects respond in such a manner as to make themselves look good

30. _____ the in-depth investigation of a single individual

31. _____ the speed of a response

32. _____ how a perceptual or cognitive process responds to a stimuli

33. _____ scientific method that involves collecting data on the electrical activity of the brain and relating them to behavior

34. _____ ethical standard that provides subjects with information about the risks and benefits regarding participation in a research study

35. _____ the misleading of research participants as to the goals of a particular study in an effort not to influence their behavior

36. _____ the extent to which data are replicable

37. _____ the extent to which the data address the research question

38. _____ the extent to which the data are free from error

39. _____ statistics that summarize the data collected

40. _____ statistics that allow researchers to determine if observed differences among groups or conditions are significant

41. _____ measure that describes a typical response

42. _____ the arithmetic average of a set of scores

43. _____ the score that falls in the exact middle of a set of scores

44. _____ the most common or frequent score in a set of scores

45. _____ measures the extent to which scores spread out across a set of scores

46. _____ the difference between the maximum and minimum scores in a set of scores

47. _____ the average difference between each score and the mean in a set of scores

48. _____ statistic that provides a measure of association between two variables

MULTIPLE-CHOICE QUESTIONS

1. Questions that can be answered through the collection and analysis of data are known as _____ questions.
   a. theoretical
   b. empirical
   c. research
   d. measurable

2. For the researcher to have confidence in the findings of psychological research, the results should
   a. be replicable
   b. be significant
   c. be as predicted
   d. not be chance

3. A group of researchers believe that an individual's environment during childhood determines how violent he or she will be in adulthood. These researchers have developed a(n)
   a. hypothesis
   b. correlation
   c. theory
   d. algorithm

4. Theories give rise to testable predictions known as
   a. proposals
   b. goals
   c. hypotheses
   d. data

5. Dr. Lange believes that television violence makes children aggressive. She proposes that exposure to 5 hr of professional wrestling will make a group of elementary-school children more physically aggressive than a group of children who watch 5 hr of Mr. Rogers. This proposal is known as a(n)
   a. hypothesis
   b. prediction
   c. theory
   d. model of behavior

6. Which best describes an independent variable?
   a. a variable that has nothing to do with the experimental hypothesis
   b. the variable manipulated by the researcher
   c. the variable that the researcher measures
   d. the variable that the researcher has no control over

7. Dr. Science is conducting an experiment to determine what effects LSD has on a person's ability to sit calmly and quietly in a green room full of wax mannequins. He gives the Group A subjects a paper cup full of LSD and Kool-Aid and gives Group B members ordinary Kool-Aid. Just 1 hr later, the Group B subjects are sitting calmly in their green room, while, in the adjoining room, the Group A subjects are yelling hysterically and attacking the mannequins. In this experiment, what is Dr. Science's dependent variable?
   a. the green room color
   b. the dosage of LSD
   c. the hour that passes during the experiment
   d. the subjects' ability to sit calmly

8. A variable that is unrelated to an experiment but that may unintentionally differ among experimental conditions is known as a(n) _____ variable.
   a. independent
   b. dependent
   c. causal
   d. confounding

9. Merija was in a hurry to complete her research on impulsivity. She assigned the first 20 people that volunteered for her study to the control condition and she assigned the next 20 subjects to the experimental condition. What potential problem has Merija introduced into her research design?
   a. a confounding variable
   b. selection bias
   c. lack of experimental control
   d. she has no clear hypothesis

10. Which of the following is a problem with correlational research?
    a. directionality problem
    b. correlation is not causation
    c. third-variable problem
    d. all of the above

11. When a researcher conducting observational research participates in the process that he or she is observing, this is known as _____.
    a. naturalistic observation
    b. modeling
    c. participant observation
    d. none of the above

12. A researcher conducts a random survey comparing how much people exercise and how satisfied they are with their jobs. The researcher finds a correlation of +0.80 between time spent exercising and the amount of job satisfaction. What can she conclude from these data?
    a. that the study is invalid because she did not use a representative sample
    b. that increases in exercise are associated with increases in job satisfaction
    c. that exercise produces increases in job satisfaction
    d. no conclusions because she did not conduct an experiment

13. Daren follows the Minnesota Vikings and records statistics for every game. He has determined that the correlation between the number of points a wide receiver scores and the yards gained by the running back is high ($r = 0.73$). If Daren wants to impress his statistically knowledgeable girlfriend, what should he say? (*Hint*: knowledge of football is not necessary to answer this question.)
    a. the point scoring of the receiver causes the running back to gain more yards
    b. the points scored by the receiver are the result yards gained by the running back
    c. when the running back gains more yards, the receiver scores more points
    d. when the running back gains more yards, the receiver scores fewer points

14. Marc was hired as director of operations at Gulp & Blow, Inc. to increase employee productivity. During his first 3 months on the job, productivity increased but then declined to previous levels. The company president was furious and hired April to fill Marc's position. Once again, there was an initial increase in productivity but eventually a return to previous levels. What is most likely happening at Gulp & Blow?
    a. the increases in productivity were the result of the Hawthorne effect
    b. the company was experiencing selective attrition in their workers
    c. Marc and April most likely failed to reward the increase in productivity, so levels declined

d. workers at Gulp & Blow were responding to the demands associated with a new director of operations

15. Sometimes the presence of an observer leads to a change in the behavior being observed. This is known as _____.
    a. reactivity
    b. responsivity
    c. observer bias
    d. expectancy effects

16. If a researcher has preconceived notions about the behavior that he or she is going to be studying, it is possible that these preconceptions can influence the interpretation of the behavior being observed. This is known as _____.
    a. reactivity
    b. observer bias
    c. experimenter expectancy effects
    d. demand characteristics

17. When a researcher treats subjects differently because of how he or she expects the subjects to react in a study, the researcher may end up influencing the behavior of the subjects in the anticipated direction. This is known as _____.
    a. reactivity
    b. observer bias
    c. situational demand
    d. experimenter expectancy effects

18. In conducting research, psychologists describe the group of interest as the _____.
    a. target group
    b. sample
    c. population
    d. research subject

19. Asking "Do you like the music of Vivaldi?" is to asking "What sort of classical music do you like?" as _____ is to _____.
    a. close ended; open ended
    b. open ended; close ended
    c. questionnaire; survey
    d. survey; questionnaire

20. One problem with self-report measures is that subjects may be reluctant to reveal certain information that might make them look bad to the researcher. This is problem is known as _____.
    a. inaccurate self-perception
    b. image manipulation
    c. social desirability
    d. response bias

21. Which of the following is NOT a self-report measure used in psychological research?
    a. survey
    b. questionnaire
    c. interview
    d. case study

22. Which research method is used to obtain extensive information about unusual phenomena?
    a. correlational method
    b. experimental method
    c. naturalistic method
    d. case study method

23. Which of the following is NOT a measure of response performance?
    a. response accuracy
    b. reaction time
    c. stimulus substitution
    d. stimulus judgments

24. Which of the following is a criticism of using response performance methodology to study cognitive processes?
    a. the tasks and stimuli used often don't have real-world validity
    b. subjects may be biased in how they respond
    c. performance measures are only indirect measures of cognitive activity
    d. all of the above

25. Polygraphs, electrophysiology, and brain imaging are all examples of what assessment technique?
    a. cognitive
    b. psychophysiological
    c. biological
    d. cerebral

26. What function do institutional review boards (IRBs) serve?
    a. provide funding for psychological research
    b. ensure that research proposals meet certain standards of science
    c. manage all of the research going on at a university
    d. review research proposals for their relevance to science

27. Which of the following is essential in conducting research with human subjects?
    a. informed consent
    b. random assignment to groups
    c. double-blind procedures
    d. random sampling methods

28. Explaining an experiment to a research subject at the end of his or her participation in a study is known as _____.

a. informed consent
b. debriefing
c. deception
d. single-blind procedures

29. Data that are consistent over time are said to be

_____.

a. valid
b. reliable
c. empirical
d. accurate

30. Data that are _____ provide clear and unambiguous information about the hypothesis being investigated.
a. valid
b. reliable
c. empirical
d. accurate

31. Data that are free from error are said to be _____.
a. valid
b. reliable
c. empirical
d. accurate

32. Which measure of central tendency should you use if you want to minimize the effects of a few extreme scores?
a. mean
b. median
c. range
d. mode

33. Which measure of central tendency defines the score that appears most frequently?
a. median
b. mode
c. mean
d. margin

34. Which of the following is NOT a measure of central tendency?
a. mode
b. range
c. median
d. mean

35. What is the best measure of central tendency for a categorical variable, like gender or handedness?
a. mode
b. mean
c. variance
d. median

36. What is the most common measure of variability?
a. range
b. variance

c. standard deviation
d. median

37. For which of the following correlation coefficients is the degree of relationship the strongest?
a. +0.52
b. +0.15
c. –0.63
d. –1.28

38. Which of the following helps determine if an observed difference occurred by chance?
a. standard deviation
b. correlation
c. descriptive statistics
d. inferential statistics

THOUGHT QUESTIONS

1. Frank and Gilovich (1988) examined the relation between how dark a hockey team's jerseys were and the number of penalty minutes that team received over the course of a season. They found a correlation of +0.48. What sort of conclusions are these researchers justified in reaching? What sort of conclusions are not appropriate?

2. A number of researchers have observed a relation between the amount of television a child watches and the amount of aggression the child displays. How would you go about proving the television violence causes children to be aggressive? Be as thorough as possible in your answer.

ANSWER KEY

Fill-in-the-Blank Questions

1. scientific method
2. empirical
3. data
4. replicate
5. theory
6. hypothesis
7. research
8. law of parsimony
9. variable
10. independent
11. dependent
12. operational
13. experiment
14. confound
15. control
16. correlational
17. random assignment
18. selection bias
19. third-variable problem
20. descriptive
21. participant observation
22. naturalistic observation
23. reactivity
24. observer bias
25. experimenter expectancy effects
26. self report
27. sampling
28. random sample
29. socially desirable responding
30. case study

31. reaction time
32. response performance
33. electrophysiology
34. informed consent
35. deception
36. reliability
37. validity
38. accuracy
39. descriptive

40. inferential
41. central tendency
42. mean
43. median
44. mode
45. variability
46. range
47. standard deviation
48. correlation

Multiple-Choice Questions

1. b Empirical questions are questions that can be answered by observing and measuring the world around us.

2. a Replication is the process by which researchers confirm the results of other investigators and leads to greater confidence in the research findings.

3. c A theory is a model or idea of how something in the world works.

4. c A hypothesis is a testable prediction of a theory.

5. a The idea that television makes children aggressive is a theory; the research proposed is a hypothesis that follows from the theory.

6. b In an experiment, the variable that is manipulated is the independent variable.

7. d The dependent variable is the variable that is measured; in this study, it is the subjects' ability to sit calmly.

8. d A confound refers to anything that affects a dependent variable and that may change across different experimental conditions.

9. b It is possible that the most impulsive people signed up for Merija's experiment first; to avoid problems of selection bias, researchers randomly assign subjects to experimental conditions.

10. d The fact that two variables are correlated with one another does not prove causation; it could be that some third variable is responsible for changes in the two variables, and if there is a causal relation that exists between the two variables, a correlation does not identify the direction this causal relation.

11. c In participant observation, the researcher is involved in the situation he or she is studying.

12. b This is a correlation design; and although the researcher cannot make conclusions about causality, she is justified in concluding that increases in exercise are associated with increases in satisfaction.

13. c Correlations allow us to say that two variables are associated with one another, we cannot conclude that one causes the other.

14. a When people know that they are being observed they tend to want to make a positive impression and thus may initially work harder; this reactivity is known as the Hawthorne effect.

15. a Reactivity effect refers to situations in which the act of observing changes the behavior being observed.

16. b Observer bias refers to systematic errors that occur due to the observer's expectations.

17. d Research has shown that the expectations of an experimenter can lead to his or her treating subjects differently, and as a result subjects performance may change as a result of that expectation.

18. c Researchers use a sample to provide information about the group of interest, which is the population that the sample was drawn from.

19. a Close-ended questions require respondents to chose among a fixed number of responses, whereas open-ended questions allow subjects to respond in as much detail as they prefer.

20. c Socially desirable responding occurs when subjects try to present themselves in the most favorable light.

21. d Surveys, questionnaires, and interviews are all self-report measures used in asking-based research methods.

22. d Case studies involve the intensive examination of one individual to document unusual psychological phenomena.

23. c Reaction time, response accuracy, and stimulus judgments are all examples of response measures.

24. d All of the choices are criticisms of response performance methodology.

25. b They are all psychophysiological assessment measures.

26. b IRBs review proposed research to determine whether they meet accepted standards of science.

27. a While all of this are important to good research, it is essential that subjects give their consent to participate in research.

28. b Debriefing involves explaining to research participants the goals of a study after they have completed their participation.

29. b Reliability refers to the consistency or stability of the data.

30. a Validity refers to whether the data obtained relate to the research question.

31. d Accuracy is the extent to which a measure is free from error.

32. b The median is used when you have a distribution with a couple of extreme scores that will dramatically effect the mean.

33. b The mode is the most frequent score in a distribution.

34. b The range is a measure of variability, not central tendency.

35. a The mode, the most common score, is the appropriate measure of central tendency when data are categorical.

36. c The standard deviation is the average variability of each score from the mean and is the most common measure of variability.

37. c Correlations range from −1.00 to +1.00, the sign indicates the direction of the correlation and the absolute value reflects the strength of the correlation.

38. d Inferential statistics allow researchers to determine if differences actually exist between different sets of numbers.

Thought Questions

1. This is a correlational design, and the researchers are able to conclude that there is indeed a relation between jersey color and penalties. They cannot, however, conclude that jersey color causes the penalties, because correlation is not causation.

2. In answering this question, you should propose an experiment; the only research design that allows for the determination of causality. You should clearly identify your independent and dependent variables. Subjects should be assigned randomly to your different groups or conditions, and you should use inferential statistics to determine if your results are statistically significant.

CHAPTER 3 | Genetic and Biological Foundations

GUIDE TO THE READING

This chapter describes the basic genetic and biological foundations of behavior and lays the groundwork for Chapter 4, which explores how the physical brain enables mind and behavior. The authors begin by discussing the influence of genes on behavior and outlining the basic process by which genetic information is transmitted from one generation to the next. Then they turn to the biological foundations of the nervous system, starting with the neuron and building to an explanation of the process by which electrochemical signals from individual neurons are transmitted across and within the peripheral and central nervous systems. The endocrine system communicates via chemicals called hormones that travel through the bloodstream, and it is the last topic covered in this chapter.

What Is the Genetic Basis of Psychological Science?

The human genome is a genetic blueprint consisting of 23 pairs of chromosomes organized into segments of DNA called genes. The basic mechanism of heredity was worked out through the careful observations of Gregor Mendel, a monk working with pea plants around 1866. As you review this material, be sure you understand the interaction between dominant and recessive genes and know the difference between an organism's genotype (its genetic makeup) and its phenotype (its observable physical characteristics). Sexual reproduction is the source of genetic variation. Be sure you can differentiate between *meiosis* (the process by which cells split to form gametes) and *mitosis* (the process by which cells divide for growth and development).

Genetic variation occurs through mutation, which includes errors in the duplication process. Behavioral geneticists study how genes and behavior interact to influence psychological activity. Some of the techniques that behavioral geneticists use are twin studies, adoption studies, and the comparison of identical twins who have been raised apart from one another. The goal of this research is to determine the heritability of a trait or characteristic. Heritability, which is not the same as heredity, refers to the amount of observed variation in a trait or characteristic that can be attributed to genetic variation. Researchers investigating the interaction of our genes and our environment have shown that the environment affects our genetic makeup and vice versa.

How Does the Nervous System Operate?

Nerve cells, also known as neurons, are the basic units of the nervous system. There are three different types of neurons: sensory neurons, which carry information from our sense organs to our brain; motor neurons, which carry signals from our brains to our muscles; and interneurons, which carry signals between neurons. While neurons come in a variety of shapes and sizes, they share the same basic structure of dendrites, cell body, axon, and terminal buttons. Communication between neurons is an electrochemical process: Prompted by an electrical signal, one neuron releases a chemical that in turn effects the electrical state an adjacent neuron. Put simply, the neuron at rest has a slight negative charge, known as a resting membrane potential. Stimulation from other neurons changes the electrical state of the neuron making it more or less negative. If there is sufficient depolarization of the neuron, an action potential is generated, which travels down the length of the axon and causes the release of neurotransmitters. These neurotransmitters then bind with receptors on the next neuron, causing changes in the electrical state of that neuron and thus beginning the process all over again. After you have read through this section of the chapter, you should be able to explain the entire process from start to finish, and you should be familiar with terms such as *propagation, temporal and spatial summation, ion channels, synaptic vesicles, ionotropic and metabotropic receptors, reuptake, autoreception,* and *saltatory conduction.*

How Do Neurotransmitters Influence Emotion, Thought, and Behavior?

Neurotransmitters are the chemicals that are released into the synapse and produce inhibitory or excitatory potentials in the postsynaptic neuron. Drugs that enhance the action of a particular neurotransmitter are known as agonists, and drugs that inhibit neuronal communication are known as antagonists. Although there are more than 60 different chemicals that are used in neuronal communication, the book focuses on just four categories of neurotransmitters: acetylcholine, monoamines, amino acids, and peptides.

- *Acetylcholine:* The neurotransmitter that is released by motor neurons. It also plays important roles in learning, memory, sleep, and dreaming.
- *Monoamines:* There are four—epinephrine, norepinephrine, dopamine, and serotonin. Epinephrine, which is also known as adrenaline, is found primarily in the body rather than in the brain. Norepinephrine is involved in vigilance and arousal. Dopamine has many functions in the brain primarily related to motivation and motor control. Parkinson disease is a movement disorder that is associated with dopamine depletion in the brain. Serotonin is involved in emotional behavior, dreaming, and impulse control.
- *Amino acids:* GABA (aminobutyric acid) is the primary inhibitory transmitter in the nervous system. Glutamate is the principal excitatory neurotransmitter in the brain.
- *Peptides:* These are long chains of amino acids, of which there are more than 30 that act as neurotransmitters or neuromodulators. Three are covered here: cholecystokinin (CCK), endorphins, and substance P. CCK is involved in exploratory behavior, learning, memory, and pain transmission. Substance P also plays a role in the transmission of pain information within the nervous system. In contrast, endorphins are involved in pain reduction and are involved in reward.

How Are Neural Messages Integrated into Communication Systems?

Neurons and neurotransmitters are part of the communication system in the body known as the nervous system. The nervous system has two distinct parts: the central nervous system (CNS), composed of the brain and the spinal cord, and the peripheral nervous system (PNS). The PNS is itself composed of two parts: the somatic nervous system and the autonomic nervous system. The somatic nervous system transmits information between our CNS and our muscles and sense organs, and the autonomic nervous system regulates our body's internal environment. There are two divisions of the autonomic nervous system. The sympathetic division activates the body, expending energy for fight or flight. In contrast, the parasympathetic division of the autonomic nervous system relaxes the body and is involved in storing energy.

Like the nervous system, the endocrine system is a communication system. However, the endocrine system uses hormones, chemicals that are secreted by glands in the body, for communication. Because hormones travel through the bloodstream to reach their targets, they take longer to exert their effects and their effects are longer lasting than signals within the nervous system. The master gland in the body is the pituitary gland, and the pituitary in turn is controlled by the hypothalamus, a structure located at the base of the brain. Thus the hypothalamus is where the nervous system and the endocrine system intersect.

Students often find the material on the biological bases of behavior to be challenging, and this is not surprising, since the material is abstract and perhaps unfamiliar. By the same token, this chapter and the next introduce many new terms and processes that serve as a foundation for later learning; careful study now will save you grief later.

FILL-IN-THE-BLANK QUESTIONS

1. _____ basic units of heredity

2. _____ genes consist of this substance

3. _____ structures within the cell made up of genes

4. _____ alternate versions of a gene

5. _____ allele expressed whenever it is present in an organism

6. _____ physical characteristics of an organism

7. _____ genetic characteristics of an organism

8. _____ process by which a cell divides into two cells, each of which contains half the chromosomes of the original cell

9. _____ process by which a cell duplicates its chromosomes and then splits into two cells

10. _____ cell that contains only half of an organism's genetic material, e.g., eggs and sperm

11. _____ scientific investigation of the interaction between genetics and the environment

12. _____ fertilized egg cell

13. _____ twins resulting from a single zygote

14. _____ twins resulting from two zygotes

15. _____ genetic transmission of traits and characteristics from parents to their offspring

16. _____ statistical estimate of the proportion of variability in a characteristic that can be attributed to genetic transmission

17. _____ basic units of the nervous system

18. _____ portion of the nerve cell that receives signals from other nerve cells

19. _____ body of the nerve cell

20. _____ portion of the neuron that sends information away from the cell body

21. _____ a collection of axons that carries information between the body and the brain

22. _____ ending of the nerve cell that releases chemicals to communicate with other nerve cells

23. _____ place where chemical communication between neurons occurs

24. _____ nerve cells that carry information about the physical world to the brain

25. _____ nerve cells that carry information from the brain to the muscles

26. _____ nerve cells that carry information between neurons

27. _____ slight negative charge of an unstimulated neuron

28. _____ electrical signal that travels down the axon and signals the release of chemicals into the synapse

29. _____ principle by which the action potential for a given neuron is always the same size

30. _____ fatty material that serves to insulate the axon

31. _____ gaps in the myelin sheath

32. _____ small gap between neurons, across which communication occurs

33. _____ chemicals that nerve cells use to communicate with one another

34. _____ specialized protein molecules that neurotransmitters bind to

35. _____ process by which neurotransmitter is taken back into the presynaptic neuron

36. _____ process by which enzymes break down neurotransmitter in the synapse

37. _____ process by which receptors on the presynaptic neuron terminate the release of neurotransmitter

38. _____ drugs that facilitate neuronal communication

39. _____ drugs that inhibit neuronal communication

40. _____ neurotransmitter that controls motor behavior at the level of the muscles; also plays a role in motivation and reward.

41. _____ neurotransmitter that controls motor behavior at the level of the brain

42. _____ neurotransmitter that plays a role in learning, memory, and attention

43. _____ class of neurotransmitters that include norepinephrine, dopamine, and serotonin

44. _____ neurotransmitter that plays an important role in arousal

45. _____ neurotransmitter that plays important roles in emotion, dreaming, and impulse control

46. _____ primary inhibitory neurotransmitter in the brain

47. _____ primary excitatory neurotransmitter in the brain

48. _____ chains of amino acids that modulate neurotransmission

49. _____ peptide that plays a role in learning, memory, pain transmission, and exploratory behavior

50. _____ peptides that play a role in pain reduction and reward

51. _____ peptide that functions as a neurotransmitter and is involved in pain perception

52. _____ portion of the nervous system consisting of the brain and spinal cord

53. _____ portion of the nervous system consisting of all nerves outside of the CNS

54. _____ separates the CNS from the rest of the body

55. _____ portion of the PNS that conveys sensory information to the CNS and transmits motor signals from the CNS to the muscles

56. _____ portion of the PNS that transmits information between the CNS and the body's internal organs and glands

57. _____ the activating portion of the autonomic nervous system

58. _____ the portion of the autonomic nervous system that relaxes the body and stores energy

59. _____ hormones that play a role in reproduction, growth, and tissue repair

60. _____ endocrine glands involved in sexual behavior

MULTIPLE-CHOICE QUESTIONS

1. A research strategy frequently used to assess the relative importance of genetic and environmental factors in human behavior _____.
   a. requires manipulation of strands of DNA
   b. relies on comparisons of differences in behaviors between grandparents and their grandchildren
   c. compares similarities and differences of monozygotic and dizygotic twinsrequires that a longitudinal method be used

2. Results from the Human Genome Project have found that humans have approximately _____ genes.
   a. 13,000
   b. 18,000
   c. 26,000
   d. 30,000

3. If a plant that has one dominant gene for red flowers and one recessive gene for white flowers, what color will the flowers be?
   a. red
   b. white
   c. pink
   d. sometimes the flowers will be red and other times they will be white

4. When genetics researchers talk of an individual's phenotype, to what are they referring?
   a. the genetic makeup of the individual
   b. the genetic makeup of the individual's parents
   c. the physical characteristics of the individual
   d. how the environment has altered the individual's genotype

5. Most traits and characteristics are determined by more than one gene. In other words they are _____.
   a. multiparty
   b. polygenic
   c. polymorphous
   d. multigenic

6. A fertilized egg cell is known as a(n) _____.
   a. gamete
   b. zygote
   c. ovum
   d. embryo

7. When a cell divides into two new cells that have only one half of the original cell's chromosomes, this is known as _____.
   a. meiosis
   b. osmosis
   c. mitosis
   d. necrosis

8. Twins who have the same genotype are known as _____.
   a. fraternal twins
   b. maternal twins
   c. dizygotic twins
   d. monozygotic twins

9. When behavioral geneticists try to determine how much of the observed variability of a trait is the result of genetic factors, they are asking a question about _____.
   a. heredity
   b. heritability
   c. coefficient of variation
   d. genetic estimation

10. The four major parts of a neuron are _____.
    a. axon, synapses, soma, myelin
    b. soma, myelin, dendrites, terminal buttons
    c. dendrites, soma, synapses, axon
    d. axon, dendrites, soma, terminal buttons

11. Which type of neurons carry information from the brain to the muscles?
    a. efferent neurons
    b. afferent neurons
    c. interneurons
    d. sensory neurons

12. Afferent is to efferent as _____ is to _____.
    a. motor; sensory
    b. sensory; motor
    c. dendrite; axon
    d. axon; dendrite

13. What type of neurons are sending information to the muscles in your hand as you circle the answers to these questions?
    a. cranial nerves
    b. interneurons
    c. afferent neurons
    d. efferent neurons

14. Richie just fell off of his bicycle and skinned his knee. What type of neurons are sending information from his knee to his brain?
    a. cranial nerves
    b. interneurons
    c. afferent neurons
    d. efferent neurons

15. Which of the following carries information toward the cell body of a neuron?
    a. axon
    b. astrocyte
    c. dendrite
    d. myelin

16. The stage at which the neuron has a slightly negative charge is called the _____.
    a. readiness stage
    b. steady-state stage

c. action potential

d. resting potential

17. The nodes of Ranvier are associated with which part of the neuron?

a. soma

b. axon

c. dendrites

d. terminal buttons

18. The electrical signal that travels down the length of the axon is known as the _____.

a. axon potential

b. action potential

c. membrane potential

d. graded potential

19. Changes in the electrical state of a nerve cell occur when sodium and potassium ions pass through _____ in the cell membrane.

a. ion channels

b. sodium-potassium gates

c. ion pores

d. permeable pores

20. Depolarization is to hyperpolarization as _____ is to _____.

a. sodium; potassium

b. potassium; sodium

c. excitatory; inhibitory

d. inhibitory; excitatory

21. The _____ is the place in a nerve cell where the action potential is generated.

a. axon hillock

b. soma

c. axon

d. nodes of Ranvier

22. After an action potential has been generated, there is a period of time when the neuron can fire only in response to a very strong signal. This is known as _____.

a. absolute refractory period

b. relative refractory period

c. postsynaptic period

d. absolute depolarization period

23. The process by which the action potential travels down the axon being regenerated at the nodes of Ranvier is known as _____.

a. propagation

b. transitory regeneration

c. saltatory conduction

d. glial propagation

24. Communication between neurons is initiated by _____.

a. ion exchange across the synapse

b. neurotransmitters being released into the synapse

c. action potentials along the dendrites

d. the opening of sodium and potassium gates

25. Whether or not an action potential becomes an inhibitory or excitatory postsynaptic potential depends on _____.

a. the effects of the neurotransmitter on the postsynaptic neuron

b. the strength of the action potential

c. the resting potential of the postsynaptic neuron

d. the total net charge of the action potentials in the postsynaptic neuron

26. Which of the following is NOT true of an action potential?

a. positively charged ions flow into the axon through ion channels

b. it regenerates itself as it travels down the axon

c. it results in the production of a graded potential in the postsynaptic neuron

d. the size of the action potential varies with the amount of stimulation the neuron receives

27. A neurotransmitter that increases the likelihood that a postsynaptic neuron will fire creates a(n) _____.

a. inhibitory postsynaptic potential.

b. excitatory postsynaptic potential.

c. postsynaptic action potential.

d. postsynaptic resting potential.

28. Multiple sclerosis (MS) destroys myelin. What effect does this have on neuronal transmission?

a. increases the strength of the action potential (increases amplitude)

b. decreases the speed of the action potential (slows communication)

c. reduces the strength of the action potential (decreases amplitude)

d. increases the speed of the action potential (speeds communication)

29. The synapse consists of all of the following EXCEPT _____.

a. terminal button

b. synaptic cleft

c. dendrite of another neuron

d. myelin

30. A receptor that indirectly affects the permeability of the cell membrane is a(n) _____.

a. ionotropic receptor

b. autoreceptor

c. metabotropic receptor

d. neuroreceptor

31. Which of the following is NOT involved in terminating a synaptic transmission?
    a. degradation
    b. enzyme deactivation
    c. autoreception
    d. reuptake

32. Which of the following is NOT an effect of an agonistic drug?
    a. increased reuptake in the synaptic cleft
    b. increased release of neurotransmitter
    c. deactivation of enzymes in the synaptic cleft
    d. activation of receptors on the postsynaptic membrane neurotransmitter has the opposite effect on neural transmission

33. While traveling through the Amazon jungle, your companion has been shot with a dart coated with curare. As paralysis sets in, you must administer an agonist of which of the following neurotransmitters if you are to save your companion?
    a. dopamine
    b. acetylcholine
    c. endorphins
    d. GABA

34. Which of the following neurotransmitters is released by efferent neurons?
    a. dopamine
    b. acetylcholine
    c. epinephrine
    d. GABA

35. This neurotransmitter has been identified as playing a role in learning, memory, and dreaming.
    a. acetylcholine
    b. serotonin
    c. dopamine
    d. endorphins

36. Smokers report that having a cigarette increases their ability to concentrate. This is probably because the nicotine in the cigarette excites the receptors for this neurotransmitter.
    a. dopamine
    b. endorphins
    c. GABA
    d. acetylcholine

37. Which of the following neurotransmitters have been identified in playing a role in Alzheimer disease?
    a. dopamine
    b. norepinephrine
    c. serotonin
    d. acetylcholine

38. Which of the following is NOT a monoamine?
    a. dopamine
    b. serotonin
    c. acetylcholine
    d. norepinephrine

39. Prozac blocks the reuptake of serotonin (5-HT). This is an example of a neurotransmitter _____.
    a. agonist
    b. antagonist
    c. mimic
    d. synthesis

40. Parkinson disease is associated with a decrease in which neurotransmitter?
    a. serotonin
    b. dopamine
    c. acetylcholine
    d. norepinephrine

41. This neurochemical is believed to be the primary neurotransmitter for sending signals about reward.
    a. endorphins
    b. serotonin
    c. cholecystokinin
    d. dopamine

42. This neurotransmitter plays an important role in attention and arousal.
    a. dopamine
    b. norepinephrine
    c. acetylcholine
    d. cholecystokinin

43. Which monoamine is found primarily in the body, outside of the brain?
    a. dopamine
    b. norepinephrine
    c. epinephrine
    d. serotonin

44. Which of the following is NOT an effect of a dopamine (DA) agonist?
    a. increase in the synthesis of DA
    b. prevention of DA reuptake by the presynaptic membrane
    c. leakage of DA from the synaptic vesicles
    d. activation of receptors that normally respond to DA

45. Dr. Reuben has developed a technique that can selectively regenerate neurotransmitter production in specific brain regions. Which brain region should Dr. Reuben target if he wants to counteract the decrease in dopamine associated with Parkinson disease?
    a. cerebellum
    b. basal ganglia
    c. substantia nigra
    d. hippocampus

46. People who take LSD experience hallucinations. These hallucinations, which are like waking dreams, probably result from LSD's effect on _____ receptors.
    a. GABA
    b. dopamine
    c. endorphins
    d. serotonin

47. Which neurotransmitter is involved in dreaming, emotion, and impulse control?
    a. serotonin
    b. GABA
    c. endorphins
    d. norepinephrine

48. Which of the following is an amino acid that acts as a neurotransmitter?
    a. GABA
    b. glutamate
    c. substance P
    d. a and b

49. The primary inhibitory neurotransmitter in brain is the amino acid _____.
    a. glutamate
    b. GABA
    c. Substance P
    d. cholecystokinin

50. Chemicals that reduce our anxiety, such as benzodiazepines and alcohol, exert their effects by increasing the binding of the neurotransmitter _____.
    a. endorphins
    b. substance P
    c. cholecystokinin
    d. GABA

51. The primary excitatory neurotransmitter in the nervous system is _____.
    a. glutamate
    b. GABA
    c. substance P
    d. norepinephrine

52. Chains of amino acids are known as _____.
    a. peptides
    b. astrocytes
    c. neuromodulators
    d. catecholamine

53. Which amino acid plays a role in satiety?
    a. endorphins
    b. cholecystokinin
    c. Substance P
    d. all of the above

54. The amino acid that is found in the highest concentrations in the brain is _____.
    a. endorphins
    b. cholecystokinin

55. Which amino acid plays a role in pain reduction and reward?
    a. endorphins
    b. cholecystokinin
    c. substance P
    d. all of the above

56. Which neurotransmitter is released when someone experiences a runner's high?
    a. acetylcholine
    b. endorphins
    c. dopamine
    d. norepinephrine

57. The administration of this amino acid has been shown to induce panic attacks in individuals with panic disorder.
    a. endorphins
    b. cholecystokinin
    c. Substance P
    d. glutamate

58. The administration of a neutral substance, such as water or a sugar pill, can produce a relief of symptoms if the person taking the substance expects that it will have an effect. This is known as the _____.
    a. Hawthorne effect
    b. endorphin effect
    c. placebo effect
    d. somatic effect

59. The release of substance P is associated with _____.
    a. the experience of pain
    b. a reduction in pain
    c. increased exploratory behaviors
    d. decreased exploratory behaviors

60. The brain and spinal cord make up the _____ nervous system.
    a. peripheral
    b. autonomic
    c. somatic
    d. central

61. Which of the following is part of the peripheral nervous system?
    a. autonomic nervous system
    b. somatic nervous system
    c. endocrine system
    d. a and b

62. When an athlete is running a race, which part of the nervous system is activated?
    a. parasympathetic
    b. sympathetic
    c. endocrine
    d. somatic

63. Activating is to relaxing as _____ is to _____.
    a. electrochemical; hormones
    b. hormones; electrochemical
    c. sympathetic; parasympathetic
    d. parasympathetic; sympathetic

64. Which of these body organs is most directly related to the functioning of the autonomic nervous system?
    a. eyes
    b. skeletal muscles
    c. heart
    d. ears

65. What division of your nervous system is responsible for the fight-or-flight response you experience when you come across a bear in the woods?
    a. somatic nervous system
    b. sympathetic nervous system
    c. central nervous system
    d. parasympathetic nervous system

66. The nervous system is to endocrine system as _____ is to _____.
    a. electrochemical; hormones
    b. hormones; electrochemical
    c. sympathetic; parasympathetic
    d. parasympathetic; sympathetic

67. Which of the following is a type of hormone?
    a. steroid
    b. amino acid
    c. peptide
    d. all of the above

68. The brain structure that coordinates the actions of the endocrine system with the central nervous system is the _____.
    a. pituitary gland
    b. amygdala
    c. hypothalamus
    d. reticular activating system

THOUGHT QUESTIONS

1. Describe the process by which a nerve cell fires, from start to finish.

2. What is the difference between ionotropic and metabotropic receptors?

3. What role do peptides play in neuronal communication?

4. How are hormones and neurotransmitters different, and how are they the same?

5. What are the different divisions of the nervous system?

6. How do agonists and antagonists exert their effects on neuronal transmission?

7. What is the difference between heritability and heredity?

ANSWER KEY

Fill-in-the-Blank Questions

1. genes
2. DNA
3. chromosomes
4. alleles
5. dominant gene
6. phenotype
7. genotype
8. meiosis
9. mitosis
10. gametes
11. behavioral genetics
12. zygote
13. monozygotic
14. dizygotic
15. heredity
16. heritability
17. neurons
18. dendrites
19. soma
20. axon
21. nerve
22. terminal button
23. synapse
24. sensory or afferent neurons
25. motor or efferent neurons
26. interneurons
27. resting potential
28. action potential
29. all or none
30. myelin
31. nodes of Ranvier
32. synaptic cleft
33. neurotransmitters
34. receptors
35. reuptake
36. enzyme deactivation
37. autoreception
38. agonists
39. antagonists
40. acetylcholine
41. dopamine
42. acetylcholine
43. monoamines
44. norepinephrine
45. serotonin
46. GABA
47. glutamate
48. peptides
49. cholecystokinin (CCK)
50. endorphins
51. substance P
52. central nervous system (CNS)
53. peripheral nervous system (PNS)
54. blood–brain barrier
55. somatic nervous system
56. autonomic nervous system
57. sympathetic division
58. parasympathetic division
59. steroids
60. gonads

Multiple-Choice Questions

1. c Twin studies are one of two important ways in which research can examine genetic contributions to behavior.

2. d We have roughly 30,000 genes-not that many more than a worm (18,000).

3. a If a dominant gene is present it will be expressed.

4. c Phenotype refers to the physical characteristics of an organism.

5. b Polygenic means that a characteristic is determined by more than one gene.

6. b A fertilized egg cell is known as a zygote.

7. a Meiosis is the process by which cells divide and form gametes.

8. d Monozygotic twins are also known as identical twins; they have the same genes.

9. d Heritability is a measure of how much of a trait's observed variation is due to genetic factors.

10. d The four major parts of the nerve cell are the dendrites, soma, axon, and terminal buttons.

11. a Efferent neurons, or motor neurons, carry information to the muscles.

12. b Sensory neurons are afferent neurons carrying information to the brain, while motor neurons are efferent neurons.

13. d Efferent neurons carry information from motor centers in the brain to the muscles in our body.

14. c Afferent neurons carry sensory information from our body to the brain.

15. c Dendrites carry information toward the cell body (soma).

16. d When a neuron is not firing it has a slight negative charge known as a resting potential.

17. b Nodes of Ranvier are the gaps in the myelin sheath along the axon.

18. b Also known as neuronal firing, the action potential is an electrical signal that travels down the axon.

19. a The selectively permeable ion channels allow sodium and potassium ions to pass through the cell membrane.

20. c Excitatory postsynaptic potentials depolarize the neuron, while inhibitory postsynaptic potentials hyperpolarize the neuron.

21. a Inhibitory and excitatory signals summate at the axon hillock, and if there is sufficient depolarization an action potential is generated.

22. b The relative refractory period is a brief period of time when further firing can occur only in response to strong stimulation.

23. c Saltatory conduction is the process by which the action potential jumps from node to node down the axon.

24. b The release of neurotransmitter by the presynaptic neuron begins the process of neuronal communication (note that answers a and c do not occur in nerve cells).

25. a It is the effect that the neurotransmitter has on the ion channels of the postsynaptic neuron that determines whether it is excitatory or inhibitory.

26. a The size of the action potential does not vary as a result of stimulus intensity; stimulus intensity is signaled by the number of neurons firing and the rate at which the neuron fires.

27. b Excitatory postsynaptic potentials depolarize the postsynaptic neuron and increase the likelihood of that neuron firing.

28. b Myelin serves to increase the speed of the action potential, thus its destruction should slow neuronal communication.

29. d Myelin is found on the axon of a neuron not at the synapse.

30. c A metabotropic receptor indirectly effects the opening of ion channels.

31. a Reuptake, enzyme deactivation, and autoreception are all events that terminate synaptic transmission.

32. a Agonists increase the effects of a neurotransmitter, and increasing reuptake of neurotransmitter has the opposite effect on neural transmission.

33. b Curare is an acetylcholine antagonist.

34. b Acetylcholine controls motor behavior at the level of the muscle.

35. a Acetylcholine is the neurotransmitter involved in sleep, dreams, learning, and memory.

36. a Nicotine is an acetylcholine agonist.

37. d Degeneration of the acetylcholine system occurs in Alzheimer disease.

38. c Dopamine, norepinephrine, and serotonin are all monoamines.

39. a By blocking reuptake, Prozac increases the amount of 5-HT in the synapse; it is an agonist.

40. b Parkinson disease is a motor disorder that results from decreases in dopamine.

41. d Dopamine is believed to be the primary neurotransmitter for communicating information about reward.

42. b Norepinephrine releasing neurons in the locus caeruleus are involved in attention and arousal.

43. c Epinephrine is found primarily outside of the brain.

44. c Leakage of DA from the synaptic vesicles results in less DA being released on neuronal firing; thus it is an antagonist effect.

45. c Parkinson disease is associated with a decline in function of the dopamine producing neurons in the substantia nigra.

46. d LSD is a serotonin agonist.

47. a Serotonin plays a role in emotional states, impulse control, and dreaming.

48. d Both GABA and glutamate are amino acids.

49. b GABA is an amino acid that is the primary inhibitory neurotransmitter.

50. d Benzodiazepines and alcohol are GABA agonists.

51. a The amino acid glutamate is the primary excitatory neurotransmitter in the brain.

52. a Peptides are chains of amino acids.

53. b Cholecystokinin promotes satiety, leading to a decrease in meal size as a result of administration.

54. b CCK is the peptide found in the highest concentrations.

55. a Endorphins are part of the body's defense against pain.

56. b The release of endorphins accompanies vigorous exercise.

57. b CCK is involved in exploratory behavior, and injections of this amino acid have been shown to trigger panic attacks in people with panic disorder.

58. c Placebos are inert substances that can provide symptom relief because the person taking the placebo expects the substance to have an effect.

59. a Substance P conveys pain information to the brain.

60. d The central nervous system is comprised of the brain and the spinal cord.

61. d The peripheral nervous system is composed of the somatic and autonomic nervous systems.

62. b The sympathetic nervous system is activated when we are expending energy.

63. d The sympathetic division of the autonomic nervous system prepares the body for action, while the parasympathetic division restores the body to a relaxed state.

64. c All of the other choices are part of the somatic nervous system.

65. b The sympathetic nervous system expends energy when we are aroused, the fight-or-flight response.

66. b The nervous system communicates via electrochemical signals while the endocrine system uses hormones.

67. d Steroids, amino acids, and peptides are the three different types of hormones in the body.

68. c The hypothalamus exerts control over the endocrine system through its connections with the pituitary gland.

Thought Questions

1. Your answer should include discussion of the neuron's resting potential and the inhibitory and excitatory postsynaptic potentials that the neuron receives along its dendrites. These electrical charges travel along the surface of the cell membrane and summate at the axon hillock. If there is sufficient depolarization and the threshold is crossed, the neuron generates an action potential. Your answer should discuss how the action potential is regenerated as it travels down the axon and how the action potential signals the release of neurotransmitter into the synaptic cleft. Finally, reuptake by the presynaptic neuron and enzymatic deactivation remove the neurotransmitter from the synapse and end the neuronal communication.

2. These are the two basic types of receptors in the nervous system. Ionotropic receptors are fast-acting receptors that directly open ion channels in the postsynaptic membrane. In contrast, metabotropic receptors are slow-acting receptors that have indirect effects on ion channels. Metabotropic receptors do this through the release of either a G protein or a secondary messenger.

3. Peptides typically modulate the effects of neurotransmitters, either prolonging or shortening the effect of the neurotransmitter on the postsynaptic neuron. A number of peptides also act as neurotransmitters. Three that are mentioned in the book are cholecystokinin, endorphins, and substance P.

4. Both the nervous system and the endocrine system are communication systems within the body. The nervous system uses electrochemical signals to communicate, while the endocrine system uses hormones. Because hormones are released into the bloodstream, they take more time before they exert their effects and their effects last longer than signals within the nervous system.

5. There is the CNS, which consists of the brain and the spinal cord, and the PNS, which consists of everything else outside of the CNS. We can then divide the PNS into the somatic nervous system and the autonomic nervous system. The somatic nervous system is the system that conveys information between our brain and our body's sense organs and muscles. The autonomic nervous system is also composed of two parts.

The sympathetic division, which activates the body, and the parasympathetic division, which calms and relaxes.

6. If you understand the process of neuronal transmission, you should be able to answer this question. Agonists are chemicals that facilitate neuronal communication and antagonists inhibit neuronal communication. Thus agonists exert their effects by acting as a mimic at the postsynaptic receptor; they increase the amount of neurotransmitter released, block reuptake, and prevent enzymes in the synapse from breaking down neuro- transmitter substance. In contrast, antagonists might block receptor sites so neurotransmitters cannot bind with the postsynaptic receptors, they might increase the action of enzymes in the synapse, speed reuptake, cause synaptic vesicles to leak, or break down neuro- transmitters in the presynaptic neuron before they are released into the synapse.

7. Heredity refers to the genetic transmission of charac- teristics from one generation to the next. Heritability is a statistical estimate of the amount of observed variability in a trait or characteristic that can be directly attributed to differences in heredity, i.e., genes.

CHAPTER 4 | The Brain

GUIDE TO THE READING

In the previous chapter the authors of the textbook outlined the biological foundations of the nervous system. Chapter 4 examines how the physical brain enables mind and behavior. The authors begin by reviewing the historical developments that laid the foundation for modern views of brain function, concluding with the modern imaging tools that have revolutionized the discipline by allowing scientists to view activity of the working human brain. At the core of this chapter is a discussion of the basic brain structures and an examination of the divided nature of the human brain. You'll want to study these sections carefully, as they build a foundation for subsequent chapters. Finally, the authors examine the brain's remarkable capacity for change over the course of development, after injury, and through daily experience.

How Have Our Views of the Brain Evolved?

Though it has been understood since ancient times that there is a relationship between the mind and the brain, our understanding of how the structures of the brain control the mind has evolved over time. One critical debate centered on the idea of *equipotentiality* versus *localization of function*. Do all parts of the brain contributing equally to mental function, or can mental functions be mapped to specific regions of the brain?

Though the idea of localization of function was carried to ridiculous extremes by the pseudoscience of phrenology, advocates of this idea were on the right track. It is now known that the brain's surface is a patchwork of many specialized areas that control rudimentary components of perception, behavior, and mental life. Throughout history our understanding of brain function has been greatly aided by the observation of patients with head injury. For instance, Paul Broca's investigation of a patient who could say only the word *tan* provided evidence that the left frontal region of the brain (Broca's area) played a crucial role in speech production, and behavior changes exhibited by Phineas Gage provided the basis for modern theories that the prefrontal cortex governs personality and self-control. More recently, functional brain imaging techniques allow us to generate maps of the healthy human brain in action. These techniques include electroencephalography (EEG) and magnetoencephalography (MEG), which both provide good temporal resolution of mental activity, and positron emission tomography (PET) and functional magnetic resonance imaging (fMRI), which both provide good special resolution of mental events.

What Are the Basic Brain Structures and Their Functions?

After providing you with an appreciation for the specialized nature of the human brain, the authors lead you through a tour of the basic brain structures that make up the central nervous system and identify the functions controlled by each structure. Though this material may seem overwhelming at first, it is helpful to remember that functioning becomes increasingly complex as you progress from the spinal cord upward through the structures of the hindbrain, midbrain, forebrain, and cerebral cortex. After studying this section you should be able to identify the location and the functions controlled by each of the following structures and substructures:

- *Spinal cord:* Be able to explain the general action of the spinal reflex and the central pattern generator. Note that the stretch reflex is just one of a number of spinal reflexes.
- *Brainstem:* Made up of the hindbrain (which itself includes the cerebellum, pons, and medulla) and the midbrain. Be able to explain the role of the reticular formation and the tectum.

- *Hypothalamus:* Explain why this structure is indispensable to an organism's survival.
- *Cerebral hemispheres:* The two halves of the fore-brain, which contain the thalamus, hippocampus, amygdala, basal ganglia. and cerebral cortex. Be able to identify the four lobes of the cerebral hemispheres and to explain the role of the corpus callosum.

Memorizing the numerous structures in the brain can be a daunting task. Being able to visualize where in the brain these structures are located will help your study of this material. In learning the function of these brain structures, think about what sort of impairments would result from damage to the various structures.

How Is the Brain Divided?

The split-brain condition has provided researchers with a wealth of information about the different roles the two cerebral hemispheres play in behavior. For most individuals, the left hemisphere is responsible for language abilities but is incapable of performing spatial tasks—a right hemisphere skill. The left hemisphere has a tendency to try to make sense out of the world, a tendency known as the interpreter. This interpreter affects how we understand and remember our world, creating a comprehensible story out of our experiences and paying attention to information that is consistent and rejecting information that is inconsistent.

How Does the Brain Change?

The brain changes throughout development and as a result of experience, a property known as plasticity. This plasticity allows the brain to recover some function after injury, though typically brain plasticity decreases with age. Changes in neuronal connections occur as a result of experience. This is the basis of learning. Neurons that fire together strengthen their connections with one another, increasing the likelihood that they will fire together in the future, a process known as Hebbian learning.

FILL-IN-THE-BLANK QUESTIONS

1. _____ the practice of determining personality characteristics by measuring bumps on the skull

2. _____ theory that states that all parts of the brain contribute equally to all mental functions

3. _____ proposed by Karl Lashley, who believed that the cortex was undifferentiated and participated equally in all behavior

4. _____ imaging technique that uses electrodes to measure brain electrical activity

5. _____ imaging technique that measures changes in magnetic fields along the surface of the scalp

6. _____ measures metabolic activity in the brain through the use of an injected radioactive isotope

7. _____ imaging technique that measures energy given off by hydrogen nuclei

8. _____ the rope of neural tissue that runs from the pelvis to the base of the skull

9. _____ neural tissue that consists mostly of cell bodies

10. _____ neural tissue that consists mostly of axons and myelin

11. _____ the thickened end of the spinal cord that consists of the hindbrain and midbrain

12. _____ a circuit that produces a rhythmic, recurring set of movements on stimulation

13. _____ the network of neurons that runs through the brainstem and plays a role in general arousal

14. _____ orienting center that sits at the back of the midbrain

15. _____ plays an important role in motor behavior; its Latin name means "little brain"

16. _____ known as the master gland; controls all other glands by the release of hormones into the bloodstream

17. _____ brain structure that regulates body temperature, circadian rhythms, glucose levels, and blood pressure

18. _____ almost all sensory information passes through this structure on the way to the forebrain

19. _____ plays an important role in memory storage

20. _____ structure near the hippocampus that plays an important role in emotional learning

21. _____ structure that plays an important role in planning and producing motor behavior; it is damaged in neurological disorders such as Huntington disease and Parkinson disease

22. _____ the outer covering of the cerebral hemispheres

23. _____ the broad band of fibers that connects the two cerebral hemispheres

24. _____ lobes at the back of the brain that receives visual input

25. _____ the primary somatosensory cortex is found at the front of this lobe

26. _____ lobes that contain the primary auditory cortex

27. _____ lobes that play an essential role in planning and movement

28. _____ rearmost portion of the frontal lobes, which sends information to the muscles

29. _____ portion of the frontal lobes that is not directly responsible for movement

30. _____ term that describes the brain's potential for change

31. _____ neurons that "fire together, wire together"

MULTIPLE-CHOICE QUESTIONS

1. Ancient cultures drilled holes in the skulls of people, possibly as a treatment for mental illness, this procedure is known as _____.
   a. trepanning
   b. lobotomy
   c. hemispherectomy
   d. evisceration

2. According to ancient Egyptians, the _____ was (were) the seat of the soul.
   a. eyes
   b. brain
   c. pancreas
   d. heart

3. The "science" of attributing personality traits and mental abilities to differences in the shape of the skull is known as _____.
   a. functional localization
   b. phrenology
   c. veneration
   d. potentialization

4. A researcher transplants a portion of the parietal lobe of a newborn rat pup to the occipital lobe of a second rat pup. When this second rat pup reaches maturity, its occipital lobe behaves just like the occipital lobes of rats who have not had transplants. This result would support the theory of _____.
   a. equipotentiality
   b. localization
   c. mind
   d. lateralization

5. Which brain imaging technique involves the injection of radioactive tracers into the bloodstream?
   a. EEG
   b. fMRI
   c. MEG
   d. PET

6. Which of the following brain imaging techniques would you use to study the time course of sentence comprehension?
   a. EEG
   b. PET
   c. rCBF
   d. MRI

7. If you were interested in examining the size of the amygdala in a group of depressed subjects, which neuroimaging technique should you use?
   a. MRI
   b. EEG
   c. PET
   d. MEG

8. The law of mass action was proposed by _____.
   a. Paul Broca
   b. Karl Lashley
   c. Jean-Pierre Flourens
   d. Jean-Baptiste Bouillard

9. The spinal cord is made up of two types of tissue: gray matter, which is composed primarily of _____, and white matter, which is composed primarily of _____.
   a. cell bodies; axons and myelin
   b. axons and myelin; cell bodies
   c. sensory neurons; motor neurons
   d. motor neurons; sensory neurons

10. A circuit that when activated produces a rhythmic set of movements is known as a(n) _____.
    a. spinal reflex
    b. orienting reflex
    c. central pattern generator
    d. corticomotor loop

11. Which brain structure is involved in controlling sleep, arousal, muscle tone, and heart rate?
    a. cerebellum
    b. brainstem
    c. thalamus
    d. basal ganglia

12. The _____ is the brain structure involved in orienting and maintains a topographic map of space.
    a. cerebellum
    b. somatosensory strip
    c. hippocampus
    d. tectum

13. The structure that runs through the brain stem and plays an important role in general arousal is the _____.
    a. reticular formation
    b. pons

c. medulla

d. cerebellum

14. Rico is experiencing problems with coordinating his arms and legs, and he also reports experiencing problems with his balance. What region would you first investigate as the source of his difficulties?
    a. basal ganglia
    b. cerebellum
    c. frontal cortex
    d. parietal lobe

15. A skilled figure skater must rely heavily on activity in the _____.
    a. reticular formation
    b. hippocampus
    c. cerebellum
    d. amygdala

16. What brain region regulates the release of hormones from the pituitary gland?
    a. amygdala
    b. thalamus
    c. hypothalamus
    d. hippocampus

17. Which gland secretes hormones that regulate and control the function of all other endocrine glands in the body?
    a. adrenal
    b. thymus
    c. pituitary
    d. parathyroid

18. A patient who has suffered a small, localized injury to the brain and who, as a result, never feels hungry and must be forced to eat has probably sustained damage to the _____.
    a. cerebellum
    b. reticular activating system
    c. thalamus
    d. hypothalamus

19. The Clark's nutcracker lives at high elevations in the Rocky Mountains. During the winter, this bird survives by eating food it stored at different locations during the summer and fall. Nutcrackers are able to remember more than 5000 different sites where they have stored food. Not surprisingly, one region of the nutcracker's brain is slightly larger than it is in other bird species that do not store food. Which region is this?
    a. hypothalamus
    b. hippocampus
    c. amygdala
    d. thalamus

20. Female rats with fetal masculinization exhibit stereotypically male mating behavior as a result of testosterone's effects on the _____.

    a. hippocampus
    b. amygdala
    c. thalamus
    d. hypothalamus

21. H. M. is unable to form new memories because surgeons removed this structure from both sides of his brain.
    a. hippocampus
    b. amygdala
    c. caudate
    d. thalamus

22. All sensory information, except for the sense of _____, pass through the thalamus on the way to the cerebral cortex.
    a. taste
    b. hearing
    c. smell
    d. touch

23. When we experience fear in response to another person's facial expressions, our _____ is activated.
    a. amygdala
    b. hippocampus
    c. medulla
    d. hypothalamus

24. A subcortical structure that plays an important role in organizing and producing motor behavior is the _____.
    a. reticular formation
    b. amygdala
    c. hippocampus
    d. basal ganglia

25. Which lobe of the cerebral cortex is involved in hearing?
    a. occipital lobe
    b. auditory lobe
    c. temporal lobe
    d. parietal lobe

26. The primary somatosensory cortex is located in the _____ lobes.
    a. temporal
    b. occipital
    c. parietal
    d. frontal

27. If you lose feeling in your left arm but you can still move it, then you probably had a mild stroke in the _____.
    a. right parietal lobe
    b. left parietal lobe
    c. right frontal lobe
    d. left frontal lobe

28. Which of the following body parts has the greatest representation (takes up the most space) on the somatosensory cortex?
    a. leg
    b. hand
    c. back
    d. arm

29. Vision is to hearing as _____ is to _____.
    a. occipital; parietal
    b. occipital; temporal
    c. frontal; temporal
    d. parietal; frontal

30. Sam refuses to wear a bike helmet. Today he had an accident and smashed his forehead on the pavement. His prefrontal brain regions don't work as well as they used to. Which of the following will Sam now have difficulty doing?
    a. listening to his teacher in class
    b. watching television
    c. breathing on his own
    d. planning his summer vacation

31. Gloria is 93 years old. She has no difficulty with verbal comprehension, but as a result of a stroke, she often has difficulty with speech production. It is likely that the stroke damaged a portion of the _____ region in her brain.
    a. left posterior
    b. right posterior
    c. left frontal
    d. right frontal

32. The two hemispheres of the brain communicate with each other primarily through a wide band of nerve fibers that pass between them called the _____.
    a. anterior commissure
    b. brainstem
    c. cortical commissure
    d. corpus callosum

33. A person with a split brain is shown an apple in their left visual field. Asked to identify what she saw, she would be able to _____.
    a. say what she saw
    b. point with her left hand to the apple
    c. point with her right hand to the apple
    d. both point to the apple and say what she saw

34. Language ability is to spatial ability as _____ is to _____.
    a. left hemisphere; right hemisphere
    b. right hemisphere; left hemisphere
    c. temporal lobe; parietal lobe
    d. parietal lobe; temporal lobe

35. The brain's ability to recover from brain damage and to change as the result of experience is known as _____.
    a. learning
    b. plasticity
    c. regeneration
    d. Hebbian learning

36. Chemical gradients play a role in brain development by _____.
    a. determining whether a neuron will be a sensory neuron, motor neuron, or interneuron
    b. determining whether cells will cortical or subcortical neurons
    c. guiding cells to congregate in one lobe or another
    d. guiding the growth of axons from one region to another

THOUGHT QUESTIONS

1. Gall and Spurzheim were correct in theorizing that different portions of the brain controlled different functions, but their theory of phrenology was rejected, why?

2. What was Karl Lashley's law of mass action? How did he test his theory, and what error did he make in his reasoning?

ANSWER KEY

Fill-in-the-Blank Questions

1. phrenology
2. equipotentiality
3. law of mass action
4. electroencephalography
5. magnetoencephalography
6. positron emission tomography
7. magnetic resonance imaging
8. spinal cord
9. gray matter
10. white matter
11. brainstem
12. central pattern generator
13. reticular formation
14. tectum
15. cerebellum
16. pituitary
17. hypothalamus
18. thalamus
19. hippocampus
20. amygdala
21. basal ganglia
22. cerebral cortex
23. corpus callosum
24. occipital
25. parietal
26. temporal
27. frontal
28. primary motor cortex
29. prefrontal cortex
30. plasticity
31. Hebbian learning

Multiple-Choice Questions

1. a Scientists are not sure why ancient cultures performed this procedure, but one hypothesis is that it represents an attempt to treat disorders such as epilepsy or psychosis.

2. d Egyptians believed that the heart was the seat of the soul.

3. b Phrenology was a pseudoscience that attributed traits and abilities to bumps on the skull.

4. a Equipotentiality held that all parts of the brain were identical and contributed equally to mental functioning.

5. d PET uses a radioactive tracer to measure metabolic activity in the brain.

6. a While EEG has poor spatial resolution, it does have good temporal resolution.

7. a MRI produces high-resolution images of brain tissue.

8. b Lashley proposed that cortex is undifferentiated and participates in all thought equally.

9. a Gray matter consists primarily of cell bodies, while white matter is composed primarily of axons and myelin.

10. c A central pattern generator produces rhythmic, recurring movements when stimulated.

11. b The brainstem controls basic life-support functions.

12. d Located at the back of the midbrain, the tectum is an orienting center.

13. a The reticular formation is a network of neurons that affects general arousal.

14. b The cerebellum plays an important role in motor behavior, including coordinating limb movements, balance and smooth pursuit eye movements.

15. c The cerebellum plays an important role in motor behavior and motor learning.

16. c The hypothalamus has direct connections to the pituitary and thus controls all hormonal function.

17. c The pituitary gland is known as the master gland.

18. d The hypothalamus is the master regulatory structure of the brain and is responsible for such fundamental drives as hunger, thirst, and aggression.

19. b The hippocampus plays an important role in the storage of new memories.

20. b The hypothalamus is one of the few brain structures that differs in organization between males and females; exposure to high levels of testosterone result in female rats have hypothalamic organization more similar to males.

21. a The hippocampus plays a crucial role in memory formation.

22. c The sense of smell is the oldest sense and has a direct route to the cortex.

23. a The amygdala plays a special role in responding to stimuli that elicit fear.

24. d The basal ganglia receives input from the entire cortex and projects to the motor centers of the brainstem.

25. c The primary auditory cortex is located within the temporal lobes.

26. c The parietal lobe receives input from the skin senses, and the somatosensory cortex is located at the front of the parietal lobes.

27. a Sensory information from the left side of the body is sent to the right hemisphere, and the parietal lobe receives somatosensory input.

28. b Area on the somatosensory cortex is allocated based on the amount of use a particular body part has.

29. b Visual input goes to the occipital lobe while auditory information goes to the temporal lobe.

30. d The prefrontal cortex is the "executive" of the brain and is involved with planning and organizing behavior.

31. c Speech is a left hemisphere function and the frontal lobe controls motor behavior; if there were difficulties in language comprehension that would indicate left posterior damage.

32. d The corpus callosum serves to connect the two cerebral hemispheres.

33. b Visual information from the left visual field goes to the right hemisphere; since the right hemisphere does not have language abilities, she would be able only to point to the apple with her left hand.

34. a Language is a left hemisphere function and the right hemisphere is specialized for spatial abilities.

35. b Plasticity refers to the brain's ability to continually change.

36. d Connections of the brain are determined in large part by chemicals that direct where axons grow to and where not to go.

Thought Questions

1. Phrenologists were unwilling to subject their theories to empirical testing, and experimental verification is needed to prove or disprove any scientific theory.

2. Lashley's law of mass action held that the cortex was an undifferentiated mass and that the more brain tissue was removed, the greater the impairment. He attempted to demonstrate this law by training rats to run mazes and then removing different portions of their brains and observing the impairments in their functioning. Lashley did not consider the fact that negotiating a maze requires a number of different skills (e.g., memory, vision, coordination of limbs), and the loss of any one of these functions would impair performance.

CHAPTER 5 | Sensation, Perception, and Attention

GUIDE TO THE READING

In the previous chapter, the authors of the textbook took you through some basic neuroanatomy and described the function of these brain structures. Chapter 5 moves outside the skull and addresses how the brain senses and perceives the external environment. The core of the chapter is the distinction between sensation and perception: the sensory properties of objects in the external environment and our ability to perceive those properties based on how they are coded into neural energy and processed by the brain. This is an incredibly complex process, and it is amazing that we have such agreement about what exists in the physical environment. The chapter explores some of the history and methods of studying sensation and perception. Then, it examines how each of the senses works as well as some basic principles of perceptual processing. For both of these, much attention is paid to the vital functions of vision and hearing. Finally, the authors look at the role attention plays in regulating perceptions.

How Are Sensation and Perception Studied?

Psychology has its roots in the philosophical debate about whether human knowledge is acquired through experience (empiricism) or whether at least some of it is innate (nativism). However, the scientific effort to understand sensation and perception did not begin in earnest until the 19th century, when Gustav Fechner developed means to quantify the relationship between physical stimuli in the external world and perceptual experience. He and other psychophysicists who followed him, including Weber and Stevens, proposed simple, but now classic, laws to describe this relationship, and you'll want to be certain that you understand these. Modern psychologists recognize that human judgment also affects our ability to detect a stimulus, also known as a signal.

What Are the Sensory Processes for Our Primary Senses?

A central part of this chapter is the section on how the primary senses work. For each of the five primary senses (vision, hearing, smell, touch, and taste) the basic sensory process works in a similar manner: A proximal stimulus triggers a response in specialized receptors, which then transduce that stimulus energy into a neural impulse that is carried to the brain.

Table 5.1 BASIC SENSORY PROCESS

Sense	Proximal Stimulus	Receptor Cell
Vision	light waves	rods and cones in the retina
Hearing	sound waves	hair cells on the basilar membrane
Smell	odor particles	receptors in the olfactory epithelium
Touch	physical pressure and and temperature (extremes)	receptors for pain, temperature, and pressure in the epidermis
Taste	substances dissolved in saliva	microvilli on taste buds

You'll want to pay special attention to the material on vision and hearing, as the sensory processes for these are covered in substantial detail. Study the figures in the text that present the anatomy of the eye (Figs. 5.6 and 5.7) and ear (Figs. 5.14 and 5.15) closely. You should also be prepared to explain the process of color vision.

In addition to spending a lot of time with the material, we've always found it helpful to consider when these sensory processes do not work. For example, what happens as people age and they need reading glasses? What are the processes involved for individuals who are color blind? How can people have operations and need no anesthesia? Why do smells evoke such powerful memories? This perspective can help make the material more meaningful for you. In keeping with the theme of the text, it is important to consider why we have developed these senses in such a way. For example, how does our vision help us survive? If you were designing the human sense of taste, what sort of features would you want us to have so that we would be able to live and thrive (e.g., detect poisons). Finally, consider how other animals have evolved based on their specialized senses. How do the specialized abilities of owls, dogs, and bats help them gather food, attract a mate, and resist predators?

What Are the Basic Perceptual Processes?

The next section begins the transition from what is out in the physical environment and its transduction into neural energy to how this information is processed in the brain. The authors begin with some localization of the various perceptual areas (e.g., primary visual cortex: V_1; primary auditory cortex: A_1, primary somatosensory cortex: S_1). Pay attention to the neuroanatomy but try not to lose sight of the big picture: The brain is a very functional organ (as you learned in Chapter 4). We have evolved an incredibly efficient system for making sense of our world. For example, we have an intricate three-dimensional knowledge of the world, even though the information that comes to our brain is inherently two-dimensional. We have learned the critical skill of depth perception by processing the binocular cues (e.g., retinal disparity) and monocular cues (e.g., occlusion, linear perspective, texture gradient). Also, the optical illusions (e.g., Ames boxes, Ponzo illusion, moon illusion) are fun to try on your friends. See whether they have difficulty with some of the figure and ground reversals. In addition, studying the phenomena of color afterimages and motion aftereffects is a good way to learn perceptual processes.

How Does Attention Help the Brain Manage Perceptions?

Finally, the authors look at the special role attention plays in perceiving the world. Your college experience should sensitize you to the fact that simply showing up for lectures does not mean that you will process and remember the material. You must attend to it in some way. Generally speaking, students vastly overestimate the amount of material to which they can attend. You cannot study effectively while also talking on the telephone and watching television. You have a limited attentional and perceptual capacity. As Pinker's research asserts, this is particularly true when trying to perform two tasks that use the same mechanisms. Visualizing a game you are listening to on the car radio can dangerously divert your attention from visual cues on the road ahead. A similar example of the limited capacity of attention (in this case, visual attention) is the *binding problem*. When observers are overextended in terms of visual attention, the brain's ability to determine what features go with what object is

compromised. However, the authors do present some interesting research that attentional selection is not an all-or-none process. There is some evidence that people can be influenced by information even though they have only minimally attended to it. The full range of implications from these findings remains to be seen.

FILL-IN-THE-BLANK QUESTIONS

1. _____ study of how our sense organs respond to external stimuli (lights, sounds, etc.) and how those responses are transmitted to the brain

2. _____ study of the further processing of sensory signals in the brain that ultimately results in an internal representation of stimuli

3. _____ holds that all human knowledge must be acquired through the senses

4. _____ holds that at least some human knowledge is innate

5. _____ the minimum intensity of stimulation that must occur before one can experience a sensation

6. _____ $\Delta I / I = k$

7. _____ $S = k \log I$

8. _____ visual receptor cells responsible for vision under high illumination and for color and detail

9. _____ region near the center of the retina where the cones are densely packed

10. _____ region of the thalamus that processes visual information

11. _____ color perception that depends on the wavelength of light

12. _____ color perception that depends on the total amount or intensity of light

13. _____ color perception that varies according to the mixture of wavelengths present in light

14. _____ sound perception that depends on the amplitude of the sound wave

15. _____ sound perception that depends on the frequency of the sound wave

16. _____ another name for the eardrum

17. _____ tiny bones of the middle ear that transfer vibrations from eardrum to the oval window

18. _____ bone of the middle ear also known as the hammer

19. _____ bone of the middle ear also known as the anvil

20. _____ bone of the middle ear also known as the stirrup

21. _____ fluid-filled tube that is also known as the inner ear

22. _____ region of the midbrain that has neurons that can inhibit pain receptor cells from carrying signals to the cortex

23. _____ specialized receptors in the nasal cavity that respond to the presence of pheromones

24. _____ short hairlike structures at the tip of each taste receptor

25. _____ location in the superior temporal lobe of the primary auditory cortex

26. _____ perceptual illusion when two or more slightly different images are presented in rapid succession

27. _____ Gestalt principle that states that the closer two figures are to one another, the more likely we are to group them together

28. _____ Gestalt principle that states that we tend to group figures according to how closely they resemble each other

29. _____ Gestalt principle that refers to the tendency to interpret intersecting lines as being continuous, rather than as changing direction radically

30. _____ Gestalt principle that refers to the tendency to complete figures that have gaps

31. _____ style of information processing wherein data are relayed from lower to high levels

32. _____ technique in which a person is presented two messages in each ear at the same time

33. _____ physical stimulus in the environment

34. _____ stimulus energy that is transduced by the sense organs

MULTIPLE-CHOICE QUESTIONS

1. John is stopped at a red light. The fact that he can stare at this light and transform its physical properties into neural impulses that are then sent to the brain (telling him to stop) is done through a process known as _____.
   a. sensory transformation
   b. perceptual mixing
   c. sensory coding
   d. psychophysical scaling

2. Virtually all sensory information (except olfaction) first goes to a structure in the middle of the brain known as the _____.
   a. hippocampus
   b. hypothalamus
   c. thalamus
   d. amygdala

3. Rob's neighbor Tom plays his music very loudly every night when Rob is trying to study. Rob asks Tom to turn it down several times. After the third or fourth time, the sound is low enough so Rob can finally concentrate, but Tom claims that he turned it down the first time Rob asked! The reason Rob didn't notice the change in volume the first time was because _____.
   a. he had a false alarm
   b. he could not localize the sound
   c. he had problems with transduction
   d. the change didn't exceed the difference threshold

4. Jorge's parents are worried that his hearing has been damaged from listening to his personal stereo too loudly. During a hearing exam, Jorge is asked to indicate whether he hears a particular auditory stimulus. Because he is worried about the consequences of failing the test he periodically detects a stimulus that isn't there. This error is known as a(n) _____.
   a. hit
   b. false alarm
   c. miss
   d. incorrect rejection

5. During your general psychology exam, you are initially angered when construction workers start using a jackhammer outside the testing room. However, by the end of the exam you barely notice this noise. This change is due to the process of _____.
   a. sensory adaptation
   b. psychophysical insensitivity
   c. correct rejection
   d. sensory fatigue

6. Mara has to take a hearing test. She is told that she will hear different tones and has to raise her hand when she hears a tone. During the test, she is not always sure if she actually hears a tone, but she raises her hand anyway. Which perspective takes into account Mara's willingness to guess?
   a. noticeable difference theory
   b. Weber's law
   c. absolute threshold theory
   d. signal detection theory

7. Carolyn was admiring Melinda's engagement ring when she was sitting across the room from her. When

Carolyn saw the ring up close she realized it was bigger than she had thought. Carolyn's first view of the ring while across the room reflected some difficulty in _____.
a. forming a proximal stimulus
b. perceiving the distal stimulus
c. visual localization
d. interposition

8. Elliot is playing with his cat one day. He notices that when his cat is outside in the bright sunlight, part of his cat's eyes appears very small. When they are inside in dim lighting, the same part of the eyes appears very large. At which part of the cat's eyes is Elliot looking?
a. cornea
b. iris
c. lens
d. pupil

9. Rita is a 40-year-old woman who is having difficulty with getting her eye muscles to thicken her lens so that she can focus on close objects. She is prescribed corrective lenses because of this natural problem in the process of _____.
a. accommodation
b. subtractive visual mixing
c. photopigmentation
d. assimilation

10. Jeremy made a candlelight dinner for his girlfriend, Ali. When she walked in the door, he could barely make out what she looked like in the dim light. Which part of his eye was responsible for his vision in this light?
a. fovea
b. tympanic membrane
c. cones
d. rods

11. The observation that almost any color can be created by combining three wavelengths (short, middle, long) of light is known as the _____.
a. subtractive law of color mixing
b. multiplicative law of color mixing
c. interactive law of color
d. three primaries law of color

12. For fun, Andre's friends have him stare at an American flag for a minute. Then they have him stare at a blank wall. Amazingly, he sees a flag but the colors are yellow, green, and black. This color afterimage is primarily due to the responses of the _____.
a. retinal cones
b. lateral geniculate nucleus
c. rods
d. retinal ganglion cells

13. The frequency of a sound wave is encoded by the receptors on the area of the basilar membrane that vibrates the most in a process known as _____.
a. temporal coding
b. place coding
c. cochlear coding
d. Bekesy coding

14. While leaving the classroom, Lyssett accidentally kicked a chair while wearing open-toed sandals. She experienced a sharp, immediate pain that was due to which of the following pain fibers?
a. A-delta fibers
b. Beta fibers
c. C fibers
d. Omega fibers

15. The influence of morphine, endorphins, and acupuncture on the periaqueductal gray (PAG) region of the midbrain supports the _____ theory of pain.
a. haptic screening
b. cutaneous diversion
c. endogenous morphine
d. gate control

16. While out on a date, Matt wears a cologne that he hopes his girlfriend will like. The smell is initially coded by receptors in the _____, and she is able to tell him how wonderful he smells.
a. olfactory bulb
b. olfactory epithelium
c. thalamus
d. nasal cortex

17. Two girls who attend the same college go home one weekend to do laundry. Accidentally, they mix their laundry together. One of the girl's moms begins sorting through the laundry and can actually identify, by smell, her daughter's clothes. What would explain this phenomenon?
a. her mother is blind and has a very unusually developed sense of smell
b. her mother recognized her daughter's pheromones
c. her mother was experiencing sensory adaptation
d. her mother has an overactive ability to habituate to smell

18. Sangsuk was trying a new candy she had gotten from the local convenience store. She specifically licked it with the side of her tongue to better assess which of the following primary taste sensations?
a. sweet
b. sour
c. salty
d. bitter

19. Cortical processing of vision begins in the occipital lobe in an area known as _____.
    a. V_1
    b. A_1
    c. PVC_1
    d. R_2

20. After suffering a stroke, Shakira is unable to perceive whether anyone is touching her. Her neurosurgeon confirms that she has damage to the primary somatosensory cortex in the anterior _____ lobe of the brain.
    a. frontal
    b. temporal
    c. parietal
    d. occipital

21. Tyler is trying to entertain himself while studying. He notes that if he puts his finger in front of his face and closes his right eye, he sees one image. However, if he closes his left eye, his finger appears to move. These differences in images are due to the depth cue of _____.
    a. binocular disparity
    b. occlusion
    c. relative size
    d. texture gradient

22. Paula and John went to Hawaii for their honeymoon. They were watching the beautiful waterfalls when Paula looked away for a moment. To her surprise, the rocks and trees appeared to move upward for a moment. Although she wondered about the wedding champagne, this actually is a common example of the phenomenon of _____.
    a. compensatory factors
    b. stroboscopic movement
    c. motion aftereffects
    d. island fatigue

23. The _____ illusion occurs when you are looking up at the sky on a cloudy night and it seems as if the moon were moving through the clouds.
    a. induced movement
    b. stroboscopic movement
    c. Ponzo
    d. Muller–Lyer

24. While Stacy was driving her little sister. Lucy, to the mall, Lucy was telling Stacy that up ahead the road was getting narrower and narrower and soon enough the road would come to an end. Which of the following depth cues did Lucy use?
    a. occlusion
    b. texture gradient
    c. linear perspective
    d. familiar size

25. Katie is driving to the beach in her brand new convertible. Katie sees a puddle about 1 mile ahead of her on the highway and becomes worried that her car will get wet. After several miles, Katie has not reached the puddle, but she can still see it. Katie is experiencing a(n) _____.
    a. optical illusion
    b. Ponzo illusion
    c. Muller illusion
    d. delusion

26. Anne and her friends are looking through remedial Waldo books. In these, Waldo is drawn very simply with only a couple of characteristics. For these simple stimuli, they find that they can find Waldo quickly, regardless of whether he is hidden among many distracters or among only one or two distracters. This finding exemplifies the phenomenon Triesman termed _____.
    a. oddball
    b. pop-out
    c. Gestalt
    d. shazaam

27. The reversible figure illusion illustrates that one of our most basic visual organizing principles is distinguishing between _____ and _____.
    a. bottom-up; top-down
    b. contours; gaps
    c. proximity; similarity
    d. figure; ground

28. The plane crash story in the beginning of the chapter in which pilots did not see a mountain because they did not expect to see one is a powerful example of which type of information processing?
    a. bottom-up
    b. top-down
    c. lateral
    d. elementary-level

29. Sandy was reporting at a recent Lakers basketball game. She noted that Shaquille appeared similarly tall both on the court and in the locker room. She found this curious because she knew that her retinal image of him would be drastically different in the two situations. Her consistent perception of his height despite differing raw sensory data is due to _____.
    a. direct perception
    b. perceptual constancy
    c. illusory contours
    d. pop-out phenomenon

30. The findings that much of the visual processing performed by the brain is innate rather than learned supports Gibson's _____ theory.

a. classic perceptual
b. direct perception
c. gestalt perception
d. holistic perceptual

31. Eileen is at a social event when she hears her name mentioned several groups over. Her ability to selectively attend to the conversation she wishes is an example of the _____ phenomenon.
    a. shadowing
    b. backward masking
    c. subliminal
    d. cocktail party

32. Research findings that individuals may extract meaning from information even though they were unaware of it supports which of the following attentional theories of information processing?
    a. Broadbent's theory
    b. filter theory
    c. early selection
    d. late selection

THOUGHT QUESTION

Consider which of your sensory processes is most vital. If you were forced to do without one sense, which one would you choose? Why? How do you believe this would compromise your ability to survive and adapt in your environment? In what ways do you believe your other senses would compensate for this loss?

ANSWER KEY

Fill-in-the-Blank Questions

1. sensation
2. perception
3. empiricism
4. nativism
5. absolute threshold
6. Weber's law
7. Fechner's law
8. cones
9. fovea
10. lateral geniculate nucleus
11. hue
12. brightness
13. saturation
14. loudness
15. pitch
16. tympanic membrane
17. ossicles
18. incus
19. malleus
20. stapes
21. cochlea
22. periaqueductal gray
23. vomeronasal organs
24. microvilli
25. Heschl's gyrus
26. stroboscopic movement
27. proximity
28. similarity
29. good continuation
30. closure
31. bottom-up
32. shadowing
33. distal stimulus
34. proximal stimulus

Multiple-Choice Questions

1. c Sensory coding is the way our sensory organs translate a stimulus's physical properties into neural impulses.

2. c Most sensory information (except olfaction) first goes to a structure in the middle of the brain called the thalamus.

3. d The difference threshold is the minimum change in volume required for you to be able to perceive that something has changed.

4. b A false alarm is when an observer erroneously detects a stimulus that is not there.

5. a If a stimulus is presented continuously, sensory adaptation is the term for the process of how the sensory response tends to diminish over time.

6. d Signal detection theory maintains that detecting a stimulus requires a judgment about its presence or absence based on inherently ambiguous information.

7. b Psychologists refer to the external stimulus as the distal stimulus and the stimulus energy that is transduced by sense organs as the proximal stimulus.

8. d The pupil, a small hole at the front of the eye, contracts or dilates to alter how much light enters the eye.

9. a Accommodation is the visual process by which the muscles behind the iris change the shape of the lens-flattening it to focus on distant objects and thickening it to focus on closer objects.

10. d The rods are receptor cells that respond at extremely low levels of illumination and are primarily responsible for night vision.

11. d The three primaries law of color refers to the observation that almost any color can be created by combining three different wavelengths of light from the short, middle, and long end of the spectrum.

12. d The retinal ganglion cells create that perception of opposite colors and are primarily involved in the phenomenon of color afterimages.

13. b Place coding for pitch is the process wherein the frequency of a sound wave is encoded by the receptors on the area of the basilar membrane that vibrates the most.

14. a Fast-conducting A-delta fibers are responsible for the processing of sharp, immediate pain.

15. d The gate control theory of pain is supported by the influence of painkillers and stimulation-induced analgesia on the PAG.

16. b The olfactory epithelium is a thin layer of tissue embedded with olfactory receptors; odorants are initially processed here before being conveyed to the olfactory bulb—the brain center for smell.

17. b Pheromones are chemicals released by animals, including probably humans, that trigger physiological or behavioral reactions.

18. b The sides of the tongue are more sensitive to sour taste sensations.

19. a The primary visual cortex, or V_1, is where the cortical processing of vision begins.

20. c Touch information from the thalamus is projected to the primary somatosensory cortex in the anterior parietal lobe.

21. a The depth cue of binocular disparity refers to the differing retinal images that arise because we have two eyes.

22. c Motion aftereffects result when direction-sensitive visual neurons become fatigued.

23. a The induced movement illusion occurs when you have an incorrect frame of reference for motion perception and explains why the moon appears to move through the clouds.

24. c The monocular depth cue of linear perspective indicates that parallel lines appear to converge in the distance.

25. a Optical illusions, such as this one, arise when normal perceptual processes result in an incorrect representation of the distal stimulus.

26. b Triesman used the term pop-out for the finding that with simple stimuli oddballs seem to stand out automatically from the crowd.

27. d The reversible figure illusion is an example of the importance of distinguishing between figure and ground.

28. b Top-down information processing refers to the observation that what we expect to see influences what we perceive.

29. b Perceptual constancy refers to the correct perception of objects as constant despite raw sensory data that could lead us to believe otherwise.

30. b Gibson's direct perception theory approaches perception from an evolutionary perspective; findings that much of visual processing is innate would support it.

31. d The cocktail party phenomenon refers to the ability to selectively attend to a single conversation at a chaotic social event.

32. d Late selection theories of information processing suggest that attentional selection is not an all-or-none process, rather we may extract meaning from information even though we are unaware of it.

Thought Question

Answers will vary.

CHAPTER 6 | Learning and Reward

GUIDE TO THE READING

Learning is the relatively permanent change in behavior that occurs as a result of experience. This chapter covers the development of learning theory over the course of the last century, beginning with the principles of classical and operant conditioning. These ideas were developed by behavioral psychologists who believed that all learning could be explained by conditioning. Yet even as these basic methodologies continue to be used by neuroscientists who study brain mechanisms, we now know not only that learning is shaped by environmental factors but also that it is an adaptive behavior shaped by evolution. As such, biology places constraints on learning, and as seen in observational or imitative learning, reinforcement does not always have to be present for learning to take place. And while the behaviorists were careful to avoid speculating as to *why* reinforcement increased behavior, our current understanding of the neurological bases of reward and the role of the dopamine system has begun to provide insights into *how* learning occurs at the neuronal level. Finally, computerized models of neural networks are also helping researchers make predictions about how complex learning might occur.

How Did the Behavioral Study of Learning Develop?

The behavioral study of learning began with the work of Ivan Pavlov, a Russian physiologist who was studying the effects of salivation on digestion. He noticed that the dogs he was using as research subjects would begin to salivate before they had received any food. Pavlov decided to investigate this phenomenon and as a result elucidated the principles of classical conditioning. In classical conditioning, a neutral stimulus is paired with a stimulus that elicits an automatic reflexive response. In Pavlov's work, food reliably produces salivation, and because no learning is required for this response, the food is called an unconditioned stimulus (US) and the salivation is called an unconditioned response (UR). The neutral stimulus or conditioned stimulus (CS) is repeatedly presented with the US, and the animal learns, or becomes conditioned, to associate the CS with the US. After repeated CS/US pairings, the CS comes to produce the behavioral response by itself. This response is known as a conditioned response (CR), because it is occurring in response to the CS.

After reading this section, you should be familiar with the principles of classical conditioning, and you should be able to define the following terms: *acquisition, extinction, spontaneous recovery, generalization, discrimination,* and *second-order conditioning.* Classical conditioning has been demonstrated to play a role in the development of phobias. It also plays a role in drug addiction, by which the environment in which the drugs are used becomes conditioned with the effects of the drugs. This helps explain why recovered drug addicts can experience cravings for their drug when they are exposed to the environmental cues associated with their past drug usage. Pavlov believed that any neutral stimulus could become conditioned, an idea known as equipotentiality. However, work by John Garcia on conditioned taste aversion has shown that humans and animals are biologically prepared to become conditioned to certain types of stimuli. A cognitive model of classical conditioning has been proposed by Rescorla and Wagner. They believe that the strength of a CR can be predicted by the extent to which the US is unexpected or novel.

How Is Operant Conditioning Different from Classical Conditioning?

Another form of learning is operant conditioning. In operant conditioning, it is the outcome of a behavior that predicts whether the behavior is likely to occur again. The study of operant conditioning began with work by Edward Thorndike, who placed cats in puzzle boxes and measured how long it took the animals to escape from the boxes. As a result of this work, Thorndike developed his Law of Effect, which states that behaviors that are followed by a positive outcome are more likely to occur, while behaviors that are followed by a negative outcome are less likely to occur. These positive outcomes are known as reinforcers, and the negative outcomes are known as punishment. Reinforcement can be positive (a positive stimulus is administered) or negative (an aversive stimulus is removed). In both cases, the behavior is strengthened, i.e., reinforced. Likewise, punishment also can be either positive (an aversive stimulus is administered) or negative (a positive stimulus is removed).

Much of the early work on reinforcement and punishment was done by Harvard psychologist B. F. Skinner, and you should be familiar with his name and with the testing device that bears his name, the Skinner box. There are different ways in which reinforcers can be delivered to a person or animal. When reinforcement follows every targeted response, it is said to be a continuous reinforcement schedule. Partial reinforcement schedules can be based on the number of responses required for reinforcement (ratio schedules) or on the time between reinforced responses (interval schedules), and these ratio and interval schedules of reinforcement can be fixed or they can vary. Biology and cognition also play roles in operant conditioning, and after reading this section, you should know what is meant by the terms *genetic drift* and *latent learning*.

How Does Watching Others Affect Learning?

Classical and operant conditioning are not the only ways through which humans and animals learn. We also learn by watching others, observational learning. Albert Bandura conducted a classic study on children's observational learning of aggression, and this study is described in the text. The authors make a distinction in the text between the acquisition of a behavioral response and the performance of the response. We can learn a response by watching others (acquisition) but we may not perform the response. One of the reasons we may not perform a response is because we have seen the consequences of that response; this is known as vicarious learning. Recent studies of neuronal activity suggest that the activity of mirror neurons may be involved in observational learning.

What Is the Biological Basis of Reward?

Research investigating the rewarding properties of intracranial self-stimulation (ICSS) has identified dopamine as the neurotransmitter involved in reward. Regions in the brain that support ICSS, known as pleasure centers, overlap with known dopamine systems in the brain. The dopamine system involved in reward is the mesolimbic dopamine system, which projects from the ventral tegmental area to the nucleus accumbens. It is dopamine activity in the nucleus accumbens that is involved with the experience of pleasure we have when we engage in behavior. This section of the text concludes with a discussion of different types of drugs and drug addiction. Individuals may become addicted to drugs because they have developed either a physical or a psychological dependence on the drug. The use of drugs is associated with both positive and negative reinforcement. The pleasure associated with drug use is positively reinforcing, whereas the escape from the negative symptoms of withdrawal or the escape from problems and stress is negatively reinforcing.

How Does Learning Occur at the Neuronal Level?

Psychological scientists have long believed that learning must be associated with changes at the neuronal level, or as Donald Hebb put it, that "cells that fire together, wire together." Eric Kandel's work with the aplysia (a sea slug) has demonstrated that habituation and sensitization, simple forms of learning, are associated with changes in the function of the synapse. This work has led to the study of long-term potentiation, the process by which repeated stimulation of one neuron leads to an increased likelihood of firing by a connecting postsynaptic neuron. In examining learning at a number of different levels, psychologists have also developed computer models of neural networks. These networks are often referred to as connectionist models of learning because they are based on the idea that neurons are connected with one another. Perhaps the best known connectionist model is the parallel-distributed processing model.

FILL-IN-THE-BLANK QUESTIONS

1. _____ a relatively permanent change in behavior that occurs as a result of experience

2. _____ an approach to psychology that focuses on observable behavior rather than on internal mental processes

3. _____ happens when a neutral stimulus produces a previously unconditioned response

4. _____ a reflexive, automatic behavior that occurs in the absence of learning

5. _____ a stimulus that automatically elicits a reflexive behavior

6. _____ a previously neutral stimulus that produces a reflexive behavior as a result of learning

7. _____ the automatic reflexive behavior that occurs in response to a conditioned stimulus

8. _____ occurs when a conditioned stimulus no longer elicits a response

9. _____ the reinstatement of an extinguished behavior to a conditioned stimulus in the absence of any further training

10. _____ occurs when a CR occurs in response to a stimulus that is similar to the CS

11. _____ the differentiating among similar stimuli such that the UR occurs only in response to the CS

12. _____ the pairing of a neutral stimulus with a CS so as to produce a CR

13. _____ the fact that conditioning occurs more easily in response to some stimuli than in response to other stimuli

14. _____ model of conditioning stating that the strength of the conditioning depends on the extent to which the US is unexpected

15. _____ theory stating that any behavior that leads to a positive outcome will be strengthened whereas behaviors that lead to negative outcomes will be weakened

16. _____ the process of learning by which the outcomes of a behavior affect the probability of the behavior being repeated in the future

17. _____ the rewarding of successive approximations of a desired behavior

18. _____ reinforcements that satisfy biological needs

19. _____ objects or events that become reinforcing through the process of conditioning

20. _____ a behavioral outcome that results in the removal of an aversive stimulus

21. _____ a behavioral outcome that results in the administration of an aversive stimulus

22. _____ a behavioral outcome that results in the removal of a pleasurable stimulus

23. _____ when behavior is rewarded intermittently

24. _____ a schedule of reinforcement by which the delivery of reinforcement is based on the number of responses

25. _____ a reinforcement schedule based on the time between rewarded responses

26. _____ a reinforcement schedule in which the number of responses necessary for reinforcement or the interval between reinforced responses does not vary

27. _____ a reinforcement schedule in which the reinforcement is delivered at different times or at different rates

28. _____ the resistance to extinction that occurs when behavior is rewarded intermittently

29. _____ learning that occurs in the absence of reinforcement

30. _____ learning that occurs through watching others perform a behavior

31. _____ the imitation by an animal or human of a behavior that has been observed

32. _____ learning the consequences of a behavior by observing the outcomes others receive when they perform the behavior

33. _____ nerve cells in the prefrontal cortex that are activated when an individual watches another perform a task

34. _____ regions in the brain that support intracranial self-stimulation

35. _____ the decrease in responsiveness to repeated presentations of nonthreatening stimuli

36. _____ the increased responsiveness that occurs following exposure to a threatening stimulus

37. _____ the strengthening of a connection between neurons that makes it easier for the postsynaptic neuron to fire

MULTIPLE-CHOICE QUESTIONS

1. Which term describes the process by which a neutral stimulus develops the ability to elicit a conditioned response through repeated pairings?
   a. conditioning
   b. acquisition
   c. associationism
   d. behaviorism

2. When studying classical conditioning, Pavlov's dogs would often salivate at the sight of the pan where food was kept. In this case, the sight of the pan is an example of _____.
   a. an unconditioned stimulus
   b. an unconditioned response

c. a conditioned stimulus

d. a conditioned response

3. When studying classical conditioning in dogs, Pavlov would sound a bell and then give the animal food. The dog would salivate when it had received the food. This salivation is a(n) _____.

a. unconditioned stimulus

b. conditioned stimulus

c. unconditioned response

d. conditioned response

4. A subject is shown a flashing light followed by a mild shock. After several pairings of the flashing light and shock, the subject is presented only with the flashing light. The subject flinches in anticipation of the shock. The flashing light is an example of a(n)

_____.

a. unconditioned stimulus

b. unconditioned response

c. conditioned stimulus

d. conditioned response

5. A subject is shown a flashing light followed by a mild shock. After several pairings of the flashing light and shock, the subject is presented only with the flashing light. The subject flinches in anticipation of the shock. The subject's flinching is an example of a(n) _____.

a. unconditioned stimulus

b. unconditioned response

c. conditioned stimulus

d. conditioned response

6. A subject is shown a flashing light followed by a mild shock. After several pairings of the flashing light and shock, the subject is presented only with the flashing light. The subject flinches in anticipation of the shock. The electric shock is an example of a(n)

_____.

a. unconditioned stimulus

b. unconditioned response

c. conditioned stimulus

d. conditioned response

7. The process by which a conditioned stimulus gradually loses the ability to evoke a conditioned response when it is no longer followed by the US is called

_____.

a. backward conditioning

b. spontaneous recovery

c. reconditioning

d. extinction

8. One of Pavlov's dogs had stopped salivating at the sound of the tone. The next day the tone was presented again and the dog began salivating. This is an example of _____.

a. extinction

b. spontaneous recovery

c. stimulus generalization

d. positive reinforcement

9. Due to classical conditioning, your dog salivates every time he hears the electric can opener you use to open his dog food. You switch to dry dog food. You continue to use the can opener, but not for dog food. After repeatedly hearing the can opener but not getting fed, your dog's salivation to the sound of the can opener should _____.

a. decrease because of spontaneous recovery

b. decrease because of extinction

c. increase because of blocking

d. increase because of instinctive drift

10. Laurie's cat, Sadie, runs into the kitchen when she hears cat food being poured into her bowl. Lately, Sadie has started running into the kitchen when Laurie is getting breakfast and pouring cereal into her cereal bowl. Sadie's running into the kitchen in response to the cereal being poured is an example of _____.

a. second order conditioning

b. stimulus generalization

c. stimulus discrimination

d. spontaneous recovery

11. Although Laurie's cat, Sadie, used to run into the kitchen when she heard cereal being poured into a bowl, she now runs into the kitchen only when she hears cat food being poured into her dinner bowl. Sadie has demonstrated _____.

a. extinction

b. second order conditioning

c. stimulus generalization

d. stimulus discrimination

12. A young coyote is taught by his parents that small furry field mice make a tasty meal. As the young coyote becomes older, he eats any small furry object that crosses its path. This is called _____.

a. second order conditioning

b. stimulus generalization

c. stimulus discrimination

d. spontaneous recovery

13. Following a severe scratching by a Siamese cat, Ian becomes very anxious whenever he sees any kind of cat. His reaction can best be explained on the basis of

_____.

a. instinctive drift

b. response substitution

c. stimulus generalization

d. biological constraints

14. When you go to take your dog for a walk, you put open the closet, put on your coat, and then take down

the leash. Your dog has always come as soon as you get down the leash, but lately your dog is coming as soon as you open the closet door. This is an example of _____.
a. second order conditioning
b. stimulus generalization
c. stimulus discrimination
d. response substitution

15. Helping people overcome their fears by having them do something pleasurable while they are exposed to their feared stimulus is a process known as _____.
a. stimulus discrimination
b. response substitution
c. systematic conditioning
d. counterconditioning

16. The therapist who developed the technique of systematic desensitization is _____.
a. John Watson
b. Joseph Wolpe
c. B. F. Skinner
d. Albert Bandura

17. Hakeem can't really wake up until he's had his first cup of coffee in the morning. One morning he discovers that all he has left in the house is decaffeinated coffee. He makes a cup, and is surprised to discover that he feels just as stimulated as when he has regular caffeinated coffee. Hakeem's response to the decaffeinated coffee can best be explained by _____.
a. operant conditioning
b. counterconditioning
c. stimulus generalization
d. classical conditioning

18. When you first started drinking beer, you would get drunk after just one beer, but now you need to drink three beers just to get the same feeling. You have developed _____.
a. tolerance
b. maturation
c. psychological dependence
d. physical dependence

19. Pavlov and early behavioral psychologists believed that any stimuli could become a conditioned stimulus as a result of pairing with an unconditioned stimulus. This view is known as _____.
a. stimulus generalization
b. biological preparedness
c. equipotentiality
d. counterconditioning

20. From an evolutionary standpoint, which paired stimulus-response chain would condition most readily?
a. sweetened water paired with nausea
b. a loud buzzing paired with nausea

c. an electric shock paired with nausea
d. sweetened water paired with an electric shock

21. Based on the work of Garcia and Koelling dealing with conditioned taste aversion, which of the following pairings would produce the strongest conditioning?
a. a taste and a foot shock
b. a taste and nausea
c. a tone and nausea
d. a tone and a foot shock

22. Why does backward conditioning, the presentation of the CS after the US, not work?
a. the CS provides too much information about the US, and the animal becomes confused
b. previously conditioned responses spontaneously emerge, confounding new learning
c. the CS does not provide any new information about the US
d. the animal cannot tell the difference between the CS and the US

23. The Rescorla–Wagner model of classical conditioning that states that the strength of the association between the CS and US can be explained based on _____.
a. the extent to which the US is unexpected
b. the extent to which the CS is unexpected
c. the magnitude of the US
d. the magnitude of the CS

24. Which of the following produces the strongest conditioning?
a. the simultaneous presentation of the CS and US
b. presentation of the US followed immediately by presentation of the CS
c. presentation of the CS followed immediately by presentation of the US
d. all of the above

25. The process by which an organism learns to repeat behaviors that yield positive outcomes, or avoids negative outcomes, is called _____.
a. stimulus generalization
b. classical conditioning
c. forward conditioning
d. operant conditioning

26. Any behavior that leads to a positive outcome will be more likely to occur, while any behavior that leads to a negative outcome will be less likely to occur. This is known as _____.
a. Skinner's Theory of Reinforcement
b. Pavlov's Law
c. Thorndike's Law of Effect
d. Watson's Principals of Behavior

27. Training pigeons to play Ping-Pong requires establishing new responses by reinforcing the desired

behavior by successive approximation. This is an example of _____.

a. shaping
b. stimulus discrimination
c. positive reinforcement
d. stimulus control

28. Which of the following is an example of a primary reinforcer?

a. money
b. being hugged by your father
c. a gold star from your teacher
d. a glass of water

29. Which of the following is an example of a negative reinforcer?

a. getting grounded because you broke curfew
b. getting a low grade on an exam because you did not study
c. paying $15 for a CD you did not like
d. cleaning your room to avoid your mother's nagging

30. Researchers studying stimulus discrimination in blue jays use operant conditioning. A correct response is followed by a food reward and an incorrect response is followed by a time delay in which the bird does not have an opportunity to earn a food reward. This time delay is _____.

a. negative punishment
b. positive punishment
c. negative reinforcement
d. positive reinforcement

31. Researchers studying stimulus discrimination in blue jays use operant conditioning. A correct response is followed by a food reward and an incorrect response is followed by a time delay in which the bird does not have an opportunity to earn a food reward. This food reward is _____.

a. negative punishment
b. positive punishment
c. negative reinforcement
d. positive reinforcement

32. Reuben and Simon are always calling each other names like "poop head" and "stupid." Their parents decide that the way to deal with this is to make each child pay 10 cents each time they call the other a bad name. This is an example of _____.

a. positive reinforcement
b. negative reinforcement
c. positive punishment
d. negative punishment

33. Research on punishment has shown that _____.

a. punishment is the best way to inhibit an unwanted behavior

b. punishment can replace the unwanted behavior with one that is more adaptable
c. punishment has stronger effects than rewards
d. punishment may only temporarily inhibit a behavior

34. Which of the following are given by learning theorists as to why punishment should be avoided?

a. punishment can elicit negative feelings like fear and anger
b. punishment may only lead to the behavior being hidden
c. punishment may have unintended consequences and teach the wrong lesson
d. all of the above

35. When you go to a casino and put a quarter in a slot machine, usually you do not get anything. On average, for every $10 you spend, you win a jackpot of $3. The reinforcement schedule for this slot machine is _____.

a. fixed ratio
b. variable ratio
c. fixed interval
d. variable interval

36. A person who checks the coin return of every vending machine he or she passes will probably be reinforced on which schedule of reinforcement?

a. variable interval
b. fixed interval
c. variable ratio
d. fixed ratio

37. Rachel is selling candy to pay for her class field trip. The candy company gives children prizes for every 10 boxes of candy that they sell. What type of a reinforcement schedule is this?

a. variable interval
b. fixed interval
c. variable ratio
d. fixed ratio

38. The fact that a pigeon who has been on a variable interval reinforcement schedule will continue to respond for very long periods of time after the reward is no longer available is known as _____.

a. extinction resistance
b. partial-reinforcement extinction effect
c. instinctive drift
d. none of the above

39. Animals that have been shaped to do unusual behavior may return to more natural behavior. This is called _____.

a. extinction
b. genetic drift
c. acquisition
d. shaping

40. Learning that occurs in the absence of reinforcement is known as _____.
    a. unconscious learning
    b. instinctive learning
    c. latent learning
    d. observational learning

41. Children who have watched adults behaving aggressively with an inflatable clown, later act aggressively toward the inflatable clown themselves. This is an example of _____.
    a. stimulus generalization
    b. operant conditioning
    c. observational learning
    d. latent learning

42. In Britain, milk used to be delivered to people's doorsteps. Each milk bottle was covered with a piece of tin foil to keep dust out. This worked out very well until one small bird figured out that if he pecked through the tin foil he could have a free lunch. Before long, birds across Britain were helping themselves to milk by pecking through the tin foil. How could wild birds have learned this trick?
    a. classical conditioning
    b. operant conditioning
    c. punishment conditioning
    d. observational learning

43. If you are concerned that television viewers may acquire new ways to express aggression, then a learning theorist you are most likely to be concerned with _____.
    a. observational learning
    b. blocking phenomenon
    c. systematic desensitization
    d. reinforcement schedules

44. Watching other men at a party try and start conversations with attractive women, Daren learns which approaches work and which do not. Daren is engaging in _____.
    a. insight learning
    b. vicarious learning
    c. trial-and-error learning
    d. latent learning

45. Suzanne is watching some friends play soccer. Recent research indicates that neurons in Suzanne's brain are activated while she watches the game. These neurons, which are the same neurons that would be activated if Suzanne was playing soccer, are known as _____.
    a. mirror neurons
    b. reciprocal neurons
    c. motor neurons
    d. imitation neurons

46. Regions in the brain that support intracranial self-stimulation are known as _____.
    a. reward centers
    b. pleasure centers
    c. intracranial self-stimulation centers
    d. stimulation centers

47. Which neurotransmitter plays an important role in reward?
    a. norepinephrine
    b. acetylcholine
    c. aminobutyric acid (GABA)
    d. dopamine

48. The fiber bundle that connects the ventral tegmental area to the nucleus accumbens is the _____.
    a. medial forebrain bundle
    b. mesocortical norepinephrine system
    c. mesolimbic dopamine system
    d. tegmental cortical system

49. The term *physical dependence* describes a person who uses a drug because _____.
    a. she believes that she cannot function without the drug
    b. it feels good
    c. she wishes to avoid symptoms of withdrawal
    d. her drug use has developed into an automatic behavior

50. A researcher studying drug addiction focuses on the effects of peer pressure and the desire to be popular. This researcher is looking at drug addiction from the _____ perspective.
    a. social learning
    b. disease
    c. psychodynamic
    d. cognitive

51. Stimulants such as cocaine and amphetamine exert their effects on the _____ system.
    a. aminobutyric acid (GABA)
    b. dopamine
    c. endorphin
    d. serotonin

52. Hebb's rule on the neural basis of learning can be summed up as _____.
    a. use it or lose it
    b. nothing occurs at the behavioral level without causing changes at the neural level
    c. neurons that fire together, wire together
    d. reinforcement strengthens connections, while punishment weakens connections

53. Repeated exposure to a nonthreatening stimuli leads to a decreased behavioral response known as _____.
    a. desensitization
    b. habituation
    c. sensitization
    d. discrimination

54. Repeated exposures to a threatening stimuli will produce _____.
    a. habituation
    b. exhaustion
    c. sensitization
    d. desensitization

55. When repeated stimulation of one neuron leads to a connecting neuron firing more readily it is known as _____.
    a. Hebb's rule
    b. systematic desensitization
    c. long-term potentiation
    d. parallel-distributed processing

THOUGHT QUESTIONS

1. Is negative reinforcement the same thing as punishment? Describe how each would work in a particular situation.

2. Describe the process of classical conditioning.

3. What is long-term potentiation?

ANSWER KEY

Fill-in-the-Blank Questions

1. learning
2. behaviorism
3. classical conditioning
4. unconditioned response (UR)
5. unconditioned stimulus (US)
6. conditioned stimulus (CS)
7. conditioned response (CR)
8. extinction
9. spontaneous recovery
10. stimulus generalization
11. stimulus discrimination
12. second-order conditioning
13. biological preparedness
14. Rescorla–Wagner model
15. Law of Effect
16. operant conditioning
17. shaping
18. primary reinforcers
19. secondary reinforcers
20. negative reinforcement
21. positive punishment
22. negative punishment
23. partial reinforcement
24. ratio schedule
25. interval schedule
26. fixed schedule
27. variable schedule
28. partial-reinforcement extinction effect
29. latent learning
30. observational learning
31. modeling
32. vicarious learning
33. mirror neurons
34. pleasure centers
35. habituation
36. sensitization
37. long-term potentiation

Multiple-Choice Questions

1. a Classical conditioning is the learning process being described.

2. c Through conditioning the dogs learned that the pan signaled the delivery of the unconditioned stimulus, i.e., the food.

3. c The salivation is an unconditioned response because it is occurring in response to the food, an unconditioned stimulus.

4. c The subject has become conditioned to the flashing light.

5. d The subject's flinching occurs in response to the light; it is a conditioned response.

6. a The shock is an unconditioned stimulus.

7. d When a CS is no longer paired with the US the UR gradually extinguishes.

8. b Spontaneous recovery occurs when a previously extinguished CR reappears in the absence of any further conditioning trials.

9. b Repeated presentations of the CS without the presentation of the US will lead to extinction.

10. b This example describes stimulus generalization: Sadie is coming into the kitchen because the sound of cereal being poured sounds similar to cat food being poured into her bowl.

11. d Because she only gets fed when cat food is being poured into her dinner bowl, Sadie has learned to discriminate between the similar but different sounds.

12. b The coyote is demonstrating stimulus generalization.

13. c Ian has generalized his fear response to all breeds of cats.

14. a Your dog has now learned that the opening of the closet door indicates that you are going to be getting down the leash, and has become conditioned to that sound.

15. d Counterconditioning involves teaching people to learn to be relaxed in the presence of a feared stimulus.

16. b Wolpe developed this useful behavioral treatment.

17. d Classical conditioning plays a role in drug addiction; the environment and stimuli associated with drug use can elicit the same reactions that the drug itself elicits.

18. a Tolerance is the process by which people need more and more of a drug experience the same effect.

19. c This idea is known as equipotentiality.

20. a Biological preparedness will produce the strongest conditioning with taste and nausea.

21. b Biological preparedness will produce the strongest conditioning with taste and nausea.

22. c Classical conditioning works because the CS is signaling the imminent delivery of the US.

23. a According to the Rescorla–Wagner model of classical conditioning the strength of the association between a CS and US is determined by the extent to which the CS is surprising or unexpected.

24. c Classical conditioning works because the CS is signaling the imminent delivery of the US.

25. d Operant conditioning is the process by which the outcomes of a behavior either strengthen or weaken a behavior.

26. c This is Thorndike's Law of Effect.

27. a Shaping involves the rewarding of successively closer approximations to the desired target behavior.

28. d Primary reinforcers are events or objects that directly satisfy basic biological needs.

29. d By cleaning your room your mother removes an aversive stimulus (her nagging) and thus reinforces your behavior.

30. a The removal of the chance to earn a food reward is intended to reduce the number of incorrect responses.

31. d The food reward is intended to strengthen the desired behavior.

32. d By giving up a positive stimulus like money Reuben and Simon are learning not to call one another names.

33. d The fact that punishment may only temporarily inhibit an unwanted behavior is one reason why learning theorists suggest using rewards to reinforce desired behaviors is a better way to produce changes in behavior.

34. d These are all good reasons as to why reinforcement is better at shaping behavior.

35. b It is the number of quarters you put in the slot machine that is important in this example and not the amount of time and the ratio of quarters to jackpots varies from jackpot to jackpot.

36. c It is the number of vending machines checked that is important here not the time between checking.

37. d Reinforcements are based on the number of boxes sold meaning that it is a ratio schedule, and this ratio is fixed.

38. b The partial-reinforcement extinction effect describes the resistance to extinction that occurs under intermittent reinforcement schedules.

39. b Breland and Breland used the term genetic drift to describe this tendency to return to instinctual behavior.

40. c Tolman described learning that occurred in the absence of reinforcement as latent learning.

41. c This is a description of the study Bandura did of observational learning.

42. d The birds learned to open the milk bottles by watching other birds perform this behavior.

43. a With observational learning individuals can acquire new behaviors by watching others.

44. b Vicarious learning occurs when we watch others perform a behavior and observe the consequences of that behavior.

45. a Mirror neurons are activated when we observe someone engage in goal-directed behavior; it is unclear what purpose these neurons serve, but they are the same neurons that would be activated if we were engaged in the behavior ourselves.

46. b Pleasure centers are brain regions that support ICSS.

47. d Dopamine plays an important role in reward.

48. c The mesocortical dopamine system runs through the medial forebrain bundle and connects the ventral tegmental area (VTA) and the nucleus accumbens.

49. c Physical dependence is a physiological state in which the failure to ingest the drug leads to aversive feelings of withdrawal.

50. a The social learning perspective looks at how parents, peers, and mass media influence our behavior.

51. b Stimulants are all dopamine agonists.

52. c Hebb's rule postulates that learning should be associated with an increase in neuronal connections.

53. b Habituation is a decrease in behavior resulting from repeated exposure to a nonthreatening stimuli.

54. c This is the definition of sensitization.

55. c Long-term potentiation leads to changes in the postsynaptic neuron making it more likely that the neuron will fire.

Thought Questions

1. Negative reinforcement is *not* the same as punishment. Negative reinforcement strengthens a behavior, whereas punishment weakens the behavior. Negative reinforcement involves the removal of an aversive stimulus, but punishment involves either the administration of a negative stimulus or the removal of a positive stimulus. If I wanted my roommate to clean up his room, I could punish his messy behavior by complaining and nagging him constantly (positive punishment). Likewise, I could strengthen his cleaning behavior by stopping my nagging when he had cleaned up (negative reinforcement).

2. Classical conditioning occurs when a previously neutral stimulus is repeatedly paired with an unconditioned stimulus (US). The neutral stimulus is known as the conditioned stimulus (CS). The reflexive behavioral response to the US is known as the unconditioned response (UR). When presentation of the CS by itself elicits the response, it is called a conditioned response (CR).

3. Long-term potentiation is the strengthening of synaptic connections that occurs when repeated stimulation of one neuron leads to an increased likelihood that the connecting postsynaptic neuron will be activated. Long-term potentiation is consistent with Hebb's rule that neurons that fire together, wire together.

CHAPTER 7 | Memory

GUIDE TO THE READING

In this chapter, the authors discuss the mental processes involved in memory, which is defined as the ability to acquire and retain skills and knowledge. They begin by presenting the commonly accepted modal memory model and introducing the different memory systems and the different types of information that are stored in memory. Next, the authors apply various levels of analysis to the study of memory, starting with cognitive and behavioral models for how information is processed and represented in memory. Our early understanding of the biological mechanisms involved in memory was based on the study of individuals who had suffered a traumatic injury to the brain. Newer brain imaging techniques have allowed researchers to go beyond that level of analysis and gain new insights into how memory works at the neurochemical and biological levels. Finally, the authors consider why forgetting occurs and examine the ways in which memories for past events are selectively distorted.

What Are the Basic Stages of Memory?

The most widely accepted model of memory is the modal memory model proposed by Atkinson and Shiffrin, also known as the information-processing model. In this model, memory is conceptualized as consisting of three distinct memory stores:

- *Sensory memory:* Briefly stores information perceived by our senses before transferring it to short-term memory.
- *Short-term memory (STM):* Can hold a limited amount of information (no more than seven "chunks" of information) in awareness for a brief period. Some psychologists conceptualize STM as "working memory" consisting of three parts (*central executive, visuo-spatial scratchpad,* and *phonological loop*) that processes information for transfer to long-term memory.
- *Long-term memory (LTM):* Relatively permanent and limitless. Meaningful information is stored here.

What Are the Different Memory Systems?

Researchers agree that memory is served by multiple systems; some psychologists focus on memory content as the basis for defining the different systems and others focus on the process of memory storage as the way to differentiate among systems. One such distinction in memory systems is between explicit and implicit memory. Explicit memory involves the effortful storage and retrieval of declarative information and takes two forms: episodic memory, which is our memories of our personal experiences, and semantic memory, which is our memories of facts and information. Implicit memory occurs without attention. Just as there are different types of explicit memory, there are also different types of implicit memory. Procedural memory, or motor memory, is the memory of how to do things, like riding a bike, making a sandwich, and other sorts of motor skills. Two other types of implicit memories are attitude formation and repetition priming.

How Is Information Represented in Long-Term Memory?

The process of memory is composed of three stages: encoding, storage, and retrieval. Information gets stored in memory based on its meaning. Craik and Lockhart's levels of processing model of memory demonstrates that information is encoded with more meaning when subjects engage in elaborative rehearsal, and as a result, the information is more easily retrieved than when subjects engage in maintenance rehearsal. One way in which meaning is determined is through schemas, hypothetical frameworks that help organize information about the world. Schemas play a role in memory storage and in memory retrieval: We are more likely to remember information consistent with a schema than information that is inconsistent. Meaning is also important in theories of memory organization based on networks of associations. Units of information or nodes are linked to one another based on their meaning. Activation of one node increases the likelihood that associated nodes will be activated. Thus exposure to a dog increases the likelihood that related nodes of different types of dogs or different types of pets will be activated. This process is called spreading activation.

What Brain Processes Are Involved in Memory?

The brain region that has been consistently identified as playing a critical role in memory is the medial temporal lobes. The structures in this region of the temporal lobes include the hippocampus, the amygdala, and the rhinal cortex. The case of H. M. highlights the critical role that the hippocampus plays, especially in the consolidation of memory. Data from brain imaging studies suggest that, while the hippocampus plays a role in consolidation, the actual memories are stored in the region of the brain associated with processing that information. For example, visual information is stored in cortical regions that are involved in visual processing, and there are hemispheric differences associated with the type of information being stored. In addition to consolidation, the hippocampus plays a role in spatial memory and special cells in the hippocampus, known as place cells, fire when an animal returns to a familiar environment. The frontal lobes play immensely important roles in many aspects of memory. Of particular interest is the fact that more effortful processing of information is associated with greater frontal activation. One suggestion is that the frontal lobes are involved in working memory and so are activated during both encoding and retrieval of information. Memory modulators are neurotransmitters that can either enhance or impair memory. Epinephrine is one neurotransmitter that has been shown to increase memory. This enhancement of memory appears to be related to the release of glucose that accompanies the increase in epinephrine levels and the associated increase in arousal. The final brain structure discussed in this section is the amygdala, which plays an important role in the memory of emotional material.

When Do People Forget?

Forgetting is simply defined as the inability to retrieve information from long-term memory. Most forgetting occurs because of interference, similar events, or experiences make it difficult for us to retrieve the information for which we are searching. One psychologist described interference as being similar to the process of finding a pearl in a bucket of white marbles. Sometimes our inability to retrieve long-term memories is only temporary, this is known as blocking. If you have ever experienced the tip-of-the-tongue phenomenon then you have experienced blocking. The shallow encoding of information, absentmindedness, leads to the forgetting of information because we have not paid enough attention to details. When an individual experiences memory problems as the result of brain injury, disease, or trauma, this is known as amnesia. Some individuals lose the ability to recall events or information that occurred in the past (retrograde amnesia). Others suffer from anterograde amnesia, the inability to store new memories. The case of H. M. discussed in this chapter is an example of someone with anterograde amnesia.

How Are Memories Distorted?

Our memories can be inaccurate for a number of reasons. Source misattributions happen when we misremember the circumstances involved with a memory. The false fame effect described in the chapter is an interesting example of source misattribution. Source misattribution is also involved in a phenomenon called cryptomnesia, which occurs when a person perceives the recovery of information from memory as being an original idea of their own. Plagiarism charges against musician George Harrison and writer Stephen Ambrose are examples of this phenomenon. Memory errors have significant consequences in the arena of eyewitness testimony, where misidentification can send an innocent person to jail or allow a guilty party to escape punishment. Errors in eyewitness testimony can occur when people have to identify someone from a different ethnic group. Because we have less exposure to members of other ethnic groups, we tend to lump them all together in one group and see them as looking all alike. Eyewitness testimony is also prone to error because our memories can be distorted by misinformation, this is known as suggestibility. Psychologist Elizabeth Loftus has done extensive work on this issue, and you should be familiar with her studies discussed in the chapter. Confabulation, the false recollection of episodic memory, can occur in cases of brain injury as individuals recall incorrect information and then try to provide a coherent story to fit the mistaken recollections. The authors also touch on the controversial topic of repressed memory in this section. This is a topic over which psychologists hold very different opinions, and it will probably be some time before consensus is reached on this issue.

FILL-IN-THE-BLANK QUESTIONS

1. _____ capacity to acquire and retain information over time

2. _____ model of memory proposed by Atkinson and Shiffrin

3. _____ brief memory store of information from our sensory receptors

4. _____ also known as immediate memory

5. _____ Baddeley's conceptualization of STM

6. _____ permanent memory storage

7. _____ more accurate memory for items at the beginning and at the end of a list

8. _____ ability to better recall items at the end of a list

9. _____ ability to better recall items at the beginning of a list

10. _____ process of remembering specific information

11. _____ memory content that can be verbalized

12. _____ memories of your experiences

13. _____ memories of facts and information

14. _____ memory process that occurs in the absence of attention or conscious effort

15. _____ memory of learned automatic skills

16. _____ the improvement in stimulus identification that comes from prior exposure to the stimulus

17. _____ act of remembering previously stored information

18. _____ transforming perceptual experiences into representations

19. _____ retention of representations over time

20. _____ repeating a piece of information over and over again

21. _____ encoding information in a meaningful manner

22. _____ cognitive frameworks that help organize information about the world

23. _____ proposal that any stimulus encoded along with an experience can act as a retrieval cue

24. _____ inability to store new experiences

25. _____ act of storing information in LTM

26. _____ memory for direction, location, and other aspects of our physical environment

27. _____ inability to retrieve previously stored information

28. _____ pattern of forgetting over time

29. _____ primary reason why information is forgotten

30. _____ transient inability to recall information

31. _____ shallow storage of information, often due to inattentiveness

32. _____ loss of memory

33. _____ loss of memory for previously learned information

34. _____ especially strong memories for surprising and emotionally intense events

35. _____ misremembering of circumstances associated with a particular memory

36. _____ thinking that a retrieved memory is in fact a newly generated idea

37. _____ tendency for memories to become distorted when people are provided with misleading information

38. _____ forgetting where you encountered information about an event for which you have a memory

39. _____ false recollection of episodic memory

MULTIPLE-CHOICE QUESTIONS

1. A three-stage memory system consists of _____.
   a. sensory memory, iconic memory, and echoic memory
   b. sensory memory, short-term memory, and long-term memory
   c. explicit memory, implicit memory, and declarative memory
   d. working memory, visuospatial memory, and articulatory memory

2. Iconic memory lasts for _____.
   a. 3 sec
   b. 1 sec
   c. about 1/3 sec
   d. about 1/10 sec

3. A quickly moving circle of light appears to be a continuous line because of _____.
   a. short-term memory
   b. long-term memory
   c. sensory bias
   d. sensory memory

4. The model of memory that consists of three distinct stages of memory _____.
   a. was proposed by Atkinson and Shiffrin
   b. is an information processing model of memory
   c. is known as the modal memory model
   d. all of the above

5. In comparison to sensory memory, short-term memory has a _____.
   a. smaller capacity and shorter duration

b. larger capacity and shorter duration

c. smaller capacity and longer duration

d. larger capacity and longer duration

6. Atkinson and Shiffrin's information processing model views memory as composed of _____.
   a. sensory memory, short-term memory, and long-term memory
   b. implicit memory and explicit memory
   c. only one type of memory store that differs in levels of processing
   d. semantic memory, episodic memory, and procedural memory

7. After finding a number in the phone book, you repeat it to yourself several times as you go to dial the phone. This repetition of the phone number in your head is called _____.
   a. priming
   b. consolidation
   c. declarative memory
   d. maintenance rehearsal

8. Including the number 1, plus the area code, by how many digits does a normal long-distance phone number tax the upper range of the average person's short-term memory?
   a. 1
   b. 2
   c. 3
   d. 4

9. Which of the following strategies can you use to help you overcome the limits of your STM memory when you are trying to keep a long-distance phone number in STM?
   a. chunking
   b. encoding
   c. maintenance interference
   d. retrieval

10. Baddeley's model of working memory consists of the following components?
    a. sensory memory, working memory, long-term memory
    b. episodic memory, procedural memory, semantic memory
    c. articulatory loop, visuospatial scratchpad, central executive
    d. explicit memory, implicit memory, immediate memory

11. The fact that words at the end of a list are more easily remembered than words from the middle of the list is an example of _____.
    a. the recency effect
    b. the primacy effect
    c. decay
    d. proactive interference

12. Tom's wife sends him to the market for milk, butter, carrots, bread, and peanut butter. According to the primacy effect, which item will Tom most likely remember to purchase?
    a. milk
    b. carrots
    c. peanut butter
    d. beer and chips

13. People will learn more if they use _____ practice rather than _____ practice.
    a. distributed; massed
    b. massed; distributed
    c. elaborative; structural
    d. structural; elaborative

14. Content is to process as _____ is to _____.
    a. implicit; explicit
    b. explicit; implicit
    c. declarative; explicit
    d. implicit; declarative

15. Gramps tells his grandchildren, "When I was your age, I walked 3 miles in the snow to school." What type of memory are the grandchildren hearing about?
    a. semantic
    b. personal
    c. explicit
    d. episodic

16. The memory process involved in the effortless storing of information that we cannot easily express verbally is called _____.
    a. procedural memory
    b. nondeclarative memory
    c. explicit memory
    d. implicit memory

17. Sherisa is able to ride a bicycle although she has not ridden one for a few years, thanks to her _____.
    a. priming memory
    b. episodic memory
    c. implicit memory
    d. procedural memory

18. When Mi-Kyung correctly identifies Abraham Lincoln as the 16th president of the United States, she is retrieving information from her _____.
    a. episodic memory
    b. explicit memory
    c. semantic memory
    d. implicit memory

19. The false fame effect demonstrates _____.
    a. the effect of implicit memory on behaviors
    b. the effect of explicit memory on behaviors
    c. that our episodic memories are not accurate
    d. that people can distort their memory on purpose

20. Which of the following best explains what information gets stored in long-term memory?
    a. repetition priming
    b. meaningfulness
    c. rehearsal
    d. chunking

21. The process of memory has been proposed to involve three stages or steps: encoding, storage, and retrieval. This model is linked to a general view of _____.
    a. information processing
    b. levels of processing
    c. neural networks
    d. multiple components

22. The process of transforming our perceptual experiences into representations is _____.
    a. encoding
    b. information processing
    c. storage
    d. concept formation

23. The process of storage refers to _____.
    a. the process of elaborative rehearsal
    b. the process of maintenance rehearsal
    c. the retention encoded representations over time
    d. the organization of nodes within a network of associations

24. A conceptual framework that helps us organize information about our world is a _____.
    a. node
    b. schema
    c. concept
    d. network of associations

25. Craik and Lockhart developed the levels of processing theory of memory which suggests that _____.
    a. different types of memories are stored in different levels of long-term memory
    b. explicit memories involve more active processing than implicit memories
    c. the central executive processes information in short-term memory
    d. people will better at retrieving memories if they form more associations with the material during learning

26. Simply repeating a piece of information over and over again is _____.
    a. repetition priming
    b. maintenance rehearsal
    c. storage priming
    d. repetitive rehearsal

27. Shallow is to deep as _____ is to _____.
    a. elaborative rehearsal; maintenance rehearsal
    b. implicit memory; explicit memory
    c. maintenance rehearsal; elaborative rehearsal
    d. explicit memory; implicit memory

28. If you spend time thinking through what you are studying, you will remember it better than if you simply memorize it because you have _____.
    a. spent more time working on the material
    b. put more effort into processing the material
    c. processed the material more deeply
    d. because you will have created a more elaborate schema

29. A unit of information in a network is a _____.
    a. concept
    b. node
    c. representation
    d. schema

30. A model of memory organization that is based on connections between items having similar meanings is a _____.
    a. network of associations
    b. processing network
    c. schematic network
    d. network of meaning

31. If you believe that studying in the classroom where you take your tests will help you do well on the tests, you are attempting to facilitate retention on the basis of _____.
    a. flashbulb memory
    b. state dependent memory
    c. context dependent memory
    d. elaborative memory

32. The principle which proposes that retrieval of information is successful to the extent that retrieval cues match the cues involved during learning is called _____.
    a. levels of processing
    b. automatic priming
    c. encoding specificity
    d. procedural memory

33. You studied for your intro psych exam in your dorm room, research suggests that when taking the test, you would do _____.
    a. better on the test if you think about your dorm room
    b. worse on the test if you think about your dorm room
    c. better on the test if you are in a good mood
    d. better on the test if you are in a bad mood

34. Peter drinks seven pots of espresso while studying for his psychology exam, according to the theory of encoding specificity, Peter would do best on his exam if he could take it _____.
    a. after a restful night's sleep
    b. while he was in a good mood
    c. after having a large dose of caffeine
    d. before he finally goes to sleep

35. Karl Lashley used the term _____ to refer to the physical location within the brain where memories are stored.
    a. register
    b. module
    c. node
    d. engram

36. Lashley incorrectly concluded that memory was distributed equally throughout the brain, an idea known as _____.
    a. the law of mass action
    b. parallel processing
    c. networks of association
    d. equipotentiality

37. All of the following are important structures for memory located within the medial temporal lobes EXCEPT _____.
    a. hippocampus
    b. rhinal cortex
    c. basal ganglia
    d. amygdala

38. After H. M. had surgery to control his severe epileptic seizure, it was found that _____.
    a. his intellect was impaired
    b. he could not retain any information
    c. the hippocampus is the site where memories are stored
    d. he suffered retrograde and anterograde amnesia

39. Surgeons removed H. M.'s hippocampus to control his epilepsy. Which type of memories were relatively unaffected by this surgery?
    a. episodic memories
    b. procedural memories
    c. semantic memories
    d. None, all types of memories were impaired

40. The case of H. M. suggests that _____.
    a. the hippocampus is the site where memories are stored
    b. destruction of the hippocampus produces massive retrograde amnesia
    c. the hippocampus plays an important role in the consolidation of memories
    d. all of the above

41. An inability to remember the temporal sequence of a series of events is associated with damage to the _____.
    a. frontal cortex
    b. rhinal cortex
    c. temporal cortex
    d. hippocampus

42. Cerebral imaging studies have found that the greater the activation of the _____ lobes during encoding the _____ the likelihood of the words being recalled later.
    a. temporal; greater
    b. temporal; smaller
    c. frontal; greater
    d. frontal; smaller

43. Recent work investigating hemispheric asymmetries and memory has found that left hemispheric activation is associated with _____ while right hemispheric activation is associated with _____.
    a. encoding; retrieval
    b. retrieval; encoding
    c. verbal memories; spatial memories
    d. spatial memories; verbal memories

44. An injection of epinephrine leads to an increase in arousal and a release of _____ which increases memory.
    a. acetylcholine
    b. glutamate
    c. noradrenaline
    d. glucose

45. The degree to which people remember emotionally arousing material is a function of the level of activity of the _____.
    a. amygdala
    b. hippocampus
    c. hypothalamus
    d. nucleus accumbens

46. The most important factor in forgetting appears to be _____.
    a. attention
    b. emotion
    c. interference
    d. decay

47. Devon fell off his skateboard, and landed on his head. As a result of this injury, he suffered anterograde amnesia. With this type of injury, we know that Devon will be unable to remember _____.
    a. how to ride his skateboard
    b. his date of birth
    c. the name of the nurse who helped him through rehabilitation after the accident
    d. what happened the day before the accident

48. Seth went riding his motorcycle without a helmet. It started raining and the bike spilled over on the highway. Seth received a massive concussion, and is unable to remember anything that has happened after the accident. Seth suffers from _____.

a. retrograde amnesia
b. anterograde amnesia
c. retroactive interference
d. repression

49. Being unable to recall events at your second birthday party is most attributable to _____.
a. decay
b. retroactive interference
c. childhood amnesia
d. retrograde amnesia

50. Korie has a vivid memory of where she was and what she was doing when she heard about the attack on the World Trade Center. Korie has a(n) _____ memory of this event.
a. emotional
b. flashbulb
c. episodic
d. photographic

51. Existing evidence indicates that flashbulb memories are _____ accurate than regular episodic memories.
a. less
b. no more
c. more
d. emotionally less

52. When a person cannot recall the circumstances associated with a memory, it is called _____.
a. the misattribution effect
b. source misattribution
c. cryptomania
d. circumstantial amnesia

53. Recent high-profile cases of plagiarism are likely the result of the authors involved writing what they think are original thoughts but failing to realize that they have retrieved the thought from memory, a phenomenon known as _____.
a. confabulation
b. cryptomnesia
c. source amnesia
d. implicit memory failure

54. Evidence shows that eyewitness testimony _____ juries, police, and attorneys assume.
a. is much more accurate than
b. is just about as accurate as
c. is much less accurate than
d. is totally inaccurate in contrast to what

55. People can develop biased recall of events they have witnessed based on the types of questions they are asked about the event. This is termed _____.
a. confabulation
b. suggestibility
c. source misattribution
d. eyewitness transference

56. Confabulation refers to the _____.
a. intentional distortion of memory
b. memory distortions that occur as a result of damage to the hippocampus
c. the delusional belief that family members have been replaced by impostors
d. attempt to make a coherent story out of mistakenly recalled information

57. Psychologists who challenge the accuracy of recovered memories of childhood abuse will often argue that

_____.
a. there are too few of these cases to draw any conclusions
b. misguided therapists often push these ideas on their clients
c. people are faking these claims in an attempt to get sympathy and money
d. people do not ever forget anything that happens to them

THOUGHT QUESTIONS

1. What is the Atkinson–Shiffrin model of memory?

2. What is the difference between implicit and explicit memories?

3. What is the evidence regarding the accuracy of eyewitness testimony?

ANSWER KEY

Fill-in-the-Blank Questions

1. memory
2. modal memory model
3. sensory memory
4. short-term memory (STM)
5. working memory
6. long-term memory (LTM)
7. serial position effect
8. recency effect
9. primacy effect
10. explicit memory
11. declarative memory
12. episodic memory
13. semantic memory
14. implicit
15. procedural memory
16. repetition priming
17. retrieval
18. encoding
19. storage
20. maintenance rehearsal
21. elaborative rehearsal
22. schemas
23. encoding specificity principle
24. anterograde amnesia
25. consolidation
26. spatial memory
27. forgetting
28. transience
29. interference
30. blocking
31. absentmindedness
32. amnesia
33. retrograde amnesia
34. flashbulb memories
35. source misattribution
36. cryptomnesia
37. suggestibility
38. source amnesia
39. confabulation

Multiple-Choice Questions

1. b The three stages of memory of the information processing model of memory are sensory, short-term, and long-term memories.

2. c Sperling found that iconic memories fade after about 1/3 sec.

3. d Our iconic sensory memory is responsible for our viewing these points of light as continuous.

4. d The modal memory model is an information processing model of memory proposed by Atkinson and Shiffrin and this model is composed of three distinct stages of memory.

5. c Short-term memory holds information for a longer period of time than sensory memory, but it holds much less information.

6. a The model of memory proposed by Atkinson and Shiffrin consists of three distinct memory stores: sensory, short-term, long-term.

7. d Maintenance rehearsal is the process by which we keep information in STM.

8. b There are 11 digits if we include the number 1 in a long distance phone number and Miller defined the limits of short-term memory as 7 ± 2 pieces of information.

9. a Chunking helps us overcome the limits of STM.

10. c The three pieces of working memory are central executive, articulatory loop, visuospatial scratchpad.

11. a The recency effect describes the fact that it is easier to remember items from the end of a list rather than from the middle of the list.

12. a The primacy effect is our ability to better remember information at the beginning of a list than information in the middle of the list.

13. a Distributed practice, studying spread out over a period of time, leads to better recall of what was studied.

14. c Explicit memory refers to the effortful process of storing information and declarative memories are the contents that are stored by that process.

15. d Episodic memories are memories of our personal events.

16. d Implicit memory is the process involved in the automatic storing of information.

17. d Procedural memory or motor memory is our memory of how to do tasks.

18. c Semantic memory represents our knowledge of facts.

19. a The false fame is a demonstration of the effects of implicit memory, subjects remembered the names but could not recall where they had encountered the names and so concluded that the individuals were famous.

20. b Whether or not information gets stored in LTM depends on how meaningful is the information.

21. a Theorists view memory as being analogous to information processing in a computer.

22. a Encoding is the first of three memory processes and involves transforming our experiences into representations.

23. c Storage is the retention of information over time.

24. b Schemas are hypothetical cognitive structures that help guide our attention and sort out incoming information about the world.

25. d The more meaning that a piece of information has the easier it will be to retrieve that information.

26. b Maintenance rehearsal is the simple repeating of information over and over again.

27. c Elaborative rehearsal involves deeper processing than maintenance rehearsal.

28. c By engaging in elaborative rehearsal there will be a greater depth of processing leading to better memory for the material studied.

29. b Nodes are individual units of information within a network of associations.

30. a The idea of a network of associations is an important model of how memory is organized.

31. c Context dependent memory refers to the fact that our retrieving memories in the location where the memories were stored provides cues that aid in retrieval.

32. c Any stimulus that is encoded with a memory can aid in the retrieval of that memory.

33. a Context-dependent memory suggests that thinking about where you studied will help you retrieve information during the exam.

34. c State dependent memory says that our retrieval of information will be better if we have the same internal state at retrieval as we did during encoding.

35. d The engram is the term Lashley used to specify where in the brain memories were stored.

36. d Equipotentiality refers to the idea that all regions of the brain have an equal role in memory storage.

37. c The hippocampus, amygdala, and rhinal cortex are all found within the medial temporal lobe.

38. d The bilateral removal of portions of H. M.'s temporal lobes resulted in his experiencing minor retrograde amnesia and a massive anterograde amnesia.

39. b H. M.'s behavior shows that he can learn tasks even though he has no conscious memory of ever having done the task.

40. c H. M. suffered massive anterograde amnesia as a result of his surgery; however, he still has most of his memories of past events.

41. a The frontal lobes play many important roles in memory, including the ability to remember the time sequence of events.

42. c A study by Wagner et al. (1998) found that words that were remembered later were associated with greater the activation of the frontal lobes at the time of encoding.

43. c While early work suggested that there were hemispheric differences in encoding and retrieval, recent work suggests that it is the nature of the material that determines hemispheric activation.

44. d The release of epinephrine produces a release of glucose which in turn enhances memory.

45. a Activation of the amygdala plays an important role in emotional memory.

46. c Competition among memories or interference seems to be the most important factor in forgetting.

47. c Anterograde amnesia results in an inability to recall new events.

48. b Anterograde amnesia is the inability to remember new events.

49. c Childhood amnesia refers to the general inability to remember events from the first three years of life.

50. b Flashbulb memories are particularly intense memories for the circumstances surrounding the events in which one first learns of a surprising or emotionally intense event.

51. b Research indicates that flashbulb memories are not any more accurate than other types of memory.

52. b Source misattribution involves an inability to recall the circumstances associated with a particular memory.

53. b The phenomenon being described is cryptomnesia, a type of source misattribution.

54. c There are a number of factors that make eyewitness testimony not very accurate.

55. b Elizabeth Loftus has demonstrated that memories for events can be altered depending on the types of questions asked about the event; this is what Schachter would term the sin of suggestibility.

56. d Confabulation has been described as honest lying; individuals mistakenly recall information and try to construct a coherent story that makes sense of these mistaken recollections.

57. b While the topic of repressed memories is highly controversial, some of the techniques suggested by therapists to recover these memories are likely to lead to the recall of events that never occurred.

Thought Questions

1. The Atkinson–Shiffrin model of memory is an information-processing model of memory and consists of three distinct memory stores: sensory memory, short-term memory, and long-term memory. Your answer should include information about the time course of each memory system as well as how much information each memory store holds.

2. Implicit and explicit memories are memory processes, as opposed to the contents of memory. Explicit memories are processes that involve effort, while implicit memories do not require conscious effort. Examples of explicit memories are episodic and semantic memories, while examples of implicit memories are procedural memories and repetition priming.

3. Eyewitness testimony should be viewed with caution as there is evidence to suggest that these memories are prone to error. Among the factors involved are difficulties in making cross-ethnic identification, suggestibility, and the fact that eyewitnesses' confidence in their testimony does not predict the accuracy of their testimony.

CHAPTER 8 | Cognition

In Chapter 8, the authors of the textbook deal with one of the most vexing of all psychology issues—cognition. How do we think about things in our mind? How can we share this with others? How can we study the mind scientifically? We all have a sense of personal awareness, but it is difficult to share that sense with others. It also is difficult to explain how phenomenal awareness arises from the workings of individual neurons and various sensory systems. Although rooted in psychological science, the study of cognition is central to the interests of philosophers, computer scientists, evolutionary biologists, and statisticians. You will see that the study of cognition is a work in progress. The authors address this complex issue by considering four different aspects of higher cognitive function: how the mind represents information, how humans solve problems and make decisions, what intelligence reflects, and how consciousness is studied.

How Does the Mind Represent Information?

The initial section of the chapter looks at how the brain represents information or, rather, what is there when we are thinking? The popular view is that these representations take the form of *picturelike images*. Other researchers have found limitations to this view and contend that the representations are *propositional;* that is, they are based on factual knowledge of the world. The answer probably includes both ideas and the notion that representations exist at different hierarchical levels. It is known that these mental representations activate different patterns of neural activity and that learning involves the strengthening of the *connectionist networks*. Having information stored in these networks likely has an adaptive capacity in that we are not as susceptible to damage to individual neurons. The authors also address how we or-

ganize our knowledge based on *defining attributes* and *prototype models*. This promotes *cognitive economy* and reduces the amount of information we need to store in long-term memory. Finally, it also is apparent we store information in *schemas* or *scripts* based on appropriate behavior in a situational context.

How Do We Solve Problems and Make Decisions?

The authors investigate problem solving and decision making as other ways psychological science can shed light on the issue of cognition. They present the Gestalt perspective that making decisions is influenced by how one structures the problem and then realizes the solution (i.e., insight). Their contention that people tend to view problems from narrow perspectives and that insight occurs when one restructures the problem in a novel way is captured in today's business cliché to Think outside the box. Information-processing models of decision making emphasize that problems have a defined *solution space,* or number of pathways that can be taken toward achieving a solution. It is interesting that they characterize humans as *limited capacity* thinkers who must use heuristics, or shortcuts, to solve problems. *Normative theories* of decision making suggest that we are rational beings who come to solutions based on objective as well as subjective probabilities. However, even those theories recognize our inherent limitations. For example, *Bayes's theorem* demonstrates how we underestimate the impact of new information in making decisions, a fact that will later explain how we continue to maintain prejudicial ideas despite evidence to the contrary. Finally, *descriptive theories* of decision making illustrate how we are not always rational in our assessment of problems and how we are heavily influenced by issues of loss aversion and regret.

What Does Intelligence Reflect?

The next section addresses intelligence and its assessment, one of the more controversial issues in psychology. The authors trace the history of the IQ test from Galton's Anthropometric Laboratory to various modern views of intelligence. As you study the different approaches to defining intelligence, summarized in the table below, pay special attention to the skills that each approach defines as relevant and adaptive.

Table 8.1 DEFINING INTELLIGENCE

Intelligence Perspective	Skills Assessed
Galton	neural speed, sensory acuity
Traditional IQ tests (e.g., Binet)	verbal, quantitative, analytical
Cattell	fluid and crystallized intelligence
Gardner	musical, verbal, mathematical/ logical, spatial, kinesthetic, intrapersonal, interpersonal

A salient problem with IQ tests is that they were originally designed to predict success in school. As they tend to measure the abilities that are associated with school performance, they still are fair predictors of this criterion. Unfortunately, the term *intelligence* has gotten tied up with overall "smartness" and societal worth. No single test could measure up to this relative standard, and it is a flawed view to believe that a single score could accurately represent the broad range of human cognitive abilities. Finally, it is apparent that both genes and environment contribute to intelligence as measured by IQ scores (i.e., the nature versus nurture debate). When comparing individuals raised in the same culture and socioeconomic class, genes probably contribute more to differences in IQ scores. When comparing individuals across cultures and socioeconomic classes, environment is the better predictor.

Can We Study Consciousness?

The authors present a final view of cognition by comparing the study of the mind versus the brain. The view of *dualism,* championed by Descartes, is that the mind and brain are separated entities. The view of *physicalism,* or *materialism,* which is necessary for an empirical study of cognition, is that the mind and brain are a unitary system. While investigators have proposed several elements of consciousness to facilitate its investigation, research into *unconscious processes* has begun to shed some light into its functioning. Studies of *subliminal perception* indicate that we can be influenced by stimuli of which we are not fully aware. This may be the mechanism for the classic Freudian slip. In addition, the phenomenon of blindsight—visual capacities without visual awareness—suggests that awareness may not be located in a single brain area.

FILL-IN-THE-BLANK QUESTIONS

1. _____ the act of thinking

2. _____ memory for factual knowledge

3. _____ idea that mental representations are based on factual knowledge of the world

4. _____ understanding neural implementation of mental representations by looking at patterns of activation

5. _____ grouping objects together based on shared properties reduces the amount of objective knowledge that must be held in memory

6. _____ model in which each concept is defined by a list of necessary features an object must have to be categorized under that concept

7. _____ common situations can be broken down into a series of linked events and people have specific roles within the situational context

8. _____ school of psychology that emphasizes insight and problem structure as aspects of human problem solving

9. _____ viewing a problem in a new way

10. _____ overall number of different paths that can be taken toward finding a solution to a problem

11. _____ maximum amount of information and operations a system can handle

12. _____ shortcuts to problem solving

13. _____ model of decision making that focuses on tendency to misinterpret and misrepresent underlying probabilities

14. _____ principle that the rational decision maker will always choose the most desirable alternative

15. _____ principle that decisions between alternatives are based on differences between them and that factors common to both are ignored

16. _____ statistical probabilities that can be computed for a given alternative

17. _____ individual's impression of probabilities that may or may not coincide with reality

18. _____ predicted frequency of an event occurring

19. _____ unequal weighting of costs and benefits in decision making

20. _____ global term that includes a range of different abilities that can be equated with how one measures on a particular ability scale

21. _____ IQ test pioneer who linked intelligence to speed of neural responses and sensory acuity

22. _____ determined by comparing a given child's test score with the average score for children of each chronological age

23. _____ intelligence that is associated with the ability to understand relationships between things in the absence of overt experience with them

24. _____ intelligence that reflects knowledge acquired through experience

25. _____ originator of idea that we have at least seven intelligences

26. _____ assertion that the mind is a thing physically distinct from the brain

27. _____ assertion that the mind and brain are an inseparable, unitary system

28. _____ subjective, phenomenological properties of our conscious awareness

29. _____ information processing in the brain that is outside one's sentient, mental awareness

30. _____ stimuli to which one's sensory system responds but never enters into consciousness

31. _____ unconscious thoughts are suddenly expressed at inappropriate times

MULTIPLE-CHOICE QUESTIONS

1. One compromise to the debate over the form of mental representations is that _____ is analogous to a higher-level programming language whereas _____ is more similar to a lower-level machine language.
   a. visual imagery; propositional knowledge
   b. distributed representation; propositional knowledge
   c. visual imagery; phenomenological representation
   d. distributed representation; phenomenological representation

2. Jen, Bill, and Todd were having their morning orange juice before class. They were discussing how, despite being incredibly tired from a long night of studying, they were able to perform the fairly complex activity of drinking juice without any problems. Jen, the smart one, suggested that it was likely due to the fact that they had performed this act many times and thus had developed strong _____.
   a. prototype models
   b. connectionist networks
   c. defining attributes
   d. neural propositions

3. Freddie knows that Toyotas, Hondas, Buicks, and Fords are all cars. Despite their differences, he knows that all are forms of transportation that get him somewhere quickly; therefore, he doesn't need to store this information in his brain for each and every car. This natural and efficient tendency to group items into categories promotes _____.

   a. phenomenological understanding
   b. insight
   c. cognitive economy
   d. problem structure

4. Freddie can instantly recognize that Camrys, Accords, Centurys, and Festivas are cars because they share the same necessary features such as four tires, doors, a steering wheel, internal combustion engine, etc. His ability to classify them based on their necessary features characterizes the _____ model of object categorization.
   a. defining attribute
   b. prototype
   c. exemplar
   d. distributed

5. Freddie also recognizes that Jeeps, pickup trucks, Hummers, and sports utility vehicles are cars even though they may not be as representative of that category as a four-door family sedan. This ability to be flexible in classifying cars reflects the development of _____ models for object categorization.
   a. attribute
   b. prototype
   c. connectionist
   d. defining features

6. Gunther is going to miss his general psychology exam because he is having an operation. He knows he must contact his professor before the exam, arrange a make-up time, and bring her written documentation of his surgery. His knowledge of how to act appropriately in this situation is predicted by _____.
   a. insight theory
   b. prototype models
   c. script theory
   d. defining attribute models

7. Wilson was stranded on a deserted island with no shoes. It suddenly occurred to him that he could wrap thick leaves around his feet and tie them off with vines as a crude substitute. This sudden realization of a solution to a problem is termed _____.
   a. flashbulb phenomenon
   b. holistic understanding
   c. Gestalt solution
   d. insight

8. Often people have difficulty because they tend to view problems from narrow perspectives. The current cliché to think outside the box illustrates the importance of _____, which concerns how one views or conceptualizes a problem.
   a. problem structure
   b. heuristics
   c. descriptive models
   d. perspect analysis

9. When *Apollo 13* malfunctioned and the astronauts were dangerously stranded in space ("Houston, we have a problem"), flight engineers had to focus on a number of different paths toward solving the problem and the sequential steps it would take for a solution. This emphasis on the solution space of a problem is characteristic of the _____ model of problem solving.
   a. Gestalt
   b. information-processing
   c. semantic
   d. structural

10. Chipper is a player on a local semiprofessional baseball team. To be able to hit well, he should consider the angle of the pitcher's arm, speed of the baseball, spin of the baseball, mass of the ball, etc. However, he just guesses where it will be and swings toward that spot. These shortcuts, which minimize the step-by-step thinking necessary to solve a problem, are known as _____.
    a. holistics
    b. heuristics
    c. synergistics
    d. mnemonics

11. Drew is diligently hunting for a lifelong partner. A _____ model of decision making would limit this search to someone who is kind, shares Drew's values, and has sufficient financial resources to contribute to the relationship.
    a. descriptive
    b. normative
    c. holistic
    d. insightful

12. _____ theory is an example of a normative model in which decisions are made by pure reason using the five basic principles of ordering of alternatives, dominance, cancellation, transitivity, and invariance.
    a. base rate
    b. expected utility
    c. descriptive
    d. vulcanistic

13. Medhi grew up in an environment in which people did not help each other. As he has grown older and moved away from home, he has seen many more instances of helping behavior; however, he continues to doubt the altruistic actions of others. This tendency to underestimate the effect of new information on updating base rates is predicted by _____ theorem.
    a. Neumann's
    b. Tversky's
    c. Seinfeld's
    d. Bayes's

14. John is involved in a romantic relationship with Tina. The costs for the relationship (time, effort, money) are about the same as the benefits (companionship, support, future wife); however, he is thinking about breaking up with her. The greater effect of the costs in his analysis is predicted by the _____ theory of decision making.
    a. prospect
    b. social exchange
    c. aversiveness
    d. masculine

15. Matt is deciding whether to study for his general psychology exam or go to a great party. He can imagine the different outcomes for each decision and how he might feel in a process known as _____.
    a. elation theory
    b. anticipatory reasoning
    c. counterfactual reasoning
    d. gambler's cognitions

16. Madeline is a contestant on a popular game show. She already has won $5,000 but has the opportunity to go for the grand prize of $25,000. However, if she fails she will wind up with nothing. She decides to play it safe and stick with the $5,000. This behavior is predicted by the _____ theory of decision making.
    a. regret
    b. counterfactual
    c. conservative
    d. conflict avoidance

17. Which of the following situations inspired Alfred Binet to develop the first modern intelligence test?
    a. he was trying to assess which French schoolchildren needed extra attention and instruction
    b. he was trying to determine which members of the U. S. military were officer material for World War I
    c. he was trying to develop a test for giftedness for the Stanford school system
    d. he was trying to develop an admissions exam to pick students for Stanford University

18. Pete is having his IQ tested to see if he deserves the title of convenience store Employee of the Month. Pete has a mental age of 20 and a chronological age of 10. Using Binet's formula, we calculate his IQ as _____.
    a. 50
    b. 200
    c. 100
    d. we don't have enough information to calculate his IQ

19. Stacy is tired of being called a "loser," so she decides to take an intelligence test. She gets her results back and goes to show them to her friends to prove how worthy she is. They tell her that, at best, IQ scores can predict only which of the following?

a. occupational success
b. intelligence in one's ethnic group
c. intrapersonal intelligence
d. success in U.S. schools

20. Charlie has such incredible mathematical and spatial abilities that he can multiply 10-digit numbers in his head as well as compute the weekday of a date 200 years from now. However, he cannot care for his daily needs and must live in an institution. Individuals like this who are highly proficient in one area yet terribly inadequate in others are known as _____.
    a. prodigies
    b. imbeciles
    c. autistics
    d. savants

21. John is taking an IQ test when he is asked the definition of a *bush hog*. Fortunately, he grew up on a farm and knows that it is a term for a mower deck that is pulled by a tractor. This test item, which concerns knowledge acquired through experience, is assessing John's _____ intelligence.
    a. fluid
    b. crystallized
    c. linguistic
    d. kinesthetic

22. Brandon and his friends are arguing about the greatest basketball player of all time. Brandon contends that it is Michael Jordan because he had such exceptional body control while shooting the ball. Brandon says that if there were such a measure, Michael Jordan would be near the top of Gardner's _____ type of intelligence.
    a. vestibular
    b. spatial
    c. kinesthetic
    d. athletic

23. A controversial topic within psychology is whether genetics or the environment plays a greater role in determining intelligence (as measured by IQ scores). This controversy is also known as the _____ debate.
    a. intellectual dualism
    b. mind–body
    c. psychophysiological
    d. nature versus nurture

24. Dr. Wechsler and Dr. Binet are arguing about the role that genes and the environment play on IQ scores. Wechsler presents research that indicates the genes are playing the greater role in IQ scores. The most reliable population for this finding is _____.
    a. identical twins who were reared in the same or different households
    b. unrelated people who were reared in the same familial environment due to adoption

c. individuals who have been raised in the same culture and socioeconomic class
d. individuals who have been raised in different cultures and socioeconomic classes

25. Dr. Wechsler and Dr. Binet are arguing about the role that genes and the environment play on IQ scores. Binet presents research that indicates the environment is playing the greater role in IQ scores. The most reliable population for this finding is _____.
    a. identical twins who were reared in the same or different households
    b. unrelated people who were reared in the same familial environment due to adoption
    c. individuals who have been raised in the same culture and socioeconomic class
    d. individuals who have been raised in different cultures and socioeconomic classes

26. Crystal is interested in going to graduate school in psychology. Her primary interest is in the scientific study of consciousness. Which of the following philosophical stances toward consciousness is she most likely to adopt?
    a. dualism
    b. materialism
    c. existentialism
    d. Platonic

27. Romeo is hopelessly in love. He is sickening his friends with the description of his beautiful Juliet. He is trying to describe the blueness of her eyes as a river, as the sky, as the color azure. He gives up, and the conversation takes a more scientific turn when he tells his friends they can never share the _____ or properties of his subjective, phenomenological experience.
    a. physicalism
    b. qualia
    c. blindsight
    d. icons

28. Which of the following is not one of the aspects of consciousness that allows its empirical study?
    a. sentience
    b. unitary experience
    c. dualism
    d. intentionality

29. In the throes of passion, Julie accidentally called her boyfriend by her previous boyfriend's name. She said there was nothing to this. Her boyfriend stated that there may be some scientific evidence that her Freudian slip was not accidental from research on _____.
    a. blindsight
    b. subliminal perception
    c. subconscious processing
    d. paranormal processing

30. Steve is blind due to damage to his primary visual cortex. It is interesting that when he is presented a moving dot in his blind field, he reports that he sees nothing but can reliably guess which way the dot was moving. This rare phenomenon of vision without awareness is known as _____.
    a. optic neuralgia
    b. tachistoscopic vision
    c. hysterical blindness
    d. blindsight

THOUGHT QUESTION

Suppose your were asked to construct an intelligence test for the following groups of children: (1) one from inner-city Philadelphia, (2) one from a rural town in Iowa, and (3) one from a remote area in Africa. Instead of predicting success in school, your test is to find the smartest, most adaptive, and most useful children in each group. What types of test questions would you include and why? How would the questions differ for the three groups? Relate your test questions to some of the problems in IQ testing today.

ANSWER KEY

Fill-in-the-Blank Questions

1. cognition
2. semantic memory
3. propositional
4. distributed representation
5. cognitive economy
6. defining attribute model
7. script theory
8. Gestalt
9. restructuring
10. solution space
11. capacity limits
12. heuristics
13. descriptive
14. dominance
15. cancellation
16. objective probabilities
17. subjective probabilities
18. base rate
19. loss aversion
20. intelligence
21. Sir Francis Galton
22. mental age
23. fluid
24. crystallized
25. Howard Gardner
26. dualism
27. materialism
28. qualia
29. unconscious
30. subliminal perception
31. Freudian slip

Multiple-Choice Questions

1. a A hierarchical view of mental representations is that visual imagery is like a higher-level programming language, whereas propositional knowledge is more similar to a lower-level machine language.

2. b Strong connectionist networks result from frequent patterns of neural activation.

3. c The tendency to group items together based on shared properties promotes cognitive economy.; this reduces the amount of object knowledge that must be held in memory.

4. a The defining attribute model indicates that each concept is defined by a list of necessary features an object must have to be categorized under that concept.

5. b The more natural approach of prototype models recognizes that some members of a category are more representative than others.

6. c Script theory proposes that we develop schemas as to how to act appropriately in various situations.

7. d Insight is the term for suddenly realizing the solution to a problem.

8. a The Gestalt notion of problem structure relates to how one views or conceptualizes a problem.

9. b Information-processing model of problem solving is based on a solution space.

10. b Heuristics are shortcuts to problem solving that minimize the thinking necessary to move from step to step in a solution space.

11. b Normative models focus on rational behavior and humans as optimal decision makers.

12. b Expected utility theory is an example of a normative model of decision making in which decisions are made using pure reason.

13. d Bayes's theorem is a formula that predicts that humans tend to underestimate the impact of new information on updating base rates.

14. a Prospect theory addresses the unequal weighting of costs and benefits such that the concern over costs typically has a larger impact.

15. c Counterfactual reasoning allows one to imagine the different outcomes of a decision.

16. a Regret theory states that we make decisions based on which imagined outcome will produce the greatest elation and least regret.

17. a Binet was commissioned by the French Ministry of Education to identify schoolchildren who needed extra attention and instruction.

18. b Binet's formula for IQ is mental age ÷ chronological age × 100; therefore, Pete's IQ is 200.

19. d Because it assesses similar abilities, IQ scores continue to be a good predictor of success in U.S. schools; however, it has not been correlated with

other indices or been a representative measure of the gamut of human intellectual capacities.

20. d Savants are individuals who show exceptional abilities in one area but minimal intellectual capacities in most domains.

21. b Crystallized intelligence concerns knowledge that is acquired through experience.

22. c Gardner used the term *kinesthetic intelligence* to refer to individuals with exceptional body control.

23. d The controversy over whether genetics or the environment plays a greater role in IQ is also known as the nature versus nurture debate.

24. c The most consistent research that genes play a greater role in IQ comes from individuals who have been raised in the same culture and socioeconomic class.

25. d The most consistent research that the environment play a greater role in IQ comes from individuals who have been raised in different cultures and socioeconomic classes.

26. b The scientific approach to consciousness is based on the philosophical stance of materialism, that is, that one can study the mind through studying the brain.

27. b Qualia are the properties of one's subjective, phenomenological awareness.

28. c The aspects of consciousness that allow its empirical study are sentience, access to information, unitary experience, self-knowledge, and intentionality; dualism is not one of those.

29. b Research on subliminal perception reveals that we are frequently unaware of the myriad different things that can affect our decisions about what we say and do and that may underlie the classic Freudian slip.

30. d Blindsight is the continuance of some visual capacities in the absence of any visual awareness.

Thought Question

Answers will vary.

CHAPTER 9 | Motivation

GUIDE TO THE READING

In Chapter 9, the authors present an overview of the topic of motivation, or the processes that energize and sustain behavior. Motivation has a long history within psychological science as an attempt to answer the question of why we do the things we do. Be forewarned that explanatory terms like *instincts, motives, needs, drives,* and *rewards* can sound very similar in that they all are involved in regulating behavior. The authors address this vagueness by considering the cognitive, social, and cultural context for each concept. In addition, they present recent findings from behavioral neuroscience to illuminate which neural systems are involved in motivation. Evidence from each area continues to support the adaptive and purposeful function of most of our behavior. Finally, the authors take a more detailed look at eating and sleeping, two of our more basic processes that energize and sustain a substantial amount of activity.

How Does Motivation Activate, Direct, and Sustain Action?

The chapter begins with a general overview of motivation and describes the four essential qualities of motivational states: They *energize* and *direct* behaviors, help the organism to *persist* toward a goal, and exist in varying *strengths*. Most motivational theories view behaviors as a way of maintaining equilibrium, and several aspects of this process (homeostasis, negative feedback model, set point) are explored. Pay special attention to the difference in emphasis between the more biologically based idea of *instincts* versus the psychologically based idea of *needs*. Both concepts involve the initiation of behavior; however, instincts focus more on unlearned, automatic actions, whereas needs allow more leeway for environmental influence. *Hedonism,* the tendency to seek

pleasure and avoid pain, is a general motivational principle that extends back at least to the time of the ancient Greeks. The idea was integrated into Freudian motivational theory with the concept of the *pleasure principle*. Finally, the authors present several examples of how hedonism is adaptive in that it promotes survival and reproduction.

How Do Cognitive, Social, and Cultural Factors Influence Motivation?

The next section of the chapter moves further away from the idea of motivation as simple biological instincts and considers additional environmental influences that activate and sustain behavior. We are motivated by *extrinsic* factors such as incentives and rewards. However, we also are motivated by *intrinsic* factors such as novelty, play, and creativity. A surprising research finding in this area is Mark Lepper's contention that rewards can actually undermine intrinsically motivated behavior. Psychological scientists continue to investigate the ramifications of this for education, business, and child-rearing. Individuals are also motivated to attain personal *goals,* and the *self-regulation* of behavior is the process by which people initiate, adjust, or stop actions in this pursuit. Goals that are challenging, difficult, and specific seem to be the most productive. They also give rise to feelings of self-efficacy or the expectancy that your efforts will lead to success. Self-awareness of one's personal standards also serves to regulate behavior. The process of *deindividuation* occurs when self-awareness is low, and it can result in some surprising disinhibited behavior (e.g., spring break, athletic events). Finally, the self-regulatory process of delay of gratification is investigated. The understanding of this crucial, adaptive function has increased with recent advances in behavioral neuroscience.

What Neural Systems Are Involved in Motivation?

The idea of neural mechanisms underlying motivation is continued in the next section, and the authors give you an idea of where future research in motivation is headed. *Dopamine reward* pathways strongly influence motivation as they satisfy drive states. Structures in the limbic system are involved in emotion, and the hypothalamus regulates several survival behaviors. Damage to the hypothalamus results in problems with eating, aggression, and sexual behavior. The frontal lobes are strongly involved in formulating goals, plans, and strategies. A fascinating research finding discussed in this section is Antonio Damasio's work on *somatic markers* that influence decision making. There are numerous examples in literature and contemporary language of going with your gut feeling instead of clearly rational processes when making decisions. Damasio's work supports the idea that there is a bodily reaction that occurs when contemplating outcomes and that these feelings serve an adaptive function. It just *feels* right!

What Factors Motivate Human Eating Behavior?

Eating is presented as a basic motivational behavior that is strongly biologically based for survival; however, it also is heavily influenced by cultural factors. The motivation for variety ensures a healthy diet, but acquired taste aversions protect us from potential danger. The hypothalamus is the brain area with the greatest influence on eating, and damage to this structure can result in severe overeating (*hyperphagia*) or undereating (*aphagia*). The influence of the brain on eating is particularly evident in gourmand syndrome, in which neural damage results in an obsession with food and its preparation. The conflict between scientific data on eating and societal views is seen with the *stigma of obesity*. In addition, extreme standards of thinness that are presented in the media are difficult, if not impossible, for most people to obtain. This can lead to the dangerous and mostly futile behavior of dieting. Fewer than 1% of individuals who lose weight are able to maintain it over 5 years. Part of this is attributable to the body's tendency to maintain a set point as a natural defense against weight loss. In addition, chronic dieters or restrained eaters tend to easily abandon their diets and go on bouts of overeating. Finally, chronic dieting and incorporation of unrealistic societal messages can lead one to develop the eating disorders of anorexia nervosa, bulimia nervosa, and binge eating disorder.

What Is Sleep?

The final section of the chapter has a more detailed look at the complex topic of sleep. When one considers the amount of time we engage in this activity, it is truly surprising that most of the scientific information on sleep is fairly recent. Sleep is an altered state of consciousness that is initiated by biological processes. Our brain waves become slower and more rhythmic as we progress from stage 1 to stage 4 sleep. After about 90 min of sleep, we venture into the cycle of *REM sleep,* also known as paradoxical sleep because of the discrepancy between a sleeping body and an activated brain. Although many view it as a nuisance, sleep appears to be an important survival behavior. Restorative theory suggests that sleep allows the body to rest and repair itself. Circadian rhythm theory proposes that sleep keeps animals quiet and inactive during times of the day when they are in greatest danger. Substantial research also indicates that sleep is important for the consolidation of learning. Students should pay particular attention to the research finding that learning new information occurs only after 6 hr of sleep. This brings into question the efficiency of cramming all night for an exam. Finally, the chapter investigates the perplexing topic of *dreaming,* which, like all of sleeping, is highly regulated by biological factors. The brain actually sends signals to paralyze the body during REM sleep that aid in preventing us from acting out our dreams. People have been interested in the meaning of dreams since ancient times, and there are many historical examples of discoveries and decisions made on the basis of them. Three dream theories are presented along with their supporting evidence. It is interesting that the Freudian theory of dream analysis, which is very well known among the general public, has virtually no scientific support.

Table 9.1 THEORIES OF DREAM INTERPRETATION

Dream Theory	Proposed Meaning of Dreams
Sigmund Freud	symbolic representation of hidden conflicts
Activation–synthesis hypothesis	mind making sense of random neural firings
Evolved threat rehearsal	allow people to rehearse coping strategies

FILL-IN-THE-BLANK QUESTIONS

1. _____ area of psychological science that is concerned with how behavior is initiated, directed, and sustained

2. _____ desired outcome associated with some specific object or future behavioral intention

3. _____ the tendency for body functions to maintain equilibrium

4. _____ unlearned, automatic actions that are triggered by external cues

5. _____ states of deficiency that lead to goal-directed behaviors

6. _____ area of psychology in which people are viewed as holistic beings who strive toward personal fulfillment

7. _____ generic term used to describe physiological activation or increased autonomic responses

8. _____ mental representations of future outcomes

9. _____ motivation that emphasizes the external goals toward which an activity is directed, such as drive reduction or reward

10. _____ involves constructing novel images, synthesizing two or more disparate ideas or concepts, and applying existing knowledge to solving new problems

11. _____ process by which people initiate, adjust, or stop actions in order to attain personal goals

12. _____ desire to do well relative to standards of excellence

13. _____ test-operate–test-exit

14. _____ process of transcending immediate temptations to achieve long-term goals

15. _____ brain area that releases dopamine in response to objects that satisfy drive states

16. _____ theory that there are excitatory and inhibitory centers in the hypothalamus that regulate motivated behaviors

17. _____ chemical process by which food is converted into energy

18. _____ diminished eating behavior that leads to weight loss and eventual death

19. _____ specialized receptors that monitor the extent to which glucose is taken into the cells to be used for energy

20. _____ theory that proposes a set point for body fat such that deviations initiate compensatory behaviors

21. _____ chronic dieters who are prone to excessive eating in certain situations

22. _____ eating disorder associated with an excessive fear of becoming fat and a refusal to eat

23. _____ eating disorder associated with alternations between dieting, binge eating, and one or more compensatory behaviors

24. _____ eating disorder wherein individuals engage in binge eating but do not purge

25. _____ brain wave pattern characteristic of being awake

26. _____ brain wave pattern characteristic of stage 1 sleep

27. _____ brain wave pattern characteristic of stage 3 and 4 sleep

28. _____ sleep disorder in which people's mental health and ability to function is compromised by their inability to sleep

29. _____ another term for REM sleep, given because of disparity between a sleeping body and an activated brain

30. _____ type of sleep in which cerebral hemispheres take turns sleeping

31. _____ theory that sleep has evolved to keep animals quiet and inactive during times of the day when there is greatest danger

32. _____ region of the hypothalamus that regulates the biological clock for sleeping

33. _____ region of the brain stem that sends signals to the spinal cord that block movements during REM sleep

34. _____ altered state of consciousness in which images and fantasies are confused with reality

35. _____ evolutionary theory wherein dreams allow individuals to simulate threatening events and practice coping strategies

MULTIPLE-CHOICE QUESTIONS

1. Which of the following is NOT one of the essential qualities of motivational states?
   a. motivational states maintain homeostasis
   b. motivational states are energizing
   c. motivational states directive
   d. motivational states help the organism persist toward a goal

2. Tiffany is doing some outdoor work and begins to perspire. This regulatory mechanism that helps the body cool down and return to a specific set point is an example of a _____.
   a. releasing stimulus
   b. directive pheromone
   c. thermostatic instinct
   d. negative feedback model

3. When Peter Parker turned into Spiderman, he immediately began capturing his enemies by spinning them in webs. This automatic action that is triggered by external cues is known as a _____.
   a. set point
   b. fixed-action pattern
   c. releasing stimulus
   d. growth need

4. Mahatma is an old man who is evaluating his life. His dreams and aspirations have been achieved as he has raised a wonderful family, contributed to his

community, and made the world a little better place to live. According to humanistic psychology, Mahatma has achieved _____.
a. nirvana
b. peak experience
c. self-actualization
d. flow

5. Martin is working on his personal growth by taking continuing education classes at the local college. However, when he loses his job, he has to quit school to pursue work and engage in other activities to make ends meet. His behavior in which survival needs take precedence over personal growth needs is an example of the Maslowian concept of a _____.
a. triangular pattern
b. need hierarchy
c. humanistic shift
d. personal growth obstacle

6. According to Hull's drive theory, the likelihood that a behavior will occur is due to both drive and _____.
a. motivation
b. goals
c. need
d. habit

7. The Greeks originated the general motivational principle of _____ in which individuals seek pleasure and avoid pain.
a. id fantasies
b. drive reduction
c. hedonism
d. epicureanism

8. Dexter's friends are trying to understand his motivation for studying so much. Although they come up with different theories, they agree that getting A's on his exams serves as a huge _____.
a. incentive
b. drive reduction
c. intrinsic motivator
d. fixed-action pattern

9. Many professional athletes talk about how they would play their sport even if they were not getting paid. When talking like this, they are referring to their _____ motivation for playing.
a. extrinsic
b. deficiency
c. growth
d. intrinsic

10. Caleb is doing well in school and enjoys learning for its own sake. His overinvolved father decides to reward him by giving him $20 for every A he brings home. Based on Lepper's research on rewarding intrinsically

motivated behaviors, which of the following would we predict from Caleb?
a. his school performance would improve due to the reward
b. his school performance would stay the same as rewards do not influence intrinsically motivated behavior
c. his school performance would worsen as rewards tend to undermine intrinsically motivated behavior
d. he would experience a greater sense of personal control and competence due to the rewards

11. Susan is motivated to do well on her exams. However, she notices that if she arrives too early for an exam she starts to get anxious because of all the panic around her. This anxiety tends to interfere with her test performance; therefore, she arrives right when class begins. Susan's performance as a function of her level of arousal is predicted by the _____.
a. hedonic value theory
b. Maslow–Rogers theory of deficiency motivation
c. negative feedback theory of arousal
d. Yerkes–Dodson law

12. Tiger believes that if he works on the mechanics of his swing, practices his putting, and visualizes every shot, he will be successful at golf and win many tournaments. When it comes to golf, Tiger has a high level of _____.
a. self-esteem
b. self-efficacy
c. deindividuation
d. self-awareness

13. Karen attends Mardi Gras in New Orleans and is shocked by the wild behavior exhibited in the streets. Some of her friends act in ways they never would back at school. It seems that the crowd and their party masks have lowered their self-awareness of personal standards in a process known as _____.
a. cold cognitions
b. deindividuation
c. reveler's phenomenon
d. optimal level of arousal

14. When it comes to delay of gratification, hot cognitions are to the amygdala as cold cognitions are to the _____.
a. reticular formation
b. hypothalamus
c. thalamus
d. hippocampus

15. The area of the prefrontal cortex that is involved in demanding tasks, particularly those that are novel or involve personal choices is the _____.
a. hippocampus

b. amygdala

c. anterior cingulate

d. hypothalamus

16. April is downloading copyrighted music off the Internet. While she knows that all of her friends are doing it, she has a gut feeling that she is doing something wrong. This bodily reaction is also known as a _____.

a. somatic marker

b. conversion reaction

c. psychophysiological trace

d. dorsolateral consequence

17. Which of the following is NOT one of the three types of energy from food that is made available to the body?

a. lipids

b. antioxidants

c. amino acids

d. glucose

18. Reggie the Rat is growing extremely obese. He suspects that Dr. Scalpel has been doing a little surgery on him while he is sleeping. Because he continues to eat great quantities of food, he thinks Dr. Scalpel may have lesioned the _____ region of his hypothalamus.

a. dorsolateral

b. orbitofrontal

c. ventromedial

d. lateral

19. Emeril suffered a stroke that resulted in damage to his limbic system and right frontal lobes. He previously was interested in accounting but now his life revolves around fine food and its preparation. We suspect that Emeril may be suffering from _____.

a. gourmand syndrome

b. hyperphagia

c. chef's compensation disorder

d. la belle indifference

20. Albert's physician is concerned about Albert's weight. He wonders whether Albert would qualify as obese so that he might receive insurance reimbursement for his treatment. His physician computes a ratio of Albert's body weight to his height in a measure known as the

_____.

a. actuarial cutoff technique

b. body mass index

c. weight-density indicator

d. scale of morbid obesity

21. According to a National Institutes of Health (NIH) study on weight-loss treatment, what percentage of individuals who lose weight manage to keep it off for > 5 years?

a. < 1%

b. 5%

c. 20%

d. 50%

22. Which of the following eating disorders is the most potentially deadly?

a. anorexia nervosa

b. bulimia nervosa

c. bulimarexia

d. binge eating disorder

23. Which of the following is NOT a characteristic of REM sleep?

a. dreaming

b. muscle paralysis

c. genital arousal

d. brain inactivation

24. After a long day of classes, Ron can't wait to get back to his dorm room to take a quick nap. He believes that he needs sleep to recover from the day's physical, cognitive, and emotional stresses. With which sleep theory does Ron's belief about sleep most closely resemble?

a. restorative theory

b. activation–synthesis theory

c. circadian rhythm theory

d. Cannon–Bard theory

25. Jane was exhausted from studying for her general psychology exam. She had stayed up all night and then drove to school for the exam. She suddenly realizes that she just dozed off for a few seconds and then awoke. Jane has just experienced _____.

a. circadian sleep

b. the Dement effect

c. microsleep

d. cerebral hyperplasia

26. Nathan has been suffering from a mild form of depression all semester. Eugene, his psychology major roommate, suggests that he cut his sleep time in half in an effort to improve his mood. Eugene knows that this technique sometimes works because sleep deprivation results in the increased activation of which of the following neurotransmitters?

a. dopamine

b. norepinephrine

c. serotonin

d. acetylcholine

27. In a freak accident, Professor Slumber slips, and her precision sharpened pencil flies through the air hitting a student in the pineal gland. This student would now most likely have difficulty _____.

a. using the rest room

b. riding a bicycle

c. falling asleep

d. having lucid dreams

28. Eileen is dreaming that she is being attacked by a monster and is hitting it back with an oversize salami. Unfortunately, Eileen's husband (who is in bed next to her) is getting punched repeatedly as she acts out what she is dreaming. From which of the following sleep disorders is Eileen suffering?
    a. REM behavior disorder
    b. sleep apnea
    c. cataplexy
    d. narcolepsy

29. Mike has a big date planned for this weekend. On Thursday night, he dreams about a limp flower. No matter how much he waters it, the flower refuses to grow. Kristen tells him the dream represents his fear of poor sexual performance on the date. Kristen is describing the _____ content of Mike's dream.
    a. activation–synthesis
    b. manifest
    c. latent
    d. real

30. Which of the following is MOST accurate regarding the Freudian theory of dreams?
    a. there is virtually no empirical evidence to support the theory
    b. it remains the most influential view of dream analysis in contemporary psychology
    c. dreams are considered to be epiphenomena of mental processes
    d. it is highly consistent with the activation–synthesis model of dreaming

31. As of late, Sara has dreamed of fireworks erupting throughout the darkened sky every single night. She appears concerned at first, but soon realizes the dreams are just the result of her mind's way of making sense of the neural firings of her brain. This explanation is consistent with which of the following theories of dreaming?
    a. Freudian theory
    b. activation–synthesis hypothesis
    c. circadian theory
    d. evolved threat–rehearsal theory

THOUGHT QUESTION

It has been estimated that individuals slept an average of 10 hr per day at the beginning of the 20th century. Today, people average a little over 7 hr per night. Speculate about the various causes for this change. Also, considering the seemingly adaptive nature of sleep and dreaming, consider how this change has influenced our society. What do you think will happen if this reduction in sleep continues?

ANSWER KEY

Fill-in-the-Blank Questions

1. motivation
2. goal
3. homeostasis
4. instincts
5. needs
6. humanistic
7. arousal
8. expectancies
9. extrinsic
10. creativity
11. self-regulation
12. achievement motive
13. TOTE unit
14. delay of gratification
15. nucleus accumbens
16. dual center
17. metabolism
18. aphagia
19. glucostats
20. lipostatic
21. restrained eaters
22. anorexia nervosa
23. bulimia nervosa
24. binge eating disorder
25. beta
26. theta
27. delta
28. insomnia
29. paradoxical
30. unihemispherical
31. circadian rhythm
32. suprachiasmatic nucleus
33. pons
34. dreams
35. evolved threat rehearsal

Multiple-Choice Questions

1. a Motivational states energize and direct behaviors, help the organism to persist toward a goal, and exist in varying strengths; homeostasis is not one of these.

2. d Negative feedback models describe how people respond to deviations from equilibrium.

3. b Fixed-action patterns, also known as instincts, are unlearned actions that are triggered by external cues.

4. c Self-actualization is the humanistic term for the state that occurs when one's personal dreams and aspirations are achieved.

5. b Maslow's need hierarchy predicts that survival needs will have priority over personal growth needs.

6. d Hull's drive theory states that the likelihood that a behavior will occur is due to both drive and habit.

7. c Hedonism is the general motivational principle in which individuals seek pleasure and avoid pain.

8. a Incentives are external objects that motivate behaviors, rather than internal drives.

9. d Intrinsic motivation refers to the value or pleasure that is associated with an activity but that has no apparent biological goal or purpose.

10. c Lepper's research is part of consistent evidence that extrinsic rewards undermine intrinsic motivation

and decrease the likelihood that individuals will perform the rewarded behavior.

11. d Yerkes–Dodson law dictates that behavioral efficiency increases with arousal up to an optimum point, after which it decreases with increasing arousal.

12. b Self-efficacy represents the expectancy that your efforts will lead to success.

13. b Deindividuation is the process in which people lose inhibitions and personal standards when their self-awareness is low.

14. d Using Mischel and Metcalfe's terminology as to how information is processed in the brain, the hot system is amygdala based and the cold system is hippocampus based.

15. c The anterior cingulate region of the prefrontal cortex has consistently been found to be involved in tasks that are demanding.

16. a Somatic markers are bodily reactions that arise from contemplating the outcomes of self-regulatory actions and decisions.

17. b Most foods contain lipids, amino acids, and glucose to use as energy sources for the body.

18. c Lesions to the ventromedial hypothalamus (VMH) cause animals to eat great quantities of food and become obese.

19. a Gourmand syndrome is the disorder in which individuals become obsessed with food and its preparation as a result of damage to the limbic system or right frontal lobes.

20. b Body mass index (BMI) is a commonly used measure of obesity in which a ratio of body weight to height is obtained.

21. a According to the NIH, < 1% of individuals who lose weight manage to keep it off for > 5 years.

22. a Although all eating disorders are serious, anorexia nervosa is the most potentially deadly as about 15–20% of individuals eventually die from the disorder.

23. d The brain is very active during REM sleep; dreams, muscle paralysis, and genital arousal are REM sleep characteristics.

24. a Restorative theory of sleep emphasizes that the brain and body need to rest and that sleep allows the body to repair itself.

25. c Microsleeps occur when individuals fall asleep during the day for brief periods of time ranging from a few seconds to as long as a minute.

26. c Sleep deprivation sometimes works as a treatment for mild depression due to the increased activation of the neurotransmitter serotonin.

27. c Pineal gland secretes melatonin and is involved with falling asleep.

28. a REM behavior disorder occurs when the normal muscle paralysis that accompanies REM is absent.

29. c Latent content is the Freudian term for the symbolic aspects of a dream.

30. a It is surprising that, given the amount of attention it receives, there is virtually no experimental evidence to support the Freudian theory of dreaming.

31. b Activation–synthesis hypothesis proposes that dreams are the side effect of the mind trying to make sense of brain activity.

Thought Question

Answers will vary. Ideas for reasons why we sleep less may include the invention of the electric light bulb and that there are more available activities at night, including television, and the Internet. The effect of less sleep on society is unclear, but one might address how this undermines the adaptive function of sleeping (rest and repair, consolidation of learning) that took thousands of years to evolve. Other possible influences may be increased stress, loss of coping mechanisms (e.g., road rage), sleep-related errors (e.g., work and vehicle accidents), and bodily breakdown (e.g., immune problems, cancer, coronary heart disease). Either we will need to concede the need for more sleep or other bodily systems will have to pick up these functions.

| Emotions, Stress, and Coping

In Chapter 10, the authors present the current state of psychological science in regard to the topic of emotion. Emotions are perplexing in that they nearly defy verbal description yet everyone understands that certain feeling. Complex emotions like love have motivated a considerable proportion of the art, literature, and music of our civilization. For all the importance and phenomenological understanding ascribed to these feelings, psychological scientists have come to a reasonable understanding of emotions only recently. Early psychologists often overlooked their role, instead preferring to view the organism as a rational information-processing machine. A more recent evolutionary perspective has proven more fruitful in integrating the motivating and sustaining forces of emotion with animal behavior. In addition, recent advances in behavioral neuroscience have clarified and improved earlier theories. The authors address this topic by considering how emotions are adaptive, how people experience emotions, the neurophysiological basis of emotion, and how people cope with stress.

How Are Emotions Adaptive?

The chapter begins with a consideration of how emotions serve a survival function. *Emotions,* immediate responses to environmental events, are distinguished from *moods,* which are diffuse and long-lasting emotional states. The evolutionary basis of emotion is supported by the cross-cultural recognition of the facial expression of emotions. The authors present Ekman and Friesen's classic studies in which the facial expressions of anger, fear, disgust, happiness, sadness, and surprise were recognized in diverse cultures. Subsequent research has continued to provide support for the cross-cultural congruence in identification of facial expressions. While recognition

of facial expression appears universal and adaptive, the *display rules,* or norms, for the exhibition of emotions differ dramatically. The adaptive nature of emotion is also seen in their influence on cognitive functions. They serve as heuristic guides in decision making, capture our attention, and aid in memory. They also strengthen interpersonal relations. Even seemingly negative emotions such as guilt, shame, and jealousy strengthen social bonds, renew commitments to relationships, and motivate positive behavior. *Embarrassment* may help reaffirm close relationships after a transgression.

How Do People Experience Emotions?

The next section looks at attempts to define and quantify the phenomenological experience of emotion. Psychological scientists have agreed on three components that accompany emotions: a subjective experience, physical changes, and cognitive appraisals. There are three main theories of emotion that differ in their emphasis on these components.

Table 10.1 THEORIES OF EMOTION

Theory of Emotion	Process of Experiencing Emotion
James–Lange	specific patterns of physical changes give rise to the perception of associated emotions
Cannon–Bard	processed in subcortical pathways resulting in two experiences: emotion and physical reaction
Two-factor	situation evokes physiological response (arousal) and a cognitive interpretation (emotion label)

The subjective nature of emotions is illustrated by the difficulty in verbally describing them. *Self-reports* are a common technique to get at the trait (how do you feel in general?) and state (how do you feel right now?) descriptions of emotion. The physiological changes associated with emotion are exemplified by the *facial feedback hypothesis,* the idea that facially mimicking an emotion will activate the associated emotion. Actors portraying emotions experience similar physiological changes (heart rate, skin temperature) as individuals experiencing the emotion. There also is a cognitive component or labeling of emotion from environmental information. The importance of this process is seen when one actually mislabels or *misattributes arousal. Excitation transfer* is an example of misattribution in which the arousal from one event is transferred to a new stimulus. The authors give some useful advice in that one should take a date to an arousing movie so that those feelings of arousal might be misattributed to positive emotions about you! Individuals use a variety of emotion-regulation processes every day. *Humor* and *distraction* are two excellent techniques for regulating negative affect.

What Is the Neurophysiological Basis of Emotion?

Recent advances in behavioral neuroscience have substantially improved our understanding of emotions. It has long been known that emotions are associated with activation in the autonomic nervous system. However, it is now clear that there is tremendous overlap in autonomic activity among the various emotions. James Papez and Paul MacLean contributed much understanding of emotion in their research on the *limbic system,* a term used for the neural circuit involved in emotional processing. Ironically, two areas they did not deem important—the amygdala and the orbitofrontal cortex—have been found to be highly involved with emotion. The amygdala has been associated with fear conditioning and perception of social stimuli, particularly fearful faces. The orbitofrontal cortex is also involved in the processing of emotional cues, especially those related to interpersonal interactions. It also has been shown that there is a *cerebral asymmetry* in emotional activation. It appears that right hemisphere activity is associated with negative affect and left hemisphere activity is associated with positive affect.

How Do People Cope with Stress?

The final section of the chapter deals with stress and the emotional/behavioral responses of coping. Hans Selye formulated the *general adaptation syndrome* (GAS) to describe the stages of physiological coping with stress. He identified a consistent pattern of responding in the alarm stage, resistance stage, and exhaustion stage. Other investigators focused on the particular *stressors,* or environmental events, that lead to stress and coping. These have been divided into the categories of *major life stressors* and *daily hassles.* The field of psychoneuroimmunology has advanced our understanding of how psychological factors can compromise our immune systems. Personality traits (e.g., hostility) and stressor characteristics (e.g., intensity, novelty, predictability) have been found to influence the perception of stress. A number of styles for coping with stress have been articulated, including emotion-focused coping, problem-focused coping, and positive reappraisal. One of the most important variables in coping is the use of *social support.* This seems to help people experience less stress overall as well as lessen the negative effects of the stress that occur (the buffering hypothesis).

FILL-IN-THE-BLANK QUESTIONS

1. _____ refers to feelings that involve subjective evaluation, physiological processes, and cognitive beliefs

2. _____ diffuse and long-lasting emotional states that influence rather than interrupt thought and behavior

3. _____ pattern of behavioral and physiological responses to events that match or exceed an organism's abilities

4. _____ govern how and when emotions are exhibited

5. _____ negative emotional state associated with anxiety, tension, and agitation

6. _____ occurs in humans after social events such as violations of cultural norms, loss of physical poise, teasing, and self-image threats

7. _____ category of disorders such as depression in which individuals experience such strong emotions they can become immobilized

8. _____ emotions such as anger, fear, sadness, disgust, and happiness

9. _____ emotions such as remorse, guilt, submission, and anticipation

10. _____ theory of emotion in which the felt emotion is the result of perceiving specific patterns of bodily responses

11. _____ theory of emotion that posits that information from an emotion-producing stimulus is processed in subcortical structures, causing the experience of two separate things at roughly the same time: an emotion and a physical reaction

12. _____ theory of emotion that proposes a situation evokes both a physiological response, such as arousal, and a cognitive interpretation, or emotion label

13. _____ term used when an emotion label is derived from the wrong source

14. _____ the way in which one thinks about an event

15. _____ simple method of regulating negative emotions that results in an improved immune system and the release of hormones, catecholamines, and endorphins.

16. _____ mistaken method of emotion regulation in which individuals attempt not to respond to or feel the emotion at all

17. _____ mistaken method of emotion regulation in which individuals think about, elaborate, and focus on undesired thoughts or feelings

18. _____ according to Zajonc, type of emotion that results from cooling the brain

19. _____ MacLean's term for the extended neural circuit of emotion

20. _____ syndrome following removal of the amygdala in which animals display fearless behavior

21. _____ hemisphere of the brain that is more involved with the interpretation and comprehension of emotional material

22. _____ environmental event or stimulus that threatens an organism

23. _____ response made by an organism to avoid, escape from, or minimize an aversive stimulus

24. _____ response that describes the physiological preparation of animals to deal with any attack

25. _____ stage of GAS in which an emergency reaction prepares the body to fight or flee

26. _____ stage of GAS in which the defenses are prepared for a longer, sustained attack against the stressor

27. _____ stage of GAS in which a variety of physiological and immune systems fail

28. _____ hormone secreted by the hypothalamus during a stress response

29. _____ hormone secreted by the pituitary that causes the adrenal cortex to release cortisol

30. _____ category of stressors that involves changes or disruptions that strain central areas of people's lives

31. _____ motivational state that occurs when demands are perceived to outweigh resources

32. _____ motivational state that results when resources are perceived to approximate or exceed demands

33. _____ personality type that describes a relaxed, noncompetitive, accommodative person

34. _____ field that studies the response of the body's immune system to psychological variables

35. _____ the body's mechanism for dealing with

invading microorganisms, such as allergens, bacteria, and viruses

36. _____ coping that occurs before the onset of a future stressor

37. _____ cognitive process in which people focus on possible good things in their current situation, the proverbial silver lining

38. _____ refers to having other people who can provide help, encouragement, and advice

MULTIPLE-CHOICE QUESTIONS

1. Jon is on his first date with a woman he really likes. She is being very polite, but he wonders how she really feels about him. Based on research on nonverbal displays of emotion, Jon should look at her _____ for clues about her inner states, moods, and needs.
   a. eyebrows
   b. eyes
   c. cheek muscles
   d. mouth

2. Which of the following basic emotions is most easily recognized in facial expressions across cultures?
   a. happiness
   b. sadness
   c. fear
   d. disgust

3. Jean-Claude is at the movies with his girlfriend. Because he lost a bet, they are watching a chick-flick love story. When the heroine dies at the end of the movie, Jean-Claude feels tears rush to the corners of his eyes. He tries to look away and subtly wipe his eyes because crying would violate the _____ in his culture for how emotions are exhibited by tough guys like him.
   a. affective standards
   b. mood guidelines
   c. display rules
   d. feelings norms

4. Portia is at the mall when she asked to evaluate a new soft drink, a combination of vanilla, cherry, and cola. Portia is fairly neutral about the beverage, but she gives it a positive evaluation because she is in a good mood, and it is nice to be out of the house. This behavior, in which individuals use their current emotional state to make judgments and appraisals is predicted by the _____.
   a. affect-as-information theory
   b. somatic marker hypothesis
   c. emotional heuristic theory
   d. affective information guide

5. Which of the following negative emotions is most highly influenced by the social environment?
   a. fear
   b. disgust
   c. anger
   d. guilt

6. Which of the following is NOT one of the components of emotion?
   a. language
   b. subjective experience
   c. physical changes
   d. cognitive appraisals

7. Leonard was in a car accident and suffered damage to his prefrontal cortex. Suddenly, he seemed detached from his problems and his relationships and job fell apart because he does not experience the subjective component of emotions. Leonard most likely suffers from _____.
   a. antisocial personality disorder
   b. affective constriction
   c. alexithymia
   d. asocial traits

8. Carl is in a psychology research study on the effect of emotions on decision making. He is given a questionnaire that asks him about his emotional traits, or how he feels in general, as well as his emotional _____, or how he feels right now.
   a. phenomenology
   b. state
   c. affects
   d. percepts

9. Excitement is an affective state that can be described by its valence (high pleasantness) as well as its activation (high arousal). This description in which two basic factors of emotion are arranged in a circle around intersections of the core dimensions of affect is an example of a(n) _____.
   a. alexithymic report
   b. circumplex model
   c. phenomenological taxonomy
   d. dysthymic description

10. Augustus is a gloomy, pessimistic individual. He always sees the glass as half empty and generally exhibits an unpleasant affect. Relative to others, Augustus probably shows an increase in which of the following neurotransmitters related to these negative activation states.
    a. dopamine
    b. norepinephrine
    c. acetylcholine
    d. serotonin

11. While Sara was on safari in Africa, the Land Rover in which she was riding was charged by a lion. Before she could even think that she was safe in the car, her heart began pounding and her brain received specific physiological feedback from her body, so she automatically knew she was experiencing fear! This experience supports the _____ theory of emotion.
    a. James–Lange
    b. Cannon–Bard
    c. Schachter two-factor
    d. Solomon opponent process

12. Wes was in a really bad mood because he got fired from his job, and he had been frowning all day. That evening his friends were attempting to cheer him up. Finally, one friend suggested that if he smiled, the change in his facial expression would produce a corresponding change in his mood. This process the friend suggested Wes use to feel better is called _____.
    a. the opponent process theory
    b. the facial feedback hypothesis
    c. the emoticon-activation hypothesis
    d. misattribution

13. Lenny is at a local comedy club. The comedian is doing some very cruel jokes about men and women and also is making fun of people in a recent tragic event. Lenny is unsure how he feels about this, but everyone around him is laughing hysterically. Because of this environmental influence, he finds the comedian uproariously funny also. Lenny's reaction is best predicted by which theory of emotion?
    a. James–Lange
    b. Cannon–Bard
    c. two-factor
    d. state trait

14. Corey is pumping iron at the gym and really gets her heart rate up. Afterward, she is cooling down and doesn't even realize that she is still aroused. Just then she bumps into a guy and notices that she is very attracted to him. Which of the following processes explains why she is highly attracted to this guy she does not even know?
    a. counterfactual thinking
    b. adaptation level theory
    c. excitation transfer
    d. opponent-process theory

15. Max and Evan were looking at their general psychology exam scores, and they both received an 85%. Max was ecstatic because he finally passed an exam in the class, but Evan was disappointed because he earned an A on the two earlier exams. Why did they react differently to the same score?
    a. they were exhibiting counterfactual thinking
    b. they were exhibiting cognitive distribution

c. they were exhibiting the social comparison effect

d. they were exhibiting the contrast effect

16. Which of the following is NOT one of the emotion-regulation processes proposed by Gross?
    a. situation selection
    b. attentional deployment
    c. use of humor
    d. cognitive change

17. Klaus is a juror in a high-profile murder case. At one point, the defense lawyer states that the victim was a prostitute who was once convicted for spousal abuse. In response to the prosecutor's objections, the judge has this comment stricken from the record as irrelevant and orders the jurors to ignore it. In spite of his best efforts, this is all Klaus can think about for the rest of the day. This common failure of thought suppression is known as the _____.
    a. rebound effect
    b. rumination tendency
    c. response modulator
    d. attentional deployment failure

18. Courtney's roommates are worried about her. She was crushed by the revelation that her boyfriend was cheating on her. She has been miserable and unable to eat or attend classes. Courtney's roommates should recommend which of the following techniques to help her regulate her mood?
    a. thought suppression
    b. distraction
    c. rumination
    d. rebound effect

19. Several people in the dorms are playing charades. They are showing high levels of arousal acting out the emotions as evidenced by increased heart rate and pupil dilation. Although they may have some differential patterns of responding for the various emotions, there is tremendous overlap in terms of the activity of their _____ nervous systems.
    a. parasympathetic
    b. limbic
    c. somatic
    d. autonomic

20. Niles, a local psychologist, is diagnosed as having brain damage, but he is still performing psychotherapy. However, since the brain damage occurred, he can no longer recognize when his clients are experiencing fear or very highly intense emotions. Which of the following brain structures is most likely damaged?
    a. amygdala
    b. hypothalamus
    c. hippocampus
    d. medulla

21. Kathi is watching a television special about puppies and kittens. She thinks they are adorable and feels happy when she watches them. Based on studies of cerebral asymmetry, we would expect an increase in activation in which of the following cortical brain areas?
    a. right prefrontal
    b. left prefrontal
    c. anterior parietal
    d. posterior temporal

22. Mike is driving along the interstate when a huge 18-wheeler truck drifts into his lane right in front of him. His heart begins to pound and his blood pressure escalates as he swerves to avoid the truck. At this point, Mike is in which stage of the general adaptation syndrome?
    a. alarm
    b. reactive
    c. resistance
    d. exhaustion

23. Beth is walking through the woods when she comes upon a venomous snake. Her body goes into action secreting a type of steroid hormone from the adrenal glands to break down protein and convert it into glucose to meet immediate energy needs. These substances, often referred to as cortisol, are _____.
    a. hypothalamic–pituitary–adrenal (HPA) axes
    b. corticotropin-releasing factor (CRF)
    c. adrenocorticotropic hormone (ACTH)
    d. glucocorticoids

24. Monica is on her way to class when traffic is slowed by an accident. She is already late for class when she finds there are no parking spaces near her building. When she finally arrives at class and gets an annoyed stare from her professor, she finds she has nothing to write with. These stressors that are part of day-to-day irritations are known as _____.
    a. major life stressors
    b. daily hassles
    c. eustress
    d. petit stressors

25. Lori is a very busy person, and she always speed walks through campus never stopping to talk to people. When she does stop to talk, she speaks rapidly and interrupts the other person constantly. She also is very frustrated and hostile, especially when waiting in line or competing with other students. Lori can best be described as having which type of personality?
    a. type A
    b. type B
    c. type C
    d. hardy

26. Which of the following is NOT one of the types of lymphocytes?
    a. B cells
    b. C cells
    c. T cells
    d. natural killer cells

27. The people who live in the apartment next to Britney play hiphop music at annoyingly high levels. Britney wants to complain, but she likes to crank up her pop music periodically. The neighbors agree that loud hip-hop music can be played from 8:00 to 9:00 P.M. and loud pop music can be played from 9:00 to 10:00 P.M. This agreement is an example of how _____ is a factor that moderates the effects of stress.
    a. intensity
    b. novelty
    c. predictability
    d. categorizing

28. Xavier has four exams and a paper due in the next week. He also has an athletic event and a party that he should attend. He sits down and constructs a schedule that will allow him to get his work done as well as meet his social obligations. This evaluation of response options and potential coping behaviors is an example of _____.
    a. primary appraisals
    b. secondary appraisals
    c. emotion-focused behaviors
    d. positive reappraisals

29. Raoul is trying to get a class he needs to graduate next December, and he just found out that it won't be offered until next spring. Although he is very upset, he realizes that there is nothing he can do about it and that the situation is out of his control. So he just gripes about it to his friends, who comfort him and tell him they will all have a good time next year anyhow. What course of action is Raoul taking to deal with his stress?
    a. thought suppression
    b. anticipatory coping
    c. problem-focused coping
    d. emotion-focused coping

30. Melinda was upset about the grade she received in her psychology course. The combination of exams and papers resulted in an 89.6% average. However, her professor refused to round this number up and gave her a B rather than an A. She was whining about the un-fairness of it all when a student came by crying because he had flunked out of school. Oh well, she thought, at least I am not in that situation! This is an example of the positive reappraisal process of _____.
    a. downward comparisons
    b. creation of positive events
    c. Pollyanna cognitions
    d. delusional thinking

31. Meg, a hard-working CEO, is committed to her work and family. She enjoys the challenges she experiences in her job and in her personal life. She has a sense of being in control of her life and of her destiny. Overall, she doesn't experience much stress despite her busy life. Meg is high in the personality characteristic of _____.
    a. realistic pessimism
    b. neuroticism
    c. hardiness
    d. extraversion

32. Alex is having a tough time at home with his wife and children. He comes into work every day and shares many of these interactions with his colleagues who offer sympathy, advice, and support. The fact that this social support actually lessens the negative effects of stress is an example of the _____.
    a. resilience phenomenon
    b. buffering hypothesis
    c. familial intervention theory
    d. dampening phenomenon

THOUGHT QUESTION

Many college students report that their lives are very stress-ful and they predict that they are much more stressed than were their grandparents. What factors might account for the increase in perceived stress over the last two generations?

ANSWER KEY

Fill-in-the-Blank Questions

1. emotion
2. moods
3. stress
4. display rules
5. guilt
6. embarrassment
7. mood disorders
8. primary
9. secondary
10. James–Lange
11. Cannon–Bard
12. two-factor
13. misattribution of arousal
14. cognitive framing
15. humor
16. thought suppression
17. rumination
18. positive
19. limbic system
20. Kluver–Bucy
21. right
22. stressor
23. coping
24. fight or flight
25. alarm
26. resistance
27. exhaustion
28. corticotropin-releasing factor
29. adrenocorticotropic hormone
30. major life stressors
31. threat

32. challenge
33. type B
34. psychoneuroimmunology
35. immune system
36. anticipatory
37. positive reappraisal
38. social support

Multiple-Choice Questions

1. d   The lower half of the face, including the mouth, is more important than the upper half in communicating emotion, particularly for positive affect.

2. a   Happiness is the easiest emotion to recognize in facial expressions.

3. c   Display rules govern how and when emotions are exhibited.

4. a   Affect-as-information theory posits that people use their current emotional state to make judgments and appraisals.

5. d   Typically, the negative emotions have a considerable genetic component, but guilt is unique in being highly influenced by the social environment.

6. a   Subjective experience, physical changes, and cognitive appraisals are the three basic components of emotion; language is not one of these.

7. c   Alexithymia is the disorder in which people do not experience the subjective component of emotion.

8. b   Emotional state self-reports have to do with how one feels right now.

9. b   Circumplex models show two basic factors of emotion arranged in a circle around the intersections of the core dimensions of affect.

10. b   Negative activation states are associated with an increase in the neurotransmitter norepinephrine.

11. a   James–Lange theory states that emotion is the result of perceiving specific patterns of bodily responses.

12. b   Facial feedback hypothesis states that facial expressions trigger the experience of emotions, not the other way around.

13. c   Two-factor theory states that emotion is the result of a physiological response, such as arousal, and a cognitive interpretation, or emotion label.

14. c   Excitation transfer occurs when residual physiological arousal caused by one event is transferred to a new stimulus.

15. a   Counterfactual thinking is the act of imagining a possible alternative outcome that did not happen.

16. c   Gross's five categories of emotion-regulation strategies are situation selection, situation modification, attentional deployment, cognitive change, and response modulation; use of humor is not one of these.

17. a   Rebound effect is a common failure of thought suppression in which individuals wind up thinking more about something after suppression than before.

18. b   Distraction is an effective method of emotional regulation in that it avoids the problems of suppression or rumination, absorbs attention, and temporarily helps people stop thinking about their problems.

19. d   Emotions are associated with activity in the autonomic nervous system; however, the overlap in activity among emotions is so great that it is difficult to distinguish emotions based solely on autonomic responses.

20. a   The amygdala is highly involved with deciphering the meaning of affective messages, particularly those involving fearful faces.

21. b   Research in cerebral asymmetry indicates that greater activation of the left prefrontal cortex is associated with positive affect.

22. a   Alarm stage of the general adaptation syndrome is an emergency reaction that prepares the body to fight or flee.

23. d   Glucocorticoids (often referred to as cortisol) are a type of steroid hormone released from the adrenal cortex to prepare the body for a stressor.

24. b   Daily hassles is the term for small day-to-day irritations and annoyances.

25. a   Traits associated with type A personality include competitiveness, achievement oriented, aggressive, hostile, hurried, restless, and unable to relax.

26. b   The three types of lymphocytes are B cells, T cells, and natural killer cells; C cells are not one of these types.

27. c   Predictability, such as knowing when an aversive noise will occur, increases adaptive responses to stress.

28. b   Secondary appraisals involve the evaluation of response options and coping behaviors in response to a stressor.

29. d   Emotion-focused coping involves trying to prevent having an emotional response to the stressor.

30. a   Downward comparisons are a type of positive reappraisal when people compare themselves to those who are worse off.

31. c Hardiness is the personality characteristic associated with stress-resistant individuals, known for their ability to adapt to life changes by viewing the events constructively.

32. b Buffering hypothesis posits that social support aids coping because other people lessen the negative effects of the stress that occurs.

Thought Question

Answers will vary but students should consider issues of the causes of stress and potential methods of coping. Humans experience more stress than other animals because most human stressors are social rather than physical. With increasing urbanization, we are in closer proximity with each other. Students might consider the adaptiveness of the flight-or-fight response system as many social stressors cannot be dealt with in this fashion. Problems in this type of responding are seen in high rates of cardiovascular disease in industrialized nations. Students might also relate increases in stress to changes in available coping resources. Increasing numbers of families are fragmented and people often move away from the nuclear family, thus compromising an important area of social support. Increasing amounts of available information and increased societal expectations have also been suggested as causal factors.

CHAPTER 11 | Cognitive and Language Development

In Chapter 11, the authors address the issues of how we develop to be the individuals we are now. It is obvious that we do not come into the world with fully formed adult abilities, so how do we change over time? And are most of our abilities innate or do they come from interaction with the environment? And if our skills do come from environmental interaction, is there a critical time during which these skills must be developed? The authors look at both ends of the developmental spectrum: infancy and old age. As language and cognition are critically important in the development of adult skills, these processes receive considerable attention. Jean Piaget's classic model of cognitive development is presented along with considerable research from psychological science on the development of particular skills. The entire topic of how cognition and language develop throughout the life span is addressed in the following areas: infant cognition, object knowledge, memory, language, and adult cognition.

How Does Cognition Develop in Infancy?

The initial section of the chapter investigates how cognition develops in infancy. Researchers and theorists have long wondered how much our genetic inheritance influences cognitive development (*nature*) and how much is attributable to the environment (*nurture*). This clash between heredity and the environment has long been termed the *nature–nurture debate*. Recent discoveries from behavioral neuroscience suggest that we have more innate abilities than was previously believed. Infants come into the world with a number of basic reflexes, including the *orienting reflex, rooting reflex,* and *grasping reflex*. The process of *brain myelination* increases the speed at which the neurons are able to transmit signals and sets the stage for early learning. This brain mat-

uration is likely highly correlated with the different stages of development and their characteristics. Research using the *preferential looking technique* has given us new information on the development of skills in infants, such as *visual acuity, depth perception,* and *auditory perception*. The final part of the section presents Piaget's *theory of cognitive development* and the stages at which critical cognitive skills are developed. While recent research has challenged the ages at which these abilities are acquired, Piaget''s ideas have had tremendous influence on our understanding of child development.

Table 11.1 PIAGET'S STAGES OF DEVELOPMENT

Stage	Critical Cognitive Tasks
Sensorimotor (0–2 years)	object permanence
Preoperational (2–7 years)	conservation of quantity
Concrete operational (7–12 years)	concrete logic
Formal operational (12+ years)	hypothetic–deductive reasoning

Does Object Knowledge Develop in Infancy or Is It Innate?

In the next section, the authors continue to weigh the nature–nurture debate through the development of *object knowledge* in infants. Recent research indicates that perception, action, and reasoning are built-in abilities that develop together over time. Again, it is likely that brain maturation allows the exhibition of inborn skills via interaction with the environment. Data from psychological science support the contention that infants have innate knowledge about *physics, math,* and *reasoning/problem solving*. David Premack addressed an additional cognitive skill that he termed *theory of mind*. This refers to the unique human ability to explain and predict behavior in terms of mental states. It appears that all of these skills develop independently and are enhanced by exposure to the world and formal instruction.

Do Children Have Good Memory Systems?

The next section provides an overview of the development of children's memories. For years, investigators accepted the Freudian notion of *infantile amnesia.* That is, since adults are unable to remember events before the age of three, then children must be unable to form memories before that time. Recent advances in experimental techniques have revealed that some rudimentary forms of memory are evident as early as 18 months. However, young children still are easily confused as to the source of their knowledge (*source amnesia*). They also are easily manipulated by *repeated, suggestive questioning.* All of these memory characteristics seem to be related to the development of the *frontal lobes,* which do not fully mature until adolescence or later.

How Does Language Develop?

Research on the acquisition of language is another area in which it seems that many developmental functions are innate. While it appears that we are responding to the environment in a trial-and-error fashion, we actually are preprogrammed to display speech in a specified progression through *grunts, cooing, babbling, first words,* and *telegraphic speech.* This same progression is seen across cultures and languages. However, information gained from language-deprived individuals does make it evident that there is a *sensitive period* during which we need environmental input for normal language to develop. This also has implications for learning a foreign language, as evidence suggests that your chances for fluency are increased with earlier exposure. Research also indicates that we are innately programmed to learn the *grammar* of a language. It is astonishing how quickly children pick up the complexities of the *phonology, morphology,* and *syntax* of their native tongue. Even children who grow up in a multilingual culture and mix the existing languages into a new one (*creole*) will then impose universal grammar rules on the new language.

How Does Cognition Change after Childhood?

The final section of the chapter addresses the issue of cognitive development with an overview of the research on changes that occur after childhood. It is apparent that adolescence marks the beginning of one's ability to reason abstractly about the environment and the future as well as to think about one's own thoughts (*metacognition*). The changes in cognitive functions that occur in the elderly provide perplexing obstacles to our understanding of development. Aging is commonly associated with a *slowing of mental processing speed* and *difficulty with short-term memory tasks* involving multiple pieces of information or divided attention. Fortunately, relatively few people exhibit the dementia or major memory loss that stereotypes the elderly. Many maintain or enhance the knowledge associated with *crystallized intelligence,* particularly if they remain mentally active.

FILL-IN-THE-BLANK QUESTIONS

1. _____ concerned with how humans acquire knowledge and understanding about the world during the course of their lives

2. _____ studies that follow changes in the same individuals over time

3. _____ tendency of humans, even from birth, to pay more attention to novel stimuli than to a stimuli to which they have become habituated

4. _____ process that develops in infants between 3.5 and 6 months of age that allows depth perception

5. _____ process in which neural connections that are frequently used are preserved, while those that are not are removed

6. _____ automatic sucking that infants engage in when a nipple or similar object is near their mouths

7. _____ the brain's ability to repair itself when one part is damaged; the ability to make new neuronal connections

8. _____ developmental stage during which young animals are able to acquire specific skills or knowledge; if not, then it cannot be acquired later

9. _____ disorder in infants characterized by low birth weight, face and head abnormalities, slight mental retardation, and later behavioral/cognitive problems that results from excessive consumption of alcohol during pregnancy

10. _____ Piaget's term for mental patterns that children form at each stage of development

11. _____ process through which a schema is adapted or expanded to incorporate new experiences

12. _____ Piagetian stage from birth until age 2 in which infants acquire information about the world only through their senses

13. _____ unique human ability to explain and predict behavior in terms of people's mental states—such as wanting, believing, or pretending

14. _____ Freudian term for theory that since adults cannot recall memories of their childhood from before about age 3, infants younger than this must not have developed memory skills.

15. _____ term used for children's confabulation of memories because they believe that what they are saying is true

16. _____ Lenneberg's original term for the idea that there are biologically determined time periods when a

child must be exposed to language to achieve normal brain development

17. _____ system of rules that characterizes the structure of a given language

18. _____ study of the set of meaningless sounds and the rules by which people combine them to make all the words and sentences in language

19. _____ highly restricted set of sounds from which every natural language is derived

20. _____ system of rules of combining the smallest meaningful units of language into words

21. _____ system of rules by which words are combined into phrases and phrases are combined to make sentences

22. _____ study of the system of meanings that underlie words, phrases, and sentences

23. _____ study of the way we use language to get what we want and to influence listeners

24. _____ study of the systematic ways by which we engage in conversations

25. _____ wordlike sounds that are learned in a context, and that a baby may not be using to represent a meaning

26. _____ Chomsky's term for babies' innate ability to narrow and deduce a theory of grammar for their native language

27. _____ strategy when mothers talk about objects that already are part of child's ongoing actions and objects of joint attention

28. _____ the mixing of words from two or more native languages in a population made of groups that speak different languages

29. _____ tendency to use simple sentences and repeat words when parents speak to their young children

30. _____ type of intelligence associated with speed of mental processing that tends to decline with age

MULTIPLE-CHOICE QUESTIONS

1. Maria, the school psychologist, is interested in the effects of parental divorce on overall intelligence. She decides to take samples of 1st graders, 7th graders, and 12th graders all at the same time and compare the results. What type of research is Maria conducting?
   a. longitudinal study
   b. age-related study
   c. cross-sectional study
   d. multicultural study

2. Baby Mario is involved in a research study. He is shown a picture of a human face and a picture of a group of shapes at the same time. The investigators compute which picture he looks at longer to gauge his preferences in a technique known as the _____.
   a. picture habituation technique
   b. orienting task
   c. milestones assessment
   d. preferential looking technique

3. Debbie heard that babies learn by repetition so she repeatedly shows her 2-month-old daughter a picture of her extended family so that the baby will recognize everyone at the family reunion they are going to attend. At first, the baby looks at the picture; however, after flashing the picture 10 times, she looks in the other direction. What most likely occurred?
   a. the baby did not know what was going on because memory does not happen until a child is much older
   b. the baby did not need to look anymore because she habituated to the picture
   c. object permanence had taken place after repeated exposure
   d. the baby stopped looking because of separation anxiety

4. Haley and Sara are about to start a brawl with each other. As Sara throws the first punch, she yells out that the reason undergraduates drink alcohol is because of the hostile environment in which they live. Haley screams that Sara is wrong because how much people drink is based on their biological background. What developmental perspectives are these angry students taking?
   a. Sara is supporting the nature perspective, while Haley is taking the nurture
   b. they are both taking the nature perspective
   c. they are both taking the nurture perspective
   d. Haley is supporting the nature perspective, while Sara is taking the nurture

5. The process of myelination occurs _____.
   a. in the first 6 months of life
   b. only in infancy
   c. only prenatally
   d. from infancy through early adulthood

6. Cassandra noticed that she has to hold her baby very close to get his attention. She is worried that her son may have some sort of visual deficit. Her friend Alicia tells her not to worry, since adult levels of visual acuity are not reached until a child is about _____.
   a. 3 months old
   b. 6 months old
   c. 1 year old
   d. 5 years old

7. When Lori was just a baby she loved to hold her mother's finger. Every time Lori's mother would touch her palm, Lori would squeeze her finger with her tiny hands. This natural reaction is known as a(n) _____.
   a. adaptation
   b. habituation
   c. grasping reflex
   d. tactile preference

8. Baby Cameron loves to nurse from his mother. As he has gotten older, he suddenly realizes that he can suck other things—a bottle, a finger, a toy, or a blanket. His new understanding that other things are suckable illustrates Piaget's concept of _____.
   a. assimilation
   b. accommodation
   c. conservation of quantity
   d. formal logic

9. Rosie is doing a study with infants. She gives the infant a toy to play with for a while and then puts it under a blanket. Rosie then watches what the infant does. Some infants look around for something else to play with while others lift up the blanket and resume playing with the toy. What can be said about the infants who lifted up the blanket?
   a. they learned separation anxiety
   b. they learned to develop conservation skills
   c. they developed object permanence
   d. they are in the formal operational stage of development

10. Yoshii is baby-sitting his neighbor's 6-year-old son. Wanting to have some fun, he takes two glasses that are the same size and fills them with soda and asks the boy which has more in it. After the youngster says that they have the same amount of soda, Yoshii pours the soda from those glasses into a tall thin glass and a short wide mug. Again, the little guy responds that both have the same amount of soda in them. What skill has this boy developed according to Piaget?
    a. object permanence
    b. visual acuity
    c. abstract thought
    d. conservation of quantity

11. Alek, a preschooler, thinks that the world revolves around him. When he gets lost at the mall, the security officer asks Alek whom he is with. Alek says, "You know, my mommie." Alek's thinking that the security officer should know whom he is with represents _____.
    a. concrete operational thinking
    b. common knowledge of security officers
    c. egocentric thinking
    d. assimilation thinking

12. When she was in high school, Buffy had to write a paper about how her life would be different if she went to a different high school. Buffy found this assignment to be fairly easy and used some imagination and abstract thought to help her write the paper. In which of Piaget's stages was Buffy?
    a. concrete operational
    b. formal operational
    c. preoperational
    d. sensorimotor

13. In which of the following areas do infants NOT seem to have innate abilities?
    a. physics
    b. math
    c. hypothetic-deductive logic
    d. problem solving

14. Mehler and Bever demonstrated that children as young as _____, if properly motivated, could understand the concept of more than or less than without using perceptual information.
    a. 6 months
    b. 2.5 years
    c. 5 years
    d. 7 years

15. Tommy brags that he can remember his second birthday when his aunt and uncle bought his mother a jogging stroller. If the truth were to be known, his memory of this event actually comes more from pictures and videotapes of his birthday rather than from his actual recollections. This confusion in memory is known as _____.
    a. source amnesia
    b. infant prevarication
    c. retrograde interference
    d. fugue states

16. Tarzan was lost as an infant in a dense jungle with only animals to care for him. He was not exposed to human language until, as an adult, he was discovered by a passing safari. Even though Tarzan now lives in a condo in Beverly Hills with many people around, his speech is still primitive and sprinkled with phrases like "Me Tarzan; you Jane!" This represents the idea that there is a _____ for learning language.
    a. critical period
    b. necessary window
    c. sensitive period
    d. brief grammatical opportunity

17. Baby George is babbling away with sounds like *b, b, b, ah, ah, ah,* and *l, l, l.* He eventually puts them together to make the word *ball.* The speech sounds that we actually say when we move our mouths to form words and sentences are known as _____.

a. morphemes
b. syntax
c. semantics
d. phones

18. Abel is testing his little brother's knowledge of sounds. He tells him, "I see a cat," and his little brother smiles and continues playing. Abel then tells him, "I see a rat," whereupon his brother starts screaming and runs from the room. The fact that his brother can distinguish the *c* sound in *cat* from the *r* sound in *rat* illustrates his recognition of _____.
    a. phonemes
    b. morphemes
    c. syntax
    d. semantics

19. Little Angelica is making a list of birthday presents she wants from her parents. She is specific about asking for toy*s*. The fact that she knows that the *s* on *toys* means more than one illustrates her understanding of _____.
    a. phonemes
    b. morphemes
    c. syntax
    d. semantics

20. Several children in a local day-care center were arguing. Some were saying, "Chuckie pushed Tommy." Others were saying, "Tommy pushed Chuckie." The fact that they know these sentences represent different ideas even though they contain the same words shows that they understand the _____ structure of the sentence, which relies heavily on word order to signal changes in meaning.
    a. objective
    b. subjective
    c. synthetic
    d. analytic

21. Galen is baby-sitting his niece. She is extremely vocal, making the following types of sounds: *ah aboo, bababababa*, and *gagaga*. What type of speech is Galen's niece demonstrating?
    a. babbling
    b. telegraphic
    c. cooing
    d. mirroring

22. Which of the following discoveries supports the idea that babbling behavior in babies is fundamentally linguistic?
    a. babies exhibit babbling, then single word speech, then telegraphic speech
    b. babies show left-mouth asymmetry during babbling
    c. babies combine vowels and consonants during babbling
    d. babies exhibit right-mouth asymmetry while babbling

23. Crystal is an anxious new mother. She has been speaking and reading to her 3-month-old infant every day but is getting nothing back. Her pediatrician tells her to relax as first words usually appear around _____.
    a. 6 months
    b. 9 months
    c. 12 months
    d. 18 months

24. Henri has been watching his son imitate him answering the phone and saying, "Hello?" Henri does not think his son understands what this means, he is simply imitating what he sees. Finally, his son points to an object and says, "Ball." This single word that is clearly meant to represent a concept is known as a(n) _____.
    a. performative
    b. morpheme
    c. true word
    d. object word

25. One day John the caveman was out hunting for his next cave partner when he saw his one friend, Ringo. When Ringo asked what John was doing he uttered, "Me hunt cave partner!" This type of speech is called _____.
    a. telegraphic speech
    b. morpheme based
    c. native tongue
    d. telephonic speech

26. Little Madeline was describing how she got lost to a local policeman. She stated, "Daddy goed to work and then I runned away." This error of speech in which she inappropriately used a grammar rule (adding *-ed* for past tense) is known as a(n) _____.
    a. joint attentional engagement
    b. overgeneralization
    c. linguistic stoppage
    d. semantic differential

27. Noam was presented with two sentences. One stated, "I am the brother of Tom," while the other one said, "Tom is my brother." The fact that Noam recognizes that the implicit meanings of these sentences are the same, despite the words and order being different, indicates that he understands the _____ of the sentence.
    a. surface structure
    b. deep structure
    c. syntax
    d. morphology

28. Surya just took a teaching job in southern Louisiana. She had always heard about the great southern cooking, but she was surprised at how some of the schoolchildren spoke what appeared to be a mixture of English and French along with some idioms that came from Canada. Surya discovered that the term for this

combination of existing languages over time is
_____.
a. cajun
b. creole
c. bayou
d. assimilation

29. Which of the following is NOT one of the qualities, described by Keating, that differentiate adolescent thought from that of younger children?
a. thinking about possibilities
b. thinking through hypotheses
c. thinking about thought
d. thinking about concrete operations

30. Pablo is an elderly gentleman who is proud of his cognitive abilities. He continues to be active, writes thoughtful articles, and is engaged in various creative activities. Which of the following changes in cognitive function should he most likely expect as he ages?
a. slowing of mental processing speed
b. increased sensitivity to contrasts
c. relatively incurable dementia
d. diminishment of crystallized intelligence

THOUGHT QUESTION

You are the president of a large toy company. You are trying to develop a series of video games that will appeal to the following audiences: 1-year-olds, 6-year-olds, 10-year-olds, and 17-year-olds. Taking into account developmental changes in cognition and language, describe the characteristics of your games.

ANSWER KEY

Fill-in-the-Blank Questions

1. cognitive development
2. longitudinal
3. orienting reflex
4. binocular disparity
5. synaptic pruning
6. rooting reflex
7. plasticity
8. critical period
9. fetal alcohol syndrome
10. schemas
11. accommodation
12. sensorimotor
13. theory of mind
14. infantile amnesia
15. honest lying
16. critical period hypothesis
17. grammar
18. phonology
19. phonemic inventory
20. morphology
21. syntax
22. semantics
23. pragmatics
24. discourse
25. performatives
26. language acquisition device
27. joint attentional engagement
28. pidgin
29. motherese
30. fluid

Multiple-Choice Questions

1. c Cross-sectional studies examine change over time by examining participants of different ages.

2. d The preferential looking technique measures the time an infant looks at one of two stimuli as a measure of preferences.

3. b Habituation is when an infant is shown a picture or object until the he or she is familiar enough with it that the amount of time he or she looks at it declines.

4. d Nature is the idea that our development is determined by our genetic makeup; nurture suggests that our development is determined by our environment.

5. d While hearing and balance areas are fully myelinated at birth; areas involved in abstract thinking may not become fully myelinated until the individual is more than 20 years old.

6. c Adult levels of visual acuity are reached when a child is about 1 year old.

7. c The grasping reflex is the natural tendency of a baby to hold your finger when presented.

8. a Assimilation is the process through which a new experience is placed into existing schemas.

9. c Object permanence is the notion that an object continues to exist even when it is hidden from view.

10. d The law of conservation of quantity states that the quantity of a substance remains unchanged, even if its appearance changes.

11. c Piaget characterized children in the preoperational stage as egocentric; they are not able to see another person's point of view.

12. b The formal operational stage involves abstract thinking and hypothetic-deductive reasoning.

13. c Infants seem to have innate knowledge about physics, math, and reasoning/problem solving. Hypothetic-deductive logic is not one of these.

14. b They demonstrated that children as young as 2.5 years could understand the concept of more than or less than.

15. a Source amnesia occurs when people can remember a fact or something that happened in the past but not the source of their knowledge.

16. c Sensitive periods reflect the idea there is an important time when an organism needs particular environmental input, but nature permits some aspects of development to occur beyond age 12.

17. d Phones are the set of speech sounds that we actually say when we move our mouths to form words and sentences.

18. a Phonemes are speech sounds that signal a difference in meaning between words.

19. b A morpheme is the smallest unit of speech that has meaning, for example, adding an *s* to a word to make it plural.

20. d English belongs to the class of languages with analytic structure, which rely heavily on word order to signal changes in meaning.

21. a Babbling is the term for the initial attempts at speech using consonants and vowels.

22. d Holowka and Petitto's discovery that babies show greater right-mouth asymmetry during babbling suggests a left hemisphere specialization that supports babbling as a fundamentally linguistic behavior.

23. c First words tend to appear when children are about 12 months old.

24. c True words are single words clearly meant to represent a concept.

25. a Telegraphic speech consists of minisentences that, though missing words and grammatical markings, actually have a logic or syntax.

26. b Overgeneralizations are errors in speech when children inappropriately apply a grammar rule.

27. b Deep structure refers to the implicit meanings of sentences.

28. b Creole describes a language that evolves over time from the mixing of existing languages.

29. d Daniel Keating's five basic qualities that differentiate adolescent thought are thinking about possibilities, thinking ahead, thinking through hypotheses, thinking about thought, and thinking beyond conventional limits; thinking about concrete operations is not one of these.

30. a Slowing of mental processing speed is one of the most consistent changes associated with aging.

Thought Question

Answers will vary but certainly should take into account Piagetian stages of cognitive development (sensorimotor, preoperational, concrete operational, formal operational). Students also should address changes in language and sensory abilities, particularly for the 1-year-old game. The limits of memory for young children could also be addressed. An interesting side discussion might be whether the games would be different for boys and girls at each age and why. It also could be extended to video games for the elderly and address changes in cognitive function that are associated with aging.

CHAPTER 12 | Social Development and Gender

GUIDE TO THE READING

GUIDE TO THE READING

The authors continue the topic of development in Chapter 12. They transition from the issues of cognition and language development discussed in the previous chapter to social development and gender identity. It is apparent that humans are social animals. The adaptiveness of this fundamental need to belong is explored throughout the chapter. The authors present the phenomenon of attachment—the bond that keeps parents and relatively helpless infants in close proximity. From the early bonds with our parents and family, we move into the larger environment and develop friendships. Much has been made over the seemingly overwhelming influence of friends over family during childhood and adolescence; however, the authors present research data indicating that both influences are important. The chapter moves on to consider the development of moral behavior. Moral behavior is crucial to the continuance of an orderly society; and, considering its adaptiveness, it is not surprising that there are physiological components underlying this behavior. Finally, the authors look at the development of gender roles and gender identity. Although the sense of being male or female seems so fundamental to our sense of self, there is evidence of considerable variation in how this develops and is experienced.

What Is Attachment?

The first section of the chapter explores social development at the time of infancy. Many young animals must be cared for by the older members of their species. The importance of this is seen in the instinctual behavior of *imprinting* in various bird species, by which they will attach themselves to a mother figure about 18 hr after hatching. Harry Harlow also showed the importance of attachment in his classic studies with rhesus monkeys, in which they preferred a terry-cloth mother over one that dispensed food.

The idea of *attachment* in humans was popularized by John Bowlby, who conceptualized it as an adaptive strategy to keep infants and caregivers in close contact. Mary Ainsworth developed a means for assessing the caregiver–infant bond and identified three styles of attachment: *secure, avoidant,* and *anxious-ambivalent.* This has proven to be a fruitful area of investigation, and each attachment style is associated with later behaviors. Finally, it appears that there is a physiological basis to attachment behaviors. The hormone *oxytocin* promotes numerous maternal tendencies that are associated with the survival of the infant.

Who Influences Social Development?

As the child develops, a wider range of behaviors must be addressed than those that ensure survival. Parents have long wondered what contributes to successful social development in their children. Chess and Thomas found that the *fit* between the child's temperament and the parents' behaviors is most important in determining social development. The implication of this is that there is no one way to raise children and that parents must be sensitive to each child's unique needs.

As children grow, peers become more important in their lives. Judith Rich Harris made quite an impact in 1995 with her *group socialization theory,* which suggested that parents have very little affect on their child's social development. Other researchers have been critical of this overstatement and presented data showing that both parents and peers are important. The value of *friends* continues through adulthood, although the nature of these friendships appears to differ between the sexes. Women's same-sex friendships are characterized more by emotional disclosure about personal issues, whereas men tend to participate in shared activities with other men. Both sexes report more friendships with the same sex as, apparently, the potential for intimacy between cross-sex friends inhibits their development.

How Does Moral Behavior Develop?

The next section of the chapter involves the critical role that *morality* plays in social development. As humans began to live in larger groups, it became increasingly important that they considered the effect of their actions on others and on the maintenance of social contracts. The authors divide moral development into *cognitive* and *affective* components. The cognitive component of *moral reasoning* has been investigated by the well-known stage theory of Lawrence Kohlberg, who classified individuals at different levels of moral reasoning (*preconventional, conventional, postconventional*) based on their answers to moral dilemmas. The *moral emotions of empathy, sympathy, guilt,* and *shame* provide an interesting insight to moral behavior. Again, these emotions appear to be adaptive in that they remind us of social contracts and encourage behaviors consistent with social norms.

Some investigators believe it is the experience of emotions produced by rewards and punishments that facilitates moral actions. As was discussed with Damasio's *somatic marker hypothesis* in Chapter 10, the visceral response associated with emotions has a tremendous influence on decision making. Recent results from behavioral neuroscience also support the idea of a physiological component to moral emotions and behavior.

What Influences Gender Development and Identity?

The final section of the chapter considers the issues of *sex, gender,* and *gender identity.* There are clear biological differences between the sexes. However, recent research suggests that gender identity, one's sense of being male or female, is the result of a combination of biological, social, and cultural forces. *Gender roles,* the behaviors that differ between men and women, are clearly determined by cultural norms. One's sense of identity was addressed by Erik Erikson in his *psychosocial theory of development.* Erikson thought that we developed in stages and that a new developmental crisis needed to be confronted at each stage. If the crisis is handled appropriately, then psychosocial growth occurs.

Table 12.1 ERIKSON'S DEVELOPMENTAL CRISES

Age	Psychosocial Crisis	Appropriate Resolution
0–1.5 years	trust vs. mistrust	strong ties with caregivers
1.5–3 years	autonomy vs. doubt	self-reliance, exploration
3–5 years	initiative vs. guilt	self-control, planning, responsibility
Grade school	industry vs. inferiority	personal efficacy
Adolescence	identity vs. confusion	sense of values and beliefs
Young adult	intimacy vs. isolation	committed friendships, romantic relationships
Middle adult	generativity vs. stagnation	producing, giving back to society
Older adult	integrity vs. despair	positive reflections

The issue of one's identity was further explored by James Marcia, who viewed identity formation as involving crisis and commitment. Marcia envisioned four possible outcomes or *statuses* to these crises: *identity achievement, identity foreclosure, identity moratorium,* and *identity diffusion.* A similar stage theory for the formation of one's *ethnic identity* (*unexamined stage, exploration stage, achievement stage*) was proposed by Jean Phinney.

FILL-IN-THE-BLANK QUESTIONS

1. _____ refers to the maturation of skills or abilities that enable people to interact

2. _____ strong, intimate emotional connection between caregiver and child that persists over time and across circumstances

3. _____ noted ethologist who worked with imprinting behavior in goslings

4. _____ noted researcher whose investigations with surrogate mothers for rhesus monkeys indicated that, in addition to food, infants needed comfort and security

5. _____ allowing an infant to cling to and hold something soft, particularly in times of threat

6. _____ Ainsworth's procedure for assessing attachment by observing infant, caregiver, and an unfamiliar adult

7. _____ attachment style in which children are not distressed by a caregiver's departure, and they ignore or snub the attachment figure on his or her return

8. _____ attachment style in which children show inconsistent or contradictory behaviors, such as smiling

when seeing the caregiver but then displaying fear or avoidance

9. _____ characterized as the *how* of behavior, the way in which it is expressed, separate from the content or the motivation for the behavior

10. _____ term for children who tend to have negative moods and trouble adapting to new situations

11. _____ style of interaction in which children sit side by side and play independently

12. _____ type of speech that occurs when children are playing near each other and talking, but not directing their speech at any individual

13. _____ Harris's theory that children learn two sets of behaviors—one for inside the home and one for outside

14. _____ social hierarchies assessment technique in which children select the classmates they most like or dislike

15. _____ smallest unit of peer interaction

16. _____ peer group that remains small enough to enable the members to be in regular interaction with one another and to serve as the primary peer group

17. _____ social unit consisting of larger groupings of people, organized by social persona, who may or may not spend a great deal of time together

18. _____ noted developer of stage theory of moral development

19. _____ level of moral development in which responses conform to rules of law and order or focus on others' disapproval

20. _____ empathy, sympathy, guilt, and shame

21. _____ emotional state involving negative feelings about a specific event or action

22. _____ involves negative feelings about the entire self and one's identity

23. _____ response by an infant to another infant's crying

24. _____ responses such as being helpful or taking reparative actions

25. _____ the testes (in males) and ovaries (in females), which are responsible for producing sperm or ova, respectively, and for secreting hormones

26. _____ term used for differences between males and females that result from socialization

27. _____ refers to commonly held beliefs about men and women

28. _____ whether you think of yourself as a man or a woman

29. _____ those who rate themselves equally on stereotypically masculine and feminine traits

30. _____ Erikson's theory of development that emphasizes age-related psychological processes and their effects on social functioning

31. _____ refers to a solid sense of one's ideologies, philosophies, values, and beliefs

32. _____ refers to the psychological association of a member of an ethnic or racial group with that group, along with awareness of the group as part of a larger society

MULTIPLE-CHOICE QUESTIONS

1. Baby Ian is pretty smooth. He puts out his arms to be lifted, smiles when he sees his parents, and expresses distress when they leave. According to Bowlby, Ian's innate repertoire of behaviors that keep his parents in close contact serves to motivate a strong _____.
   a. imprinting
   b. sense of guilt
   c. attachment
   d. instinct

2. Konrad is at the park. He sees several ducklings that have just hatched nearby. As a joke, he starts mimicking a duck by moving around in front of them and quacking loudly. To his surprise, the newly hatched ducklings begin following him around as if he were their mother. What is their behavior called?
   a. imprinting
   b. secure attachment
   c. critical periods
   d. contact comfort

3. In Harry Harlow's famous studies, infant rhesus monkeys preferred a surrogate mother who _____.
   a. was constructed of wire
   b. could give milk through an attached bottle
   c. was made of soft terry cloth
   d. could give food through an operant magazine

4. When Rosemary left her baby at the day-care center for the first time, Rosemary's baby started to cry when Rosemary left the room. Her baby is likely experiencing _____.
   a. separation anxiety
   b. separation permanence

c. concrete operations

d. conservation anxiety

5. Charity drops off her son at the day-care center. When she leaves, her son is distressed, but when she returns he is very happy. This is an example of which type of attachment?

a. secure

b. insecure

c. avoidant

d. anxious-ambivalent

6. Little Sandra is having trouble with the Strange Situation Test. She clings to her mother after first entering the room and then is inconsolably upset when her mother leaves. When her mother returns, she looks like she wants to be held but then fights to be released. These behaviors are characteristic of which of the following attachment styles?

a. secure

b. insecure

c. avoidant

d. anxious-ambivalent

7. Mr. and Mrs. Romano tend to be emotionally and behaviorally inconsistent with their children. At times they can be very giving and loving; but, at the slightest provocation, they can be cold and punishing. Their two sons are likely to have a(n) _____ attachment style.

a. secure

b. insecure

c. avoidant

d. anxious-ambivalent

8. Mr. and Mrs. Williams are very rejecting with their children. They rarely respond to their questions and punish them when they seek attention and affection. Their two daughters are likely to have a(n) _____ attachment style.

a. secure

b. avoidant

c. anxious-ambivalent

d. disorganized

9. Cheryl was always uncertain about having a baby and had to go to great lengths to conceive. However, she now is thrilled with her little bundle of joy and feels a strong bond between them. The hormone that is most associated with these maternal tendencies is _____.

a. estrogen

b. androgen

c. oxytocin

d. ptossin

10. Mr. and Mrs. Brady are having dinner with Mr. and Mrs. Connor. They are bragging about their children and how their child-rearing practices led to healthy social development in all of them. According to Chess and Thomas, which of the following is most important in determining social development?

a. overall level of positive reinforcement

b. consistent discipline from both parents regardless of reason

c. fit between the child's temperament and the parents' behaviors

d. free expression of children's and parents' affective reactions

11. Allison has arranged a play group for the children in her neighborhood. She is distressed that when they get together, the children mostly play by themselves and do not really interact. Debbie tells her not to worry because interactive friendships characterized by physical proximity and shared activities do not begin until the age of _____.

a. 9 months

b. 1 year

c. 2 years

d. 3 years

12. Which of the following is NOT one of the factors listed by Gottman as essential to the formation of friendships?

a. common-ground activity

b. clear communication

c. avoidance of conflicts

d. reciprocity

13. Ally is about to attend her high-school reunion. She is thinking back to how some of her classmates were called jocks, brains, loners, druggies, nerds, etc. These small set of stereotypic names describe the social unit called _____.

a. friendships

b. cliques

c. crowds

d. mobs

14. Ms. Rhinard's kindergarten classroom is undergoing sociometric analysis. She is concerned that some children are seen as being liked by a number of their classmates and disliked by a number as well. These students are known as _____ children.

a. popular

b. rejected

c. neglected

d. controversial

15. Which of the following is TRUE in regard to gender differences in adult friendships?

a. men tend to spend more time with their friends than do women

b. both sexes report an equivalent number of friends

c. women tend to spend more time with their friends in groups than do men

d. men are more likely to inquire about their friend's feelings

16. Which of the following is TRUE in regard to gender differences in adult friendships?
    a. women tend to have more female friends; men tend to have more male friends
    b. both sexes tend to have more female friends
    c. Women tend to have more male friends; men tend to have more female friends
    d. both sexes tend to have more male friends

17. Winona finds a wallet in the street that has obviously been lost. She takes the money from it because she wants to buy herself something really nice. According to Kohlberg, Winona is responding at the _____ level of moral reasoning.
    a. preconventional
    b. conventional
    c. postconventional
    d. narcissistic

18. Harriet Tubman was well known for breaking the law to free slaves via the Underground Railroad. According to Kohlberg, her behavior was characterized by a _____ level of moral reasoning.
    a. preconventional
    b. conventional
    c. altruistic
    d. postconventional

19. Empathy, sympathy, guilt, shame, and embarrassment are considered _____ emotions.
    a. primary
    b. self-conscious
    c. affective
    d. self-regulatory

20. Pete is a first-year college student who is struggling to get by. He is overwhelmed by the course load, stressed by his many new adult responsibilities, and depressed by the loss of his old friends and family. Arie, a senior, experiences the emotional response of _____ as he remembers how difficult it was his first year.
    a. sympathy
    b. empathy
    c. hedonism
    d. shame

21. Fred is doing his best to teach his children to be good, moral people. When his daughter turns 4, he can expect prosocial responses that are _____.
    a. hedonistic and self-centered
    b. other-oriented
    c. characteristic of notions of being "good"
    d. internally generated and mindful of social responsibilities

22. _____ reasoning by parents focuses on their children's emotions and intentions and tends to promote sympathetic attitudes, feelings of guilt, and an awareness of others' feelings.
    a. inductive
    b. deductive
    c. prosocial
    d. altruistic

23. Which of the following is NOT one of the three classes of sex organs?
    a. testes
    b. gonads
    c. internal sex organs
    d. external genitalia

24. Pat the fetus is not exposed to androgen. Into which of the following precursors to sex organs is Pat going to develop?
    a. Mullerian system
    b. Wolffian system
    c. Gonadian system
    d. Ruthian system

25. Carrie and Aidan are trying to have a baby. She is shocked to find out that the reason for her infertility is that she is biologically a man! Apparently during development, her androgen receptors failed to function, and she outwardly developed as a female, despite having the genes of a man. Carrie's unusual condition is known as _____.
    a. Mullerian failure
    b. androgen insensitivity syndrome
    c. gender identity disorder
    d. transgender dysfunction

26. When Rhett was younger, he saw his father open the door for his mother. As he got older, he noticed that his father also held the door for his sister and other women. Now that he is in college, Rhett holds the door open for his good friend Scarlett. Rhett's behavior best illustrates _____.
    a. social facilitation
    b. gender identity
    c. androgyny
    d. gender roles

27. June tells her friends that a "real" woman should act very feminine, wear frilly dresses, and not engage in sports. Men should look "ratty" because they have been doing hard work so they can try to win over women by buying them things. When she judges whether a person is acting "properly," she uses these beliefs to judge them. What is she using to make these judgments?
    a. gender schemas
    b. gender identity
    c. sexist dimorphism
    d. role diffusion

28. Chloe is a 15-month-old infant. Her parents attend to her needs and feed her when she cries. They read her stories at night and do their best to provide her with a stimulating, nurturing environment. Chloe is successfully making her way through Erikson's stage of _____.
    a. trust versus mistrust
    b. autonomy versus doubt
    c. initiative versus guilt
    d. industry versus inferiority

29. Denzell is a 40-year-old man who is quite busy in his life. In addition to his job, he volunteers at a local center for troubled adolescents. He contributes financially to a number of charitable organizations, and he coaches his girls' soccer team. Denzell is successfully making his way through Erikson's stage of _____.
    a. identity versus confusion
    b. intimacy versus isolation
    c. generativity versus stagnation
    d. integrity versus despair

30. Amanda is a 15-year-old girl who is fighting with her mother about clothes. Amanda tells her mother that if she wears the clothes her mother picked for her, then everyone will laugh at her. Erikson termed this unrealistic self-scrutiny that is characteristic of adolescence as _____.
    a. narcissism
    b. cognitive conceit
    c. egocentrism
    d. conformity

31. Trevor is a junior at a local university. He has been trying to figure out his identity since his first year. After trying several philosophies, he now feels good about his values and beliefs. Trevor is at which of Marcia's identity statuses?
    a. identity achievement
    b. identity foreclosure
    c. identity moratorium
    d. identity diffusion

32. Chang is a Korean student studying in the United States. He has totally adopted American customs and shows apathy toward his native Korean culture. Chang displays behaviors characteristic of which of Phinney's stages of ethnic identity?
    a. unexamined
    b. exploration
    c. foreclosure
    d. achievement

THOUGHT QUESTION

Consider the contention made by Judith Rich Harris that beyond choosing schools and where to live, parents contribute little to a child's social development. That is to say, peers have a much greater influence. Give examples of the roles parents and peers have played in your social development.

ANSWER KEY

Fill-in-the-Blank Questions

1. social development
2. attachment
3. Konrad Lorenz
4. Harry Harlow
5. contact comfort
6. Strange Situation Test
7. avoidant
8. disorganized
9. temperament
10. difficult
11. parallel play
12. collective monologues
13. group socialization
14. sociometric analysis
15. friendships
16. clique
17. crowds
18. Lawrence Kohlberg
19. conventional
20. moral emotions
21. guilt
22. shame
23. empathetic distress
24. prosocial
25. gonads
26. gender
27. gender stereotypes
28. gender identity
29. androgynous
30. psychosocial
31. identity
32. ethnic identity

Multiple-Choice Questions

1. c   Attachment was popularized by Bowlby as an innate means of keeping parents and infants in close contact.

2. a   Imprinting is the behavior seen in some birds, such as ducks, in which shortly after hatching they attach themselves to something in their environment (usually their mothers) and follow the object of their attachment.

3. c   Harlow's studies showed that infant rhesus monkeys preferred a surrogate mother made of terry cloth.

4. a   Separation anxiety occurs in young children, particularly 6 to 8 months of age, in which they become very upset and distressed when they cannot see or are separated from their attachment figure.

5. a   Secure attachment describes how a child is distressed when the attachment figure leaves but is happy and quickly comforted when the attachment figure returns.

6. d   Anxious-ambivalent children are anxious throughout the test, clinging to the attachment figure and becoming very anxious on her departure; however, on return, these children want to be held but then fight to be released.

7. d   Caregivers who are emotionally or behaviorally inconsistent tend to have children with an anxious-ambivalent attachment style.

8. b Caregivers who are rejecting tend to have children with an avoidant attachment style.

9. c Oxytocin plays a role in maternal tendencies, feelings of social acceptance and bonding, and sexual gratification.

10. c According to Chess and Thomas, the fit between the child's temperament and the parents' behaviors is most important in determining social development.

11. d Around age 3, interactive friendships emerge that are mainly characterized by physical proximity and shared activities.

12. c Gottman's five factors essential to the formation of friendships are common-ground activity, clear communication, exchange of information, resolution of conflicts, and reciprocity; avoidance of conflicts is not one of these.

13. c Crowds is the term for the stereotyped social unit of people who are differentiated by their interests, activities, abilities, and attitudes.

14. d Controversial children get many "like" and "dislike" nominations.

15. b In terms of adult friendships, both sexes reports an equivalent number of friends.

16. a In terms of adult friendships, women tend to have more female friends; men tend to have more male friends.

17. a The preconventional level of moral reasoning is characterized by responses pertaining to self-interest or hedonistic advantages.

18. d Postconventional level responses center around complex reasoning about abstract principles and values such as "slavery is unjust."

19. b Empathy, sympathy, guilt, shame, and embarrassment are considered self-conscious emotions because they require comprehension of the self as a causal agent and an evaluation of one's own responses.

20. b Empathy is an emotional state that arises from understanding another's emotional experiences.

21. a At age 4, children show prosocial responses that are hedonistic and self-centered.

22. a When parents use inductive reasoning it encourages children to consider the consequences of their behaviors, and facilitates empathy and understanding of others' feelings.

23. a The three classes of sex organs are gonads, internal sex organs, and external genitalia; testes is not one of these classes.

24. a In the absence of androgen, a male sex hormone, the Mullerian system develops.

25. b Androgen insensitivity syndrome leads one to develop as a woman despite having the genes of a man.

26. d Gender roles are behaviors that differ between men and women because of cultural influence or learning.

27. a Gender schemas are cognitive structures that influence how people perceive the behaviors of men and women.

28. a Erikson's first stage from birth until 18 months is concerned with how infants' needs are met by their parents, which is why it is called trust versus mistrust.

29. c Generativity versus stagnation is Erikson's stage for middle adulthood, when individuals are productive and engaging in activities that bring meaning to life.

30. c Egocentrism is Erikson's term for the unrealistic self-scrutiny that is characteristic of adolescence.

31. a Individuals who have reached identity achievement have investigated a number of philosophies and have chosen a clear identity.

32. a Phinney's unexamined stage is characterized by a preference for the dominant culture and apathy toward one's own ethnicity.

Thought Question

Answers will vary but students should consider areas of parental influence that have been discovered by other researchers. The influence of parents has also been seen on the exhibition of specific individual behaviors (e.g., prosocial responses) as well as on the child's selection of what kind of crowd to join. Parents and teachers also play a major role in realigning social groups that are consistent with family norms. Finally, students should consider the role of family support in social development. The formation of personal identity is facilitated by having a strong family support base from which to explore.

CHAPTER 13 | Self and Social Cognition

GUIDE TO THE READING

Chapter 13 is the first of two chapters historically associated with social psychology—the study of how others influence how we think, feel, and act. The authors begin by observing that humans alone seem to form an abstract representation of the self. After examining the nature of the self and the role of self-esteem, the authors consider the part that attitudes play in determining how we think about and behave toward others. Being able to work with others in groups is clearly adaptive and fundamental to our survival.

What Is the Nature of Self?

The chapter begins with a consideration of one of our more fundamental characteristics—our idea of *self*. We all have some sense of who we are and how we are unique from others. Despite considerable contradictory sensory information, we have a unitary experience of self that is continuous over time and space. Our *symbolic self* seems to be the uniquely human capacity to form an abstract mental representation of oneself through language. The beginning of this sense of self appears to begin at around 18 months with the *recognition of self* as distinct from others. At least some of the developing sense of self appears to be related to the maturation of the *frontal lobes*.

According to Higgins's *self-discrepancy theory,* our self-awareness also appears to motivate our behaviors by calling attention to the differences between who we are, how others see us, and who we would like to be. These discrepancies can lead to such strong emotions as depression, frustration, anxiety, and guilt. Also, different cultures tend to reward the development of different types of selves. *Collectivist cultures* emphasize connections to family, social groups, and ethnic groups and conformity to social norms and group cohesive-

ness. *Individualistic cultures* emphasize personal rights and freedoms, self-expression, and diversity. A quick review of one's daily activities is usually enough to identify where your culture stands on this continuum.

What Is Self-Esteem and What Is It Good For?

The next section of the chapter looks at *self-esteem.* This is the evaluative aspect of self-concept, referring to whether people view themselves to be worthy or unworthy, good or bad. The idea that children should have a high self-esteem has reached nearly cult status in recent years, leading to *unconditional acceptance* of children by their parents. More recent research suggests this is a useful idea but only in the context of relatively strict parenting and clear limit setting. Self-esteem seems to have a biological basis as it is *moderately heritable* and may be related to the neurotransmitter *serotonin.* We seem to be preprogrammed to view ourselves in a favorable fashion. Most people view themselves as *better-than-average* in many domains. We maintain *positive illusions, bask in the glow of reflected glory,* and compare ourselves socially with those who we believe are deficient compared to us (*downward social comparison*). We also tend to take credit for successes ourselves but blame failures on outside factors (*self-serving bias*). These ego-defensive distortions appear to make us feel better and prevent rejection from the group.

How Do Attitudes Guide Behavior?

The last half of the chapter concerns *social cognition* as it relates to how we make sense of other people and our social situations. It seems that we are *cognitive misers,* who make quick judgment about others based on limited information. Our evaluation of objects or ideas is known as an *attitude,* and it has *affective, cognitive,* and *behavioral components.* The *mere exposure effect* illustrates that our attitudes about an object or situation can improve simply through the process of greater familiarity. Our *implicit attitudes* can influence us unconsciously, and those whose associated memories are *easily accessible* are more predictive of behavior.

One of the classic findings in social psychology was Leon Festinger's discovery that discrepancies between attitudes and behavior can lead to *cognitive dissonance.* Generally, individuals are motivated to reduce this dissonance by either changing their attitudes or their behavior. Many disciplines are interested in how attitudes can be changed through *persuasion.* We like to think of ourselves as rational decision makers, but there is a wealth of evidence to the contrary. Richard Petty and John Cacippo's *elaboration likelihood model* indicated that there are two distinct ways by which persuasion leads to attitude change. The *central route to persuasion* is one that makes use of rational cognitive processes. The *peripheral route to persuasion* is one by which people minimally process the message and make decisions by numerous nonrational processes. The ways of influencing both routes continues to be investigated; however, the personal trait of *need for cognition* is related more to central routes of information processing.

How Do People Form Attitudes about Others?

The final section of the chapter looks at social cognition in terms of how we form attitudes about others. We seem predisposed to making *attributions* or causal explanations about why events or actions occur. And, rather than employing an objective evaluation, we tend to take shortcuts and attribute others' behaviors to personal traits but attribute our own behaviors more to situational factors (i.e., *actor–observer discrepancy*). These shortcuts continue in the arena of *stereotypes,* by which we organize social information about people based on their membership in certain groups. While efficient, negative stereotypes can lead to harmful *prejudices* and dangerous *discriminatory behavior.* Fortunately, although the information processing that leads to these attitudes appears to be innate and based on historically adaptive ideas, such as *ingroups* and *outgroups,* we can control our behavioral responses to some of our more pernicious stereotypes.

Research has indicated that *cooperation* with others, particularly in activities that have shared *superordinate goals,* can reduce the hostility between disparate groups. One educational application of this has been the *jigsaw classroom,* in which students work together in mixed-race or mixed-sex groups. The future of civilization may rest on how well we apply these ideas to broader races, nations, and cultures.

One precautionary note: It is tempting to believe that this portion of psychological science is just common sense—we all know how we deal with our friends and family. Actively fight that natural tendency. You will find that some of the research is actually counterintuitive (e.g., *cognitive disso-*

nance). Also, there are subtle distinctions among several of the social psychological terms. When answering the multiple choice questions, be sure you know why the correct answer is accurate as well as why the wrong answers are incorrect.

FILL-IN-THE-BLANK QUESTIONS

1. _____ concerned with how others influence how we think, feel, and act

2. _____ concerned with the mental processes by which we make sense of ourselves, other people, and our social situations

3. _____ involves the mental representation of personal experience and includes thought processes, a physical body, and a conscious experience that one is separate and unique from others

4. _____ also known as the narrative self, it is the uniquely human capacity to form an abstract mental representation of oneself through language

5. _____ the sense of self as the object of attention

6. _____ the ability to mentally represent the self's past and future

7. _____ controllable mental operations that help the self achieve its goals

8. _____ the cognitive aspect of the self-concept, consisting of an integrated set of memories, beliefs, and generalizations about the self

9. _____ self emphasized in individualistic cultures, encourages personal rights and freedoms, self-expression, and diversity

10. _____ from collectivist cultures, self-concepts are determined to a large extent by social roles and personal relationships

11. _____ the evaluative aspect of self-concept, referring to whether people perceive themselves to be worthy or unworthy, good or bad

12. _____ parents should love their children no matter what their children do

13. _____ an internal monitor of social acceptance/ rejection

14. _____ overly favorable and unrealistic beliefs about oneself

15. _____ individuals can be threatened when someone close to them outperforms them on a task that is personally relevant

16. _____ people evaluate their own actions, abilities, and beliefs by contrasting them with other individuals

17. _____ refers to the evaluation of an object or idea

18. _____ model that attitudes consist of three components—affect, cognition, and behavior—that become linked

19. _____ thoughts that influence one's feelings and behavior at an unconscious level

20. _____ ease with which memories related to an attitude are retrieved

21. _____ seek out attitudinal information that supports one's decision and avoid information suggesting it's a poor choice

22. _____ active and conscious effort to change attitudes through the transmission of a message

23. _____ Petty and Cacioppo's model that there are central and peripheral routes to persuasion

24. _____ route to persuasion in which people minimally process the message

25. _____ process of how first impressions influence long-term evaluations

26. _____ people's causal explanations for why events or actions occur

27. _____ cognitive schemas that organize information about people based on their membership in certain groups

28. _____ with respect to stereotypes, people believe that a relationship exists when it actually does not

29. _____ when people encounter someone who does not fit their stereotype, rather than alter the stereotype they place that person in a special category

30. _____ groups to which we belong

31. _____ groups to which we do not belong

32. _____ very strong devaluation that extends to a person's entire character

33. _____ process in which people come to behave in ways that confirm their own or other's expectations

34. _____ idea that prejudice comes from a lack of familiarity with outgroup members and that getting to know the outgroup better would reduce the negative attitudes

35. _____ shared goals that, because they require people to cooperate to succeed, reduce hostility between groups

36. _____ program in which students work together in mixed-race or mixed-sex groups in which each mem-

ber of the group is an expert on one aspect of the assignment

MULTIPLE-CHOICE QUESTIONS

1. Charles works hard at maintaining a positive public image. He does a lot of high-profile charity work, and he is careful not to lose his temper in public. He believes that other parents see him as a role model for their children. His views of what he thinks others believe about him are known as _____.
   a. reflected appraisals
   b. basked glory
   c. the collective self
   d. the minimal self

2. Cliff often holds his infant daughter in front of the mirror to she if she recognizes herself or thinks the image is a playmate. Claire, his wife, explains that self-recognition normally occurs around _____.
   a. 6 months
   b. 12 months
   c. 18 months
   d. 24 months

3. Woody is having a tough time in college. There is a substantial gap between how he sees himself and how he believes he ought to seem to others. According to Higgins's self-discrepancy theory, which of the following emotions is Woody most likely to experience?
   a. disappointment
   b. frustration and helplessness
   c. sadness and depression
   d. anxiety and guilt

4. Naomi is a normal individual. She can recognize herself in a photograph with her sisters, and she can also recognize herself in photos as a little girl. This self-recognition is associated with which of the following brain areas?
   a. parietal lobe
   b. left frontal lobe
   c. right frontal lobe
   d. basal ganglia

5. Stephanie and Said have just met at a party. Stephanie asks him to describe himself. Said states that he is a senior finance major, 22 years old, Moroccan, Muslim, a soccer player, shy, and optimistic. These things Said knows about himself are part of his _____.
   a. minimal self
   b. self-concept
   c. self-recognition
   d. reflected appraisal

6. Jennifer is at a sorority mixer talking to friends. Although engaged in conversation, she hears her name mentioned in a discussion across the room. Her tendency to process information about herself despite distractions is known as _____.
   a. shadowing
   b. the cocktail party effect
   c. prosopagnosia
   d. selective consciousness

7. Bonita and Carlos come from a close-knit family, and their parents instilled in them the values of loyalty and teamwork. They both work very well in a group and understand the importance of cooperating with their friends. Their culture places greater emphasis on the _____ self.
   a. independent
   b. personal
   c. collective
   d. individual

8. Brandy has been encouraged by her parents to attend soccer camp. They want her to develop her skills enough that she will be selected for competitive leagues, even though it will mean leaving her friends behind on the community teams. Because of this influence, Brandy's self-concept will likely be characterized by _____.
   a. independent self-construals
   b. interdependent self-construals
   c. collectivism
   d. self-discrepancy

9. Jeffrey flunked out of school, got caught cheating on his girlfriend, lost his job due to embezzlement, and was arrested for running a methamphetamine lab. The fact that his parents still love him demonstrates _____.
   a. sociometry
   b. the better-than-average effect
   c. the self-enhancement motive
   d. unconditional acceptance

10. Sam is a businessman who likes to point to the money he gives to charity as an indicator of what a good person he is. Of course, he conveniently forgets that he pays his workers a terrible wage, provides no family or health benefits, and imports many of his goods from foreign sweatshops. The fact that Sam seeks out information that supports his positive self-views illustrates _____.
    a. the better-than-average effect
    b. sociometry
    c. reflected appraisals
    d. the self-enhancement motive

11. Raymond says to his brother Charlie, "I'm a very good driver," despite the fact that he is totally inept and has never driven before. This inflated view of the self is often referred to as _____.
    a. delusional cognitions
    b. the better-than-average effect
    c. self-evaluative maintenance
    d. downward social comparison

12. Which of the following is NOT one of the domains of positive illusions?
    a. overestimate one's skills, abilities, and competencies
    b. unrealistic perception of one's personal control over events
    c. unrealistically optimistic about one's personal future
    d. unconditional acceptance of other's misfortunes

13. Jorge has a friend who just made a popular music video. As Jorge has no musical aspirations, he is experiencing a boost in self-esteem just because he knows the now-famous musician. This phenomenon is known as _____.
    a. basking in reflected glory
    b. upward social comparison
    c. self-serving bias
    d. positive illusions

14. Tara and Lynn just finished a difficult psychology exam. Lynn is very upset and expresses concern over several questions on which she felt she might have done poorly. Although Tara is mildly apprehensive about a couple of questions, she feels much better after hearing Lynn moan about her test disaster. Tara's reaction illustrates the working of _____.
    a. upward social comparison
    b. counterfactual thinking
    c. self-serving bias
    d. downward social comparison

15. Jodie got her results for two exams on the same day. She made an A on her psychology exam but received a D on her anthropology exam. She attributed her psychology grade to her hard work, but stated that her poor performance in anthropology was because her professor is a "stupid jerk who tested irrelevant information." Assuming the tests were roughly equal in difficulty, her attributions are an example of _____.
    a. downward social comparison
    b. upward social comparison
    c. a self-serving bias
    d. the better-than-average effect

16. We tend to prefer photographs of ourselves with the image reversed, but we prefer photographs of friends as we see them because of _____.
    a. the mere exposure effect
    b. social exchange theory
    c. need complementarity
    d. attitude similarity

17. Samantha and her boyfriend, Lance, decide to be participants on a couples reality-television show. Before the show, Samantha believes she is totally committed to Lance and will not give in to the temptations presented by show's premise. However, after a few dream dates with a single guy on the show, Samantha gives in to temptation and cheats on Lance. Afterward, she feels very guilty about it and suddenly realizes that she is not as in love with Lance as she thought she was. What do Samantha's latest realizations illustrate?
    a. social facilitation
    b. implicit attitudes
    c. a consensus effect
    d. cognitive dissonance

18. Leon did an experiment with a group of graduate students who were music teachers. He paid one group of teachers $100 to try to convince an alleged school board member that music education was unimportant and the funding for it should be cut. He paid the other group $1 to accomplish the same task. He found that the group to which he paid $1 actually agreed with the message more because they had _____ for lying.
    a. insufficient justification
    b. postdecisional dissonance
    c. implicit attitudes
    d. selective exposure

19. Ozzy has free tickets to a baseball game and a rock concert. He really wants to attend both, but they are at the same time. He finally decides on the baseball game. He immediately focuses on the positive aspects of the baseball game (good weather, good pitching matchup) and the negative aspects of the rock concert (poor parking, hearing loss). Ozzy is motivated by _____.
    a. peripheral routes to persuasion
    b. elaboration likelihood
    c. effort justification
    d. postdecisional dissonance

20. Rory is pledging a sorority on campus. As part of initiation, she is forced to wear silly clothes, sing silly songs, and disregard her personal hygiene for a couple of weeks. After acceptance, she tells her family it was all worth it, because the ridicule brought her pledge class much closer together. Rory is engaging in the dissonance-reducing strategy of _____.
    a. selective exposure
    b. effort justification
    c. hazing denial
    d. elaboration likelihood

21. Chris is a first-year student who has not had much luck with studying. After listening to a couple of lectures on memory and studying tips, he tells his psychology professor that he found the lecture and text material very influential. He said that because of all these good suggestions, he was beginning to study more effectively. Chris's decision-making process is an example of using _____.
    a. the central route of persuasion
    b. the peripheral route of persuasion
    c. groupthink
    d. social facilitation

22. Mario is a political candidate who is debating the merits of the death penalty. He decides to give both sides of the argument and then focus on his position. This strategy is a better idea if his audience is _____.
    a. strongly supportive of him
    b. strongly supportive of the idea
    c. skeptical
    d. gullible

23. Dominique is purchasing a car. She has been gathering information from consumer magazines and prides herself on being thoughtful and reflective. Dominique can be considered to have a high level of _____.
    a. need for cognition
    b. elaboration likelihood
    c. achievement motivation
    d. conflict tolerance

24. Holly met a guy who was very sweet to her and complimented her on how beautiful and intelligent she was. Later that week, some of her friends told her that this guy was very arrogant and demeaning to women once you got to know him. Holly did not listen to her friends, continued to see him, and found out that her friends were wrong. Holly formed her impression based on _____.
    a. the matching effect
    b. a recency effect
    c. a primacy effect
    d. normative social influence

25. A man robbed a convenience store with a gun, escaping with all the money in the register. During the course of the investigation, detectives came up with several possible reasons as to why the man robbed the store. One was that maybe the man was poor and needed money to feed his family. This explanation is an example of _____.
    a. a personal attribution
    b. a situational attribution
    c. the fundamental attribution error
    d. groupthink

26. People often have difficulty accepting that celebrities have substantial drug and alcohol problems because their television characters are so nice and sweet. This expectation that one's behavior should correspond with their beliefs and personality (even if acting) is known as the _____.

a. actor–observer discrepancy
b. intuitive cognitive system
c. correspondence bias
d. Hollywood effect

27. Patty scurries into her psychology class at the last second. Her hair is sticking straight up, she has a sock stuck to the rear of her shirt, and her notebook has a bunch of papers sticking out in every direction. Before she can explain that her electricity went haywire, her psychology professor assumes that she is disorganized and lazy. The professor's attribution is an example of the _____.
a. confirmation bias
b. self-fulfilling prophecy
c. actor–observer discrepancy
d. misattribution principle

28. Josh, a Euro-American, has negative feelings about Juo, an Asian-American. Josh has no reason for these feelings and actually has not even talked to Juo. He just dislikes him because he is from a different ethnic background. What are Josh's feelings called?
a. prejudice
b. discrimination
c. a stereotype
d. a typology

29. Since the terrorist attacks on September 11, some American citizens have taken out their fear and anger on people who look like they might be from the same ethnic group as the hijackers. This type of unjustifiable behavior is called _____.
a. prejudice
b. assimilation reaction
c. ethnic referencing
d. discrimination

30. Following the terrorist attacks on September 11, some angry Americans have lumped together all people who look even vaguely "Middle Eastern" and believe they all are linked to terrorism in some way. The beliefs of these Americans illustrate _____.
a. social categorization
b. the outgroup homogeneity effect
c. social role typing
d. ingroup favoritism

31. Sandy, Roxanne, and Carolyn are put into a group in their statistics class. Kristen, Lori, and Melinda are put into a different group. All six of these women were originally friends. However, since being put into opposing groups, they have become bitter toward those not in their group and will share notes and homework only with group members. Their reactions reflect _____.

a. egoistic realism
b. ingroup favoritism
c. outgroup homogeneity effect
d. social roles theory

32. Two groups of college women are participating in validation studies for a new test. They take the same test. One group is told that it is a general information test, the other group is told that it is a math test on which women generally struggle. Even though the groups are roughly equal in mathematical ability, the group that is primed for the math struggle does substantially worse. This apparent confirmation of a negative stereotype is known as _____.
a. confirmation bias
b. stereotype threat
c. illusory correlation
d. gender choking

THOUGHT QUESTION

You have been brought in as a consultant to a school system that is experiencing considerable racial conflict and gang violence. Considering the research on stereotypes, prejudice, and discrimination, discuss how you might address these problems.

ANSWER KEY

Fill-in-the-Blank Questions

1. social psychology
2. social cognition
3. self
4. symbolic self
5. self-awareness
6. autonoetic consciousness
7. executive functions
8. self-schema
9. personal self
10. interdependent self-construals
11. self-esteem
12. unconditional acceptance
13. sociometer
14. positive illusions
15. self-evaluative maintenance
16. social comparison
17. attitude
18. tricomponent
19. implicit attitudes
20. attitude accessibility
21. postdecisional dissonance
22. persuasion
23. elaboration likelihood
24. peripheral route
25. impression formation
26. attributions
27. stereotypes
28. illusory correlation
29. subtyping
30. ingroups
31. outgroups
32. stigma
33. self-fulfilling prophecy
34. contact hypothesis
35. superordinate goals
36. jigsaw classroom

Multiple-Choice Questions

1. a Reflected appraisals are the views we believe others have of us.

2. c At around 18 months, children show evidence that they recognize a mirror or video image as their own.

3. d According to Higgins's self-discrepancy theory, anxiety and guilt result from gaps between how we see ourselves and how we believe we ought to seem to others.

4. c The ability to recognize oneself appears to be a function of the right hemisphere frontal lobe.

5. b Self-concept is the term for everything that you know about yourself.

6. b The cocktail party effect is the tendency to process information about the self despite distractions.

7. c The collective self emphasizes connections to family, social groups and ethnic groups and conformity to societal norms and group cohesiveness.

8. a Those in individualistic cultures tend to have independent self-construals, as they are encouraged to be self-reliant and pursue personal success, even at the expense of interpersonal relationships.

9. d Unconditional acceptance is when parents love their children no matter what they do.

10. d The self-enhancement motive is when individuals are especially motivated to seek out information that confirms their positive self-views.

11. b The better-than-average effect refers to the tendency for people to describe themselves as above average in just about every possible way.

12. d The three domains of positive illusions are overestimate one's skills, abilities, and competencies; unrealistic perception of one's personal control over events; and unrealistically optimistic about one's personal future; unconditional acceptance of other's misfortunes is not one of these domains.

13. a On dimensions you do not find personally relevant, you might bask in the glow of reflected glory and experience a boost in self-esteem based on your relationship with others.

14. d In downward social comparison, people contrast themselves with others who are deficient to them on relevant dimensions.

15. c The self-serving bias is the tendency to take credit for success but blame failure on outside factors.

16. a The mere exposure effect indicates that the greater exposure we have to an item, the more positive attitude we have toward the item.

17. d Cognitive dissonance states that when there is a contradiction between an attitude and behavior, people change either their attitude or the behavior.

18. a The $1 group had insufficient justification for lying; therefore, they had to change their attitude more to reduce their dissonance.

19. d Postdecisional dissonance motivates individuals to focus on the positive characteristics of their choice and the negative aspects of the choice not made.

20. b Effort justification is when individuals resolve their dissonance by increasing the importance of the group and their commitment to it.

21. a The central route to persuasion is one in which people pay attention to arguments, consider all the information, and use rational cognitive processes.

22. c Two-sided arguments tend to be more persuasive when the audience is skeptical.

23. a Those high in need for cognition pride themselves on being thoughtful and reflective, and they tend to process information centrally.

24. c The primacy effect in impression formation occurs because the initial information alters the way that the subsequent information is interpreted.

25. b Situational or external attributions refer to outside events, such as the weather, luck, accidents, or the actions of other people that cause actions to occur.

26. c The correspondence bias is when we expect people's behavior to correspond with their beliefs and personality.

27. c In the actor–observer discrepancy, individuals are biased toward situational factors when explaining their own behavior but biased toward dispositional factors when explaining the behavior of others.

28. a Prejudice refers to the affective or attitudinal responses associated with stereotypes, and it usually involves negative judgments about people based on their group memberships.

29. d Discrimination is the unjustified and inappropriate treatment of people based solely on their group memberships.

30. b In the outgroup homogeneity effect, individuals tend to view outgroup members as less varied than ingroup members.

31. b With ingroup favoritism, individuals are more likely to distribute resources to members of the ingroup than the outgroup.

32. b Stereotype threat is when individuals do poorly when they perceive that their behavior may confirm a negative stereotype.

Thought Question

Answers will vary but might include a discussion of the contact hypothesis or idea that simply learning more about outgroups will lessen tension and hostility (it does not). Students might incorporate Sherif's ideas of disparate groups having shared superordinate goals and how this might be incorporated into school activities. In addition, they might propose a variation of Aronson's jigsaw classroom as a way of facilitating more positive attitudes toward other ethnicities. Finally, students might discuss how ingroup and outgroup formation seems to be a natural, and normally adaptive, process of social interaction.

CHAPTER 14 | Interpersonal Processes

Chapter 14 continues the topic of social psychology—how other people influence the way we think, feel, and act. In the last chapter, the authors looked at social cognition or how we process information relevant to the self and others. The focus in Chapter 14 is on personal relationships and social influence, or how other people shape our actions. One fundamental principle that runs through the entire chapter is the basic human need to belong. This clearly has an adaptive function, because in our evolutionary past, those who could live in functional groups and share the work survived. Our need to belong has a host of repercussions, including the fact that we are strongly influenced by social norms. We also try to maintain a positive self-presentation, environmental cues highly influence our prosocial behavior, and we are strongly affected by our interpersonal relationships. Our ability to interact with others continues to be one of our most basic needs as well as one of our greatest challenges.

How Social Are Humans?

The chapter begins with Baumeister and Leary's *need to belong theory* that states that the need for interpersonal attachments is a fundamental motive that has evolved for adaptive purposes. This theory is supported by the finding that people feel anxious when they face exclusion from their social groups (*social exclusion theory*). It is hypothesized that we have evolved *cheater detectors* that are especially sensitive to violations in social exchanges. Thus, although individuals may be motivated to act selfishly for short-term gain, they are inhibited by the possibility of being detected and facing long-term social punishment and rejection. Additional sup-

porting evidence of the need to belong is seen in Stanley Schachter's classic *affiliation* study. Research participants faced with an anxiety-producing situation chose to affiliate with other anxious participants. This led to Schachter's often-quoted line that "misery loves miserable company."

What Information Is Contained in Nonverbal Behavior?

The advantages of living with others resulted in the need to communicate. We are adept at forming immediate impressions of others through both verbal and *nonverbal information*. Nonverbal information is communicated through *facial expressions, gait, posture, gestures,* and *vocal cues.* However, despite our facility with these channels of data, we are poor at detecting *deception.* This leads to the interesting proposal that deception is a prerequisite for harmonious human interaction. Finally, although we appear to be innately predisposed to communicating nonverbally, the form of one's body language can vary widely between cultures as seen in the regulation of *personal space* and gestures.

How Do People Manage Their Public Impressions?

The need to belong also influences how we want to be seen by others. We want to be viewed as competent and contributing members who would be desirable to the group. Therefore, we have developed a number of strategies for positive *self-presentation.* One must be careful with *impression management* techniques because they can easily backfire, particularly among people who know us well. Individuals who are high in the trait of *self-monitoring* are especially likely to monitor and regulate their public image.

Table 14.1 SELF-PRESENTATION STRATEGIES

Strategy	Process/Goal
Ingratiation	convincing others that you are likable
Self-promotion	showing one's competence and aptitude to gain others' respect
Exemplification	convincing others that you are, by example, a morally virtuous person
Intimidation	demonstrating importance and power over others through words and actions
Supplication	stressing one's weaknesses to elicit sympathy and assistance

When Does Social Power Influence Others?

Because groups are so important to us, they exert a powerful influence over our behavior. In fact, the power of social situations is much greater than most people believe, and individuals will often act in ways that greatly contradict their personal standards. The processes of *social facilitation, social loafing,* and *deindividuation* show how groups can influence individual behavior, sometimes in dangerous ways. Groups can make terrible decisions, such as in the case of the launching the space shuttle *Challenger;* thus it is necessary for individuals to understand the tendency toward *group polarization.*

Individuals conform to *social norms,* even when there may be obvious reasons not to do so. Those aware of strategies of social influence may use the techniques of *foot in the door, door in the face,* and *low balling* to gain *compliance.* A rather frightening demonstration of the power of social influence was provided by Stanley Milgram's classic studies on *obedience* to authority. He showed that one can get others to engage in horrible, antisocial acts simply through the power of the social context and by being insistent.

When Do People Harm or Help Others?

In the next section, the authors present data from psychological science on when individuals are likely to harm or help others. *Aggression,* behavior intended to harm someone else, is related to *frontal lobe dysfunction* and low levels of *serotonin.* It also stems from *frustration* and situations that elicit negative affect. Although men are more physically aggressive than women, they show similar levels of verbal aggression. Societal factors such as a *culture of honor* also can factor into displays of aggression. On the other side, humans engage in amazingly *prosocial* and *altruistic* acts. This is particularly evident when the person in need is a relative. Surprisingly, having more people around when in need does not increase your chances of getting help (*bystander intervention effect*) due to a *diffusion of responsibility* and *fear of making social blunders.*

What Determines the Quality of Relationships?

The final section of the chapter looks at the factors that influence some of our most critical social decisions—the choice of friends and relationship partners. These choices are affected by variables such as *proximity, similarity,* and *physical attractiveness.* The controversial *sexual strategies theory* suggests that men and women differ on mating strategies based on what is evolutionarily adaptive for them. Therefore, men may seek women who look as if they could bear healthy children, whereas women search for mates who have the resources necessary to nurture offspring.

Our society places a great emphasis on love and a distinction is made between the intense longing of *passionate love* and the long-term commitment of *companionate love.* Divorce statistics indicate that making love last is a difficult proposition. Relationships are challenged by the fading of passion, jealousy from extramarital affairs, and maladaptive strategies for coping with conflict. Happy couples explain their partner's behavior through *partner-enhancing attributions,* but unhappy couples make *distress-maintaining attributions.*

FILL-IN-THE-BLANK QUESTIONS

1. _____ how other people shape our actions

2. _____ the norms, standards, and values of other people in a particular situation

3. _____ the tendency to be in social contact with others

4. _____ theory that says the need for interpersonal attachments is a fundamental motive that has evolved for adaptive purposes

5. _____ involve friends, lovers, and family members and are ruled by the expectation that there is a mutual interdependency and care for each other's needs.

6. _____ body language including facial expressions, gestures, walking style, and fidgeting

7. _____ how people walk

8. _____ gestures that expand on or explain verbal communication

9. _____ physical distance that people maintain between themselves and others

10. _____ area within about 18 inches of a person in which close friends are allowed

11. _____ also known as self-presentation, it refers to how we exhibit our personal characteristics before an audience

12. _____ convincing others that you are likable

13. _____ the more a person needs to be liked, the more sensitized the target person will be to any cues suggesting deceit or ulterior motives

14. _____ demonstrating personal importance and power over others through words and actions

15. _____ individuals stress their weaknesses and rely on others' reluctance to kick a person who is down

16. _____ when people work less hard in a group because the efforts are pooled together so that no one individual is accountable for the group's outcome

17. _____ finding that groups often make riskier decisions than do individuals

18. _____ process in which groups tend to enhance the initial attitudes of members who already agree

19. _____ people agree to do things requested by others

20. _____ people are more likely to comply with a large and undesirable request if they have earlier agreed to a small request

21. _____ when people follow orders given by an authority

22. _____ model that frustration leads to aggression because it elicits negative affect

23. _____ belief system found in the southern United States in which men are primed to be prepared to protect their reputations through physical aggression

24. _____ behavior in which someone benefits from another's actions

25. _____ people are altruistic toward those with whom they share genes

26. _____ explains altruism toward nonrelatives in which one animal helps another because the other can return the favor in the future

27. _____ in emergency situations, people expect that others who are also around will offer help

28. _____ general human fear of anything novel

29. _____ finding that the most successful romantic couples tend to be the most physically similar

30. _____ evolutionary theory that men seek women who can bear healthy children, whereas women seek men with the resources to nurture offspring

31. _____ state of intense longing and sexual desire

32. _____ strong commitment to care and support a partner that develops slowly over time

33. _____ attributions of happy couples in which good outcomes are the result of each other and bad outcomes are the result of the situation

MULTIPLE-CHOICE QUESTIONS

1. Monty is playing with his buddies in a golf tournament. However, he is playing poorly and is not contributing much to his group's success. The fact that Monty is feeling anxiety because of possible rejection from his group is predicted by _____ theory.
   a. emotional affiliation
   b. social exclusion
   c. group norms
   d. interdependency

2. In Stanley Schachter's famous affiliation experiment, research participants who were highly anxious chose to affiliate with _____.
   a. no one
   b. happy research participants
   c. neutral research participants
   d. highly anxious research participants

3. Chantal has a 2.96 cumulative grade-point average. However, she really wants to know if this is better or worse than the average student in her major. Her desire for accurate information about herself and others is an example of _____ theory.
   a. social comparison
   b. need to belong
   c. social exclusion
   d. social context

4. George is completing his federal tax form. He is tempted to exaggerate his charitable contributions and travel expenses to lower his taxes. However, he also knows that the money goes to support many necessary social programs, including some that may take care of him when he gets older. This motivational conflict between cooperating in a group and being selfish is known as a _____.
   a. Wason selection task
   b. social honesty encounter
   c. social dilemma
   d. cheater's phenomenon

5. Eileen and Connie are psychology professors. Eileen agrees to cover Connie's classes while she is in China; however, Eileen expects the same favor when she needs to be gone in the very near future. This expectation of immediate repayment for benefits given is characteristic of _____ relationships.
   a. exchange
   b. communal

c. community

d. interdependent

6. Lilith is a therapist who is very good at reading body language. She can tell a lot about her clients simply by noting their facial expressions, gestures, and tone of voice. These various sources of nonverbal information are known as _____.

a. pathways

b. channels

c. gateways

d. markers

7. Jon is going on a blind date. As he meets the woman in the lobby of his dorm, he sees his friends hiding behind a large plant. They give Jon the thumbs-up sign, indicating that they think his date is attractive. Gestures such as these that have specific meanings are known as _____.

a. illustrators

b. signage

c. markers

d. emblems

8. Dr. Jones is giving a psychology exam. He notices a lot more grumbling and sighing than usual. From this, he infers that it must be a difficult exam. These vocal cues are often referred to as _____.

a. paralanguage

b. subvocalizations

c. body language

d. gestures

9. Deception seems to be a necessary part of social interaction. For college students, the person they lie to most often is their _____.

a. professor

b. father

c. mother

d. sibling

10. Kelli is talking to her casual friend Henri. Suddenly Henri moves his face to within about 18 inches of hers and continues the conversation. Kelli is uncomfortable as Henri has exceeded the _____ zone of her personal space where most casual conversations take place.

a. intimate

b. personal

c. implicit

d. interactive

11. Julie wants to be seen as competent. Every time her boss is around, she talks about her recent accomplishments and how valuable she is to the organization. Julie is engaging in the impression management strategy of _____.

a. exemplification

b. positive reassurance seeking

c. supplication

d. self-promotion

12. Tony is a professional baseball player. He does considerable charity work with kids who are at risk for problems. Tony tries to set a good example while on the baseball field by playing hard and not showing his anger when he is frustrated. Tony is engaging in the self-presentation strategy of _____.

a. ingratiation

b. exemplification

c. supplication

d. negative reassurance seeking

13. Rachel constantly asks her roommates, "I'm not fat, am I?" and "People like me, don't they?" They did not mind this at first, but now they are getting tired of her strategy of _____.

a. negative reassurance seeking

b. self-monitoring

c. exemplification

d. social loafing

14. Bob is a smooth car salesman. He is very sensitive to what the buyer wants and can change his personality to fit the situation. He is relaxed with young people and respectful with the elderly. Bob is likely high in the trait of _____.

a. self-monitoring

b. social facilitation

c. pragmatism

d. psychopathy

15. Kristen decided to try out for the university's gymnastics team. When she performed her routine in front of team members and the coach, she did really well on an easy cartwheel. However, when she tried the really difficult double-twisted flip, she fell over and lost her shoe. Kristen's performance was affected by _____.

a. social loafing

b. deindividuation

c. the bystander effect

d. social facilitation

16. Brandy is at a music concert where she is surrounded by thousands of people. Although she is normally shy and afraid to express her feelings, she soon gets swept up in the madness around her. She joins the mosh pit and begins yelling, laughing, and dancing hysterically. Which of the following best explains her sudden loss of inhibition?

a. deindividuation

b. the bystander effect

c. social facilitation

d. emotional contagion

17. The space shuttle *Challenger* was launched despite the fact that it was a fairly cold morning and NASA had been warned about faulty O-rings on the solid-rocket booster. The term that describes this extreme form of group decision making among NASA engineers is _____.
    a. groupthink
    b. deindividuation
    c. conformity
    d. conflict avoidance

18. Dr. Smith, an American psychologist, went to a professional conference. When she greeted other psychologists, she politely said hello and firmly shook hands with them. What does Dr. Smith's behavior illustrate?
    a. social schemas
    b. ingroup rules
    c. sanction norms
    d. social norms

19. When Phoebe stopped by her friend Monica's new apartment, she noticed that the living room walls were covered by hideous orange wallpaper. However, the next day when Monica asked her group of friends if they liked her beautiful wallpaper, all the rest said yes, so Phoebe did too. Phoebe's statement is an example of _____.
    a. social facilitation
    b. groupthink
    c. deindividuation
    d. conformity

20. Ginger is interested in buying a new evening dress. She tells her mother that she will need $300 to purchase it. After her mother goes through an emotional tirade, Ginger asks for $100 to purchase the dress (which is the amount she wanted all along) and her mother agrees. Ginger is engaging in the influence tactic of _____.
    a. foot in the door
    b. door in the face
    c. low balling
    d. high rolling

21. Pedro is shopping for a car. He finally finds one at a reasonable price with all the options he wants. He agrees to buy it from the salesperson. When he goes to sign the contract, he notices a number of extras have been added (e.g., pinstripes, floor mats, keys, undercoating). Pedro believes the salesperson is trying the tactic of _____.
    a. high rolling
    b. door in the face
    c. options management
    d. low balling

22. In the famous Milgram obedience study, approximately what proportion of volunteers were willing to deliver the highest level of shock (450 volts) to the innocent volunteer/confederate?
    a. none
    b. one fifth
    c. one third
    d. two thirds

23. Which of the following is NOT an example of aggression?
    a. Shelton breaks the leg of a pedestrian he does not see and backs over
    b. because of jealousy, Mara starts a vicious, untrue rumor about a girl who talks to her boyfriend
    c. Mac pushes his professor down the stairs after getting frustrated in a psychology exam
    d. after Elliot and his girlfriend break up, he goes for a walk and knocks over the little lawn statues on everybody's lawns

24. Which of the following was NOT found in the history of 100 violent criminals studied by Jonathan Pincus?
    a. early childhood abuse
    b. psychiatric disorders such as paranoia
    c. torturing animals
    d. frontal lobe dysfunction

25. Which of the following is TRUE regarding sex differences in aggression?
    a. men are more physically aggressive than women, but women show higher levels of verbal aggression
    b. men are more physically aggressive than women, and they also show higher levels of verbal aggression
    c. men are more physically aggressive than women, but men and women show similar levels of verbal aggression
    d. women show greater levels of physical and verbal aggression

26. Lori, who was in a hurry to get to school so she could be on time for a big test, became very angry because Kristen was driving like a snail in front of her. When they stopped at a red light, Lori got out of her car and smashed Kristen's windshield. Lori's behavior can best be explained by _____.
    a. social facilitation theory
    b. the frustration–aggression hypothesis
    c. the projection hypothesis
    d. the bystander effect

27. Jerry was involved in a train crash. Although numerous cars were on fire, he rushed back into the train to save as many others as possible. This providing of help without any apparent reward for doing so is known as _____.
    a. inclusive fitness
    b. altruism
    c. hedonism
    d. reciprocity

28. Jen was leaving a house with friends after a night of partying. In the street, they see several groups and pairs of people staring and discussing a scene involving a man repeatedly slapping a woman while yelling and cursing at her. Jen experiences the bystander intervention effect, so she _____.
    a. ignores the scene and does not help the woman
    b. ignores everyone standing around and runs to help the woman
    c. immediately finds a phone and calls the police
    d. rallies a bunch of other observers to help the woman

29. Which of the following is NOT one of the reasons for the bystander intervention effect?
    a. diffusion of responsibility
    b. fear of making social blunders
    c. personal anonymity
    d. low level of moral reasoning

30. Norman found that his friends in college were the people in the dorms who lived near him. He saw them a lot and they began hanging out together. His situation illustrates the effects of _____ on friendship.
    a. matching
    b. proximity
    c. conditioned rewards
    d. propriety

31. Pam and Tommy have all the same interests. They both like wild parties, tattoos, constant stimulation, and loads of attention. Because of the effects of _____, they have become close friends.
    a. matching
    b. propinquity
    c. conditioned rewards
    d. similarity

32. When Lyle and Erik were facing charges in court, their attorney took great pains to ensure that they had fresh haircuts and were dressed as attractively as possible. Their attorney is using the _____ stereotype.
    a. door in the face
    b. what is beautiful is good
    c. birds of a feather flock together
    d. external similarity

33. Which of the following is NOT one of the components of Robert Sternberg's triangular theory of love?
    a. arousal
    b. passion
    c. intimacy
    d. commitment

34. Dennis decides to bring home some flowers to show his girlfriend, Carmen, how much he cares for her. When she sees the flowers, she flies into a rage accusing him of infidelity or doing something else that he is trying to atone for. Carmen is making _____ attributions.
    a. distress-maintaining
    b. partner-enhancing
    c. external
    d. socially destructive

THOUGHT QUESTION

You are a psychotherapist at the university counseling center. The university has instituted a policy that all students who wish to get married can come in for four sessions of free prenuptial advice. Describe how you would assess which couples were at risk for problems and how you might help the couples with future difficulties.

ANSWER KEY

Fill-in-the-Blank Questions

1. social influence
2. social context
3. affiliation
4. need to belong
5. communal relationships
6. nonverbal behavior
7. gait
8. illustrators
9. personal space
10. intimate zone
11. impression management
12. ingratiation
13. ingratiator's dilemma
14. intimidation
15. supplication
16. social loafing
17. risky-shift effect
18. group polarization
19. compliance
20. foot in the door
21. obedience
22. cognitive-neoassociationistic
23. culture of honor
24. prosocial
25. kin selection
26. reciprocal helping
27. diffusion of responsibility
28. neophobia
29. matching principle
30. sexual strategies
31. passionate love
32. companionate love
33. partner-enhancing

Multiple-Choice Questions

1. b Social exclusion theory states that individuals feel anxious when they face exclusion from their social groups due to reasons of immorality, incompetence, or unattractiveness.

2. d High-anxiety participants wanted to wait with only other high-anxiety participants; thus misery loves miserable company.

3. a Leon Festinger's social comparison theory states that people have a strong desire to have accurate information about themselves and others.

4. c A social dilemma exists when there is a motivational conflict both to cooperate within a group and to be selfish.

5. a Exchange relationships, which are typical of how people interact with co-workers or casual acquaintances, are ruled by the expectation of immediate repayment for benefits given.

6. b The various sources of nonverbal information are referred to as channels.

7. d Emblems are gestures that have specific meanings.

8. a Vocal cues are often referred to as paralanguage and include stress, intonation, pitch, and nonwords (grumbling and sighs).

9. c For college students, the person they lie to most often is their mothers.

10. b Most casual conversations take place in the personal zone of personal space, which extends several feet.

11. d Self-promotion is showing one's competence and aptitude to gain others' respect.

12. b Exemplification refers to convincing people that you are, by example, a morally virtuous person.

13. a Negative reassurance seeking occurs when individuals constantly look to others for compliments.

14. a People who are high in self-monitoring are very sensitive to cues of situational appropriateness and use these cues as guidelines for regulating self-presentations.

15. d Social facilitation is when the presence of others influences performance; it can enhance the performance for simple tasks but interfere with performance on complex tasks.

16. a Deindividuation occurs when people are not self-aware (e.g., part of a group) and, therefore, not paying attention to their personal standards.

17. a Groupthink is an extreme form of group polarization that occurs when the group is under intense pressure, is facing external threats, and is biased in a particular direction.

18. d Social norms are expected standards of conduct, such as behavior that is appropriate in a given situation.

19. d Conformity is the altering of one's behavior or opinions to match those of others.

20. b Door in the face is the influence technique in which people are more likely to agree to a small request after they have refused a large request, because the second request seems modest in comparison.

21. d Low balling is the tactic of getting people to agree to a very low price and then adding additional costs.

22. d Approximately two thirds of volunteers were willing to deliver the highest level of shock.

23. a Aggression is any behavior or action that involves the intention to harm someone else.

24. c Pincus found a combination of early childhood abuse, psychiatric disorders such as paranoia, and frontal lobe dysfunction evident in more than 90 percent of violent criminals. A history of torturing animals was not evident.

25. c Men are more physically aggressive than women, but men and women show similar levels of verbal aggression.

26. b The frustration–aggression hypothesis states that the more one's goals are blocked, the greater the frustration and thus the greater the aggression.

27. b Altruism is the providing of help without any apparent reward for doing so.

28. a The bystander intervention effect refers to the failure to offer help by those who observe someone in need.

29. d The bystander intervention effect is due to a diffusion of responsibility, fear of making social blunders, personal anonymity, and a cost-benefit trade-off; level of moral reasoning has not been correlated with it.

30. b The effects of proximity are that the more often people come into contact, the more likely they are to become friends.

31. d People who are similar in attitudes, values, interest, backgrounds, and personalities tend to like each other.

32. b The what is beautiful is good stereotype relates to the finding the physically attractive people are judged to be less socially deviant and are given lighter sentences when convicted of crimes.

33. a Sternberg's triangular theory of love consists of three components: passion, intimacy, and commitment. Arousal is not one of these.

34. a Unhappy couples make distress-maintaining attributions in which they view each other in the most negative way possible.

Thought Question

Answers will vary. In terms of assessment, students might address the issues of proximity and similarity while taking into account the phenomenon of need complementarity. The couple could also be rated on Sternberg's three components of love: passion, intimacy, and commitment. A therapist might inform the couples of evolutionary differences in mating strategies as developed by sexual strategies theory. One also could relate the differences between passionate and companionate love and the toxicity of extramarital affairs.

In terms of treatment, the therapist could attempt to alter Gottman's four interpersonal styles that lead to marital discord: being overly critical, holding the partner in contempt, being defensive, and mentally withdrawing from the relationship. One could also try to help the couple make partner-enhancing attributions as opposed to distress-maintaining attributions.

CHAPTER 15 | Personality

GUIDE TO THE READING

Chapter 15 addresses the issue of personality, one of the oldest topics in psychology. It seems to be a fundamental aspect of human nature to speculate as to why each of us is unique and what made us that way. Investigators have long debated what personality is, the correct way to study it, and how individual personality interacts with the broader social environment. The authors summarize the four traditional approaches to understanding personality (psychodynamic, trait, humanistic, cognitive-social) and the methods of personality assessment associated with each. Recent advances in the area of behavioral neuroscience have contributed greatly to our understanding of the individual person. Many of our traits have a strong genetic component, and these tendencies are relatively stable from infancy through adulthood. But while genetics and neurochemistry may set the framework for our tendencies, our interactions with the environment finalize this process based on our selections of which traits and skills are adaptive.

How Has Personality Been Studied?

The initial section of the chapter reviews what personality is and the four traditional approaches for studying it. Although researchers have disagreed about specific aspects, there is relative agreement that the term *personality* refers to a person's characteristics, emotional responses, thoughts, and behaviors that are relatively stable over time and across circumstances. *Psychodynamic* theorists, beginning with Freud, have proposed that unconscious forces influence behavior. Freud developed a topographical model of the mind in which there are three levels of mental awareness: *conscious, preconscious,* and *unconscious*. Freud described how thinking and behavior develop in five psychosexual stages (*oral, anal, phallic,*

latency, genital) based on children's interactions with their parents. Finally, he proposed a structural model of personality in which three dynamic processes (*id, ego, superego*) struggle to meet basic needs in the context of interaction with the social environment. Despite the many criticisms of Freudian theory, it served as a springboard for much of the theorizing and research of the past century.

Humanistic personality theorists objected to the determinism of Freudian (and later behavioral) models. They emphasized personal experience, or *phenomenology,* and the fulfillment of human potential (*self-actualization*). Recently, this has led to the *positive psychology movement* and the scientific investigation of the positive aspects of humanity. *Trait* theorists propose that individuals differ on broad personality dispositions. Factor analysis of these traits has led to a number of different solutions, but in the last 20 years many personality psychologists have endorsed the *five-factor theory* of personality. The *Big Five,* as they are known, are *extraversion, neuroticism, conscientiousness, agreeableness,* and *openness to experience.* Finally, *cognitive-social* theories of personality have integrated the findings of learning theory with the idea that beliefs, expectancies, and interpretations also influence the exhibition of behavior.

Table 15.1 TRADITIONAL APPROACHES TO THE STUDY OF PERSONALITY

Theoretical Approach	View of Personality
Psychodynamic	result of unconscious conflicts, usually developed in childhood
Humanistic	result of striving for fullest human potential (self-actualization)
Trait	reflected in variations of broad human dispositions
Cognitive-social	integration of learning history and cognitive expectancies and beliefs

How Is Personality Assessed and What Does It Predict?

The next section of the chapter deals with the assessment of personality. *Idiographic approaches* to understanding personality address individuals and the characteristics that make them unique. Common techniques in this approach are *case studies* and *psychobiography*. *Nomothetic approaches* focus on characteristics that are common among all people but for which individuals vary. Traditionally, assessment tools have been divided into projective and objective measures. *Projective measures*, such as *inkblots* and *the Thematic Apperception Test*, are based on psychodynamic theory. That is, it is hypothesized if you are presented with an ambiguous stimulus, you will project your unconscious conflicts onto that stimulus. Recent developments in these techniques have been more empirically based. *Objective measures* are more direct and usually consist of behavioral observations or self-report questionnaires (e.g., *NEO personality inventory*).

Walter Mischel initiated a turning point in personality study with his 1968 proclamation that the traits assessed by such measures did a poor job of predicting behavior. His theory of *situationism* suggested that the interpersonal environment had a much greater influence on behavior, which calls into question whether the construct of personality even exists. The result of this work led to much research and today's idea of *interactionism*, which maintains that behavior is the result of both broad dispositions and the unique situation.

What Is the Biological Basis of Personality?

Research into the biological basis of personality has done much to illuminate many of the classic questions of personality (e.g., Does personality exist? Can personality change?). It is now evident that personality is strongly rooted in neurophysiology, and roughly half the variance in personality traits is accounted for by genetic influences. Biological differences in personality, referred to as *temperaments*, are evident in very young children and persist throughout the life span. In direct contrast to the ideas of Freud, Stella Chess and Alexander Thomas found that many children can be divided into one of three temperaments (*easy, difficult, slow to warm up*), regardless of parental upbringing. The temperamental trait of *introversion/extraversion* has been strongly linked to neurophysiology. Introverts have an active *behavioral inhibition system* that leads them to avoid social situations in which they anticipate possible negative outcomes. Extraverts have a stronger *behavioral approach system* and are influenced more by the possibility of rewards than punishments. The results of these investigations suggest that people are different because of differing physiology. These preferences also likely reflect what has been adaptive for us over the course of human evolution.

Can Personality Change?

Sigmund Freud proposed that the personality is basically fixed by the age of 5. This infuriated people in Western cultures, because it contradicted the possibility for change and improvement that is part of our mythology. Research in temperament suggests that these early tendencies do play a pervasive and influential role in adulthood. A meta-analysis of 150 studies on personality change indicated that there is a possibility for change in childhood, but personality becomes very stable by middle age. Part of the debate concerns the definition of personality. Our *basic tendencies*, which are highly determined by biological processes, tend to be very stable. Our *characteristic adaptations* may vary in novel situations, but it is argued that our core dispositions do not change. Still, we maintain the possibility of a *quantum change* or personality transformation, but this results only from an extreme negative affect (hitting rock bottom) and/or a trigger event. A final finding that certain personality traits are strongly related to neurochemistry (e.g., *hostility* and *serotonin*) and can be manipulated leads to a host of ethical questions. If thousands of years of human evolution have led us to vary on the trait of sociability, should we take a pill that instantly would make us more sociable? Is it adaptive to make everyone more cooperative and less hostile?

FILL-IN-THE-BLANK QUESTIONS

1. _____ refers to a person's characteristics, emotional responses, thoughts, and behaviors that are relatively stable over time and across circumstances

2. _____ dispositional tendency to act in a certain way over time and across circumstances

3. _____ Freudian term for process that directs people to seek pleasure and avoid pain

4. _____ energy that drives the pleasure principle

5. _____ Freudian conflict in which boys develop an unconscious conflict to kill their fathers and marry their mothers

6. _____ Freudian principle for the ego that involves rational thought and problem solving

7. _____ approach to personality that emphasizes personal experience, belief systems, and human potential

8. _____ subjective human experience

9. _____ recent movement to use the methods of science to study the positive aspects of humanity

10. _____ general term for how much happiness and satisfaction people have in their lives

11. _____ tendency to assume that personality characteristics go together and, therefore, make predictions about people based on minimal evidence

12. _____ Kelly's term for people's understandings of their circumstances

13. _____ people's responses in a given situation are influenced by how they encode or perceive the situation, their affective response to the situation, the skills and competencies they have to deal with challenges, and their anticipation of the outcomes that their behavior will produce

14. _____ traits that are particularly descriptive of individuals as compared to others

15. _____ traits that people consider less personally descriptive or not applicable at all

16. _____ reconstructive and imaginative process in which people link together personal motives, goals, and beliefs with the events, people, and circumstances in which they find themselves

17. _____ uses personal life stories to develop and test theories about human personality

18. _____ focus on characteristics that are common among all people, but for which people vary

19. _____ requires people to sort 100 statements printed on cards into nine piles according to what extent the statement is descriptive of them

20. _____ trait referring to how much excitement you seek out of life

21. _____ trait theorists who believe that behavior is jointly determined by situations underlying dispositions

22. _____ refer to general tendencies to feel or act in certain ways

23. _____ overall amount of energy and behavior exhibited by a person

24. _____ general tendency to affiliate with others

25. _____ children who exhibit regular cycles of eating and sleeping, approach novel situations positively, and adapt to change quickly with few if any problems

26. _____ children who display irregular sleep and eating patterns, have an overall negative response to most situations and especially new situations, and have a tendency to withdraw from others

27. _____ regulates cortical arousal or alertness

28. _____ consists of the brain structures that lead organisms to approach stimuli in pursuit of rewards

29. _____ consists of the brain structures that are sensitive to punishment and, therefore, inhibits behavior that might lead to danger or pain

30. _____ system that locks a person into the trait strategy chosen to the exclusion of others that might have been pursued under different circumstances

31. _____ dispositional traits that are determined to a great extent by biological processes and, as such, are very stable

32. _____ adjustments people make to situational demands, which tend to be consistent because they are based on skills, habits, and roles

MULTIPLE-CHOICE QUESTIONS

1. Randall has been highly disruptive in college. His poor grades and antisocial behavior have eventually led him to be expelled. His therapist explains to his parents that Randall is unconsciously acting out because he did not want to attend college. The therapist is taking a _____ approach to understanding personality.
   a. psychodynamic
   b. type
   c. cognitive-social
   d. humanistic

2. Julie is introduced to her biological mother who abandoned her as an infant. As they shake hands Julie says, "It's nice to *beat* you." This Freudian slip is an example of information at the _____ level being accidentally revealed.
   a. conscious
   b. preconscious
   c. subconscious
   d. unconscious

3. Which of the following is NOT one of Freud's psychosexual stages of development?
   a. oral
   b. anal
   c. castration
   d. latency

4. As a baby, Dave did not receive sufficient gratification from his mother. Now, as an adult, he smokes, drinks excessively, and constantly chews on his fingernails. According to Freud, Dave's behavior is a result of _____.
   a. fixation
   b. projection
   c. identification
   d. compensation

5. Alexander sees a new CD that he really wants. Part of him thinks about just stealing it when the salesperson's head is turned, but part of him feels guilty for thinking in such a selfish, antisocial way. Finally, Alexander decides to do a few extra jobs to earn the money for the CD. Which Freudian personality structure is guiding his behavior?
   a. id
   b. libido
   c. ego
   d. superego

6. Eileen's son is applying for college. He really wants to go to one of the military academies but, unfortunately, gets rejected. When he gets his rejection letters he states, "I didn't want to go there anyway, those guys are just a bunch of jarheads, and their parents probably paid someone to get them in!" This represents the defense mechanism of _____.
   a. denial
   b. rationalization
   c. repression
   d. projection

7. Pete gets turned down for the convenience-store employee of the month because he did not turn in the guy who was stealing breath mints. Rather than beat his employer with a stale hoagie, Pete tells everyone what a great guy he is and how he only is trying to help him improve. This represents which ego defense mechanism?
   a. projection
   b. denial
   c. sublimation
   d. reaction formation

8. Holly tries to do her best at everything. Even though she may fail periodically, her boyfriend, Sven, sticks with her in all her endeavors. According to Rogers, Sven is demonstrating _____ toward Holly.
   a. unconditional love
   b. reciprocal determinism
   c. unconditional positive regard
   d. self-efficacy

9. Ginger's friends are trying to figure out why she would humiliate herself as a stripper at a local cabaret. They finally agree on a type/trait approach to understanding personality. Which of the following explanations best represents that approach?
   a. she is unconsciously trying to get back at her parents who were rather repressed in the area of sexuality
   b. at her stable core, Ginger is just an exhibitionist
   c. she has received attention (i.e., reinforcement) for this behavior

   d. she is trying to fulfill her potential and sees clothing as an artificial societal constraint

10. Which of the following is NOT one of the basic traits of the five-factor personality theory?
    a. extraversion
    b. psychoticism
    c. neuroticism
    d. agreeableness

11. Tyshawn gets a 75 on his first psychology exam. He decides that he will have to study harder to receive the A he desires for the class. Tyshawn is exhibiting a(n) _____ locus of control.
    a. internal
    b. external
    c. efficacious
    d. utilitarian

12. Professor Perez is trying to figure out why John is consistently disruptive during her lectures. John not only laughs throughout the class but also points and throws unmentionable items up at the stage! Professor Perez finally decides that John has been inadvertently rewarded with attention for his rude behavior, and he expects to be rewarded for it in the future. With which theory of personality does her approach most closely resemble?
    a. psychodynamic
    b. humanistic
    c. trait
    d. cognitive-social

13. Latasha is doing a case study about Karen Horney, a famous personality theorist. Latasha is investigating her background and how it contributed to her ideas about human behavior. Latasha is using a(n) _____ approach to understanding personality.
    a. idiographic
    b. nomothetic
    c. individual
    d. stratified

14. Tiffany is developing a scale called the California Conscientiousness Chart. She is hoping to describe people on this trait ranging from low to high. Tiffany is using a(n) _____ approach to understanding personality.
    a. idiographic
    b. person-centered
    c. nomothetic
    d. psychobiographical

15. Juan was trying his luck as a painter. One day in frustration, he just tossed some different paints on the blank canvas in no particular order. When he showed his "masterpiece" to his friends, they began describing

the ambiguous splotches according to their personal needs, conflicts, hopes, and fears. Unknowingly, Juan had created a(n) _____ test.
a. thematic apperception
b. projective
c. Minnesota Multiphasic Personality Inventory
d. subliminal perception

16. Andrea is in treatment when her therapist decides to do some additional personality assessment. Andrea takes a test in which she is shown an ambiguous picture and asked to tell a story about it. Andrea likely has taken a _____.
a. Thematic Apperception Test
b. Rorschach inkblot test
c. Millon personality inventory
d. NEO personality inventory

17. Ramone is administering a self-report questionnaire to his client to learn more about his personality. Ramone is using a(n) _____ measure of personality.
a. subjective
b. objective
c. projective
d. multimodal

18. Paul is taking a self-report questionnaire designed to assess the Big Five personality traits. Paul is most likely taking the _____.
a. NEO personality inventory
b. Minnesota Multiphasic Personality Inventory
c. California Q-sort
d. Millon Clinical Multiaxial Inventory

19. Wes takes a personality test when he applies for a job at a local prison, and he scores very well. However, his answers do not really reflect his behavior and his personality differs drastically from one situation to the next. His behavior relative to his measured traits supports Mischel's idea that _____.
a. prospective employees must be retested several times to get a true picture of their personality
b. behaviors are determined to a much greater extent by situations than by personality traits
c. only projective personality tests (which cannot be faked) give a true picture of individual's traits
d. several personality tests must be used to reliably predict behavior in a particular situation

20. Which of the following statements best describes the relation between the trait of self-monitoring and the consistency of personality?
a. people who are high in self-monitoring alter their behavior to match the situation, so that they exhibit low levels of consistency
b. people who are high in self-monitoring alter their behavior to match the situation, so that they exhibit high levels of consistency

c. people who are low in self-monitoring are less able to alter their self-presentations to match situations, so that they exhibit low levels of consistency
d. people who are low in self-monitoring are less able to alter their self-presentations to match situations so their personalities are relatively unpredictable

21. According to twin studies, genetic influence accounts for approximately what percent of the variance in personality traits?
a. 0–10%
b. 10–20%
c. 20–40%
d. 40–60%

22. Emily is an expressive child. The slightest offense can cause her to cry, and she is easily frightened by new situations. Emily is high in the temperament of _____.
a. affectivity
b. activity level
c. sociability
d. emotionality

23. Granny Smith is worried about her grandson. He is initially cautious and anxious when meeting her, and he is hesitant about approaching new situations. However, over time he can be engaged in conversation and generally adjusts well if given the opportunity. Chess and Thomas would classify Granny Smith's grandson as what personality type?
a. difficult
b. slow to warm up
c. easy
d. reticent

24. Cindy is doing a research study on the effects of caffeine on various behaviors. Cindy finds that several of her participants are very arousable or reactive to the caffeine. These individuals likely fit which of the following trait categories?
a. introverts
b. extraverts
c. sensation seekers
d. sociopaths

25. Dan lives an exciting lifestyle. He likes to go bungee jumping and parachuting on a waveboard. Dan seeks arousal through adventures and new experiences. He is easily bored and used to escape this boredom through the use of drugs and alcohol. Dan is high in arousal-based trait of _____.
a. sociopathy
b. psychopathy
c. extraversion
d. sensation seeking

26. Drew the extravert loves to gamble. He is more influenced by the possibility of winning the big pot

than he is by the constant punishment of losing his money. Which of the following neurological systems has the greatest affect on Drew?

a. behavioral approach system
b. behavioral inhibition system
c. ascending reticular activating system
d. early experiential calibration system

27. Farrah is in a relationship with a man who is demeaning and abusive. In response to her confrontation he tells her, "I can change!" According to a meta-analysis of 150 studies on personality change, personality becomes more stable by _____.

a. age 5
b. adolescence
c. young adulthood
d. middle age

28. Which of the following is not one of the levels of personality as classified by Dan McAdams?

a. dispositional traits
b. general typologies
c. personal concerns
d. life narratives

29. Following a divorce from an oppressive spouse, Rebecca took on an entirely new look. She suddenly became outgoing and sociable, enrolled for evening classes at a local university, signed on for a travel club, and dressed in a more flamboyant manner. Her friends said it was like she acquired a new personality. This transformation is known as a(n) _____.

a. butterfly effect
b. affective blossoming
c. quantum change
d. trigger event

30. Hannah is a hostile young woman. In response to complaints from family and friends, she enrolls in a clinical trial to test a new medication that might reduce her hostility. Hannah's medication will likely focus on which of the following neurotransmitters?

a. norepinephrine
b. γ-aminobutyric acid (GABA)
c. serotonin
d. dopamine

THOUGHT QUESTION

Suppose you found out that someone you were dating had modified his or her personality through neurochemical means. Your friend states that he or she is less hostile and more sociable when taking the medication. How would you feel about this and would you encourage your friend to continue with it? How would you determine whether the medication was necessary? What other options would you have for personality change?

ANSWER KEY

Fill-in-the-Blank Questions

1. personality
2. personality trait
3. pleasure principle
4. libido
5. Oedipus complex
6. reality principle
7. humanistic
8. phenomenology
9. positive psychology
10. subjective well-being
11. implicit personality theory
12. personal constructs
13. cognitive-affective personality system
14. central traits
15. secondary traits
16. life story
17. psychobiography
18. nomothetic approaches
19. California Q-sort
20. sensation seeking
21. interactionists
22. temperaments
23. activity level
24. sociability
25. easy
26. difficult
27. ascending reticular activating system
28. behavioral approach system
29. behavioral inhibition system
30. early experiential calibration
31. basic tendencies
32. characteristic adaptations

Multiple-Choice Questions

1. a The central premise of the psychodynamic theory of personality is that unconscious forces, such as wishes and motives, influence behavior.

2. d The unconscious mind contains wishes, desires, and motives that are associated with conflict, anxiety, or pain.

3. c Freud's psychosexual stages of development are oral, anal, phallic, latent, and genital; castration is not one of the stages.

4. a Freud stated that people become fixated at a stage during which they have received excessive parental restriction or indulgence; excessive pleasures via the mouth are characteristic of fixation at the oral stage.

5. c The ego tries to satisfy the wishes of the id while being responsive to the dictates of the superego; it accomplishes this through rational thought and problem solving.

6. b People often rationalize their behavior by blaming situational factors over which they have little control.

7. d Reaction formation occurs when people ward off an uncomfortable thought about the self by embracing its opposite.

8. c Unconditional positive regard is when individuals are accepted, loved, and prized no matter how they behave.

9. b Type and trait approaches to personality describe people by general behavioral dispositions such as exhibitionism.

10. b The basic traits of the five-factor personality theory (Big Five) are extraversion, neuroticism, conscientiousness, agreeableness, and openness to experience; psychoticism is not one of these.

11. a Individuals with an internal locus of control believe that their efforts (e.g., studying) will bring about positive outcomes.

12. d Cognitive-social theories of personality incorporate cognition into learning theories and emphasize how personal beliefs, expectancies, and interpretations of social situations shape behavior and personality.

13. a Idiographic approaches focus on individual lives and how various characteristics are integrated into unique persons.

14. c Nomothetic approaches focus on characteristics that are common among all people but for which people vary.

15. b Projective measures are tests that attempt to delve into the realm of the unconscious by presenting people with ambiguous stimuli and asking them to describe the stimulus items.

16. a The thematic apperception test requires one to tell a story about an ambiguous picture.

17. b Objective measures of personality are straightforward assessments usually made by self-report questionnaires or observer ratings.

18. a The NEO personality inventory consists of 240 items designed to assess the Big Five personality traits.

19. b Mischel proposed the theory of situationism, the idea that behaviors are determined to a much greater extent by situations than by personality traits.

20. a People who are high in self-monitoring alter their behavior to match the situation, so that they exhibit low levels of consistency.

21. d According to twin studies, genetic influence accounts for 40–60% of the variance in personality traits, including the Big Five.

22. d Emotionality describes the intensity of emotional reactions, or how easily and frequently people become aroused or upset.

23. b Slow-to-warm-up children are initially cautious and anxious in new situations but generally adjust well over time.

24. a Introverts tend to be more arousable or reactive to stimuli at all levels of intensity.

25. d Sensation seekers are easily bored and pursue arousal through adventures and new experiences.

26. a Extraverts are highly affected by the behavioral approach system, so they are more influenced by rewards than punishments.

27. d A meta-analysis of 150 studies on personality change indicated that personality does change some in childhood, but that it becomes more stable by middle age.

28. b The three levels of personality according to McAdams are dispositional traits, personal concerns, and life narratives; general typologies is not one of these levels.

29. c A quantum change is a transformation of personality that is sudden, profound, and enduring.

30. c Low levels of serotonin are associated with hostility, aggressiveness, and criminality.

Thought Question

Answers will vary but students should realize the association between neurotransmitter systems (e.g., serotonin) and personality traits such as hostility. The necessity for the medication could be addressed by the degree of impairment exhibited initially. Students might propose methods of personality change from other theories (e.g., psychodynamic, humanistic, cognitive-social). The potential for change would also depend on the age of the person, with greater stability being exhibited at middle age. The phenomenon of quantum change usually occurs in response to an extreme negative affect and/or a trigger event.

CHAPTER 16 | Disorders of Mind and Body

GUIDE TO THE READING

In Chapter 16, the authors explain how certain behaviors come to be classified as mental disorders and consider the cognitive, situational, and biological context in which these behaviors occur. The designation of behavior as "abnormal" or as a "mental disorder" is invariably a cultural judgment. In addition, within American culture, the labeling of someone with a mental disorder comes with a resulting stigma. After the chapter introduction, the authors look at common categories of mental disorders (anxiety, mood, schizophrenia, personality, childhood) and their causes. Recent advances from behavioral neuroscience have helped with the understanding of both normal and abnormal human behaviors.

How Are Mental Disorders Conceptualized and Classified?

The chapter begins with a consideration of how disorders are conceptualized and classified. Again, abnormality is a cultural judgment, and particular behaviors may be seen as deviant in one society but unremarkable in another. In American society, the symptoms of a disorder must interfere with a least one aspect of a person's life—such as work, social relations, and self-care. Health care professionals use the *Diagnostic and Statistical Manual of Mental Disorders* (DSM-IV) to identify psychological disorders. The DSM has been around for more than 50 years, and in its current fourth edition, *psychopathology* is described in terms of observable symptoms. Individuals are diagnosed on a *multiaxial* scale, including *clinical syndromes, personality disorders, general medical conditions, psychosocial stressors,* and *global assessment of functioning.* However, the DSM-IV gives little information about the cause, prognosis, or treatment of disorders.

The authors review some of the classic models of psychopathology (*psychoanalytic, family systems, sociocultural, cognitive-behavioral*). Most ideas of cause involve multiple factors and incorporate some aspect of the *diathesis-stress model.* This is the idea that disorders are the result of an underlying predisposition (diathesis) which is made evident by environmental stress.

Finally, the authors look at the differences between the psychological concept of mental disorders and the legal concept of *insanity.* Most people mistakenly believe that the insanity defense is a common strategy to avoid criminal prosecution. In actuality, *competency to stand trial* is a more common area in which one's mental functioning comes into question.

Table 16.1 DEFINITIONS OF *INSANITY*

Insanity Rule	Definition
M'Naughten	person does not know right from wrong
Durham	behavior is the result of mental illness or mental defect
American Law Institute	mental illness or defect led to a lack of capacity to appreciate the criminality of the act or to an inability to conform to the law

Can Anxiety Be the Root of Seemingly Different Disorders?

The next section begins the consideration of specific psychological disorders. The *anxiety disorders* are characterized by excessive anxiety in the absence of true danger. Within this category, the *phobias* involve excessive fear of a specific object or situation. Most students will be familiar with *specific phobias* (e.g, claustrophobia, acrophobia, hydrophobia) that involve discrete events or objects. Most students also will have empathy for the *social phobias* which involve the fear of being negatively evaluated by others, fear of public speaking, and fear of eating in front of others.

Individuals with *generalized anxiety disorder* are constantly anxious and worry about trivial matters. *Panic disorder* involves sudden and overwhelming attacks of terror and often results in *agoraphobia,* the fear of being in a public situation from which escape is difficult. *Obsessive-compulsive disorder* (OCD) involves intrusive thoughts that are dealt with through maladaptive, repetitive actions. Numerous theories have been proposed to explain the anxiety disorders, and they certainly involve the cognitive misperceptions of actual danger. Recent advances in neurophysiology have related obsessive-compulsive disorder to dysfunction in the *caudate nucleus* and panic disorder to abnormality in the *locus coeruleus.*

Are Mood Disorders Extreme Manifestations of Normal Mood?

The *mood disorders,* which involve extreme emotions, include one of the most common diagnostic categories—*major depression.* Individuals with this disorder show symptoms such as depressed mood, loss of interest in pleasurable activities, weight changes, sleep disturbances, difficulty concentrating, guilt, and suicidal ideation. A milder form of depression, *dysthymia,* involves depressed mood for at least 2 years. Moods can also swing from depression to *mania,* as is seen in *bipolar disorder*, or from mild depression to *hypomania,* as is seen in *cyclothymia.* A strong genetic component has been implicated in bipolar disorder. A genetic component has been found for major depression also, but it has not been as strong.

Major depression has been linked to the neurotransmitters *norepinephrine* and *serotonin.* Indeed, medications such as Prozac that selectively increase serotonin have had a huge impact on treatment since the early 1990s. Depression has also been associated with maladaptive cognitions (e.g., Beck's *cognitive triad*), *errors in logic,* and *learned helplessness.* Finally, *life stressors* can precipitate an episode of major depression; however, the effects of these events can be attenuated by the presence of close friends.

Is Schizophrenia a Disorder of Mind or Body?

Schizophrenia is one of the most devastating of all the mental disorders in terms of its effect on the victim and family. Although it often is erroneously referred to as "split personality," the splitting in schizophrenia is between thought and emotion. Schizophrenia is a *psychotic disorder,* characterized by alterations in thought, perceptions, or consciousness. The rate of schizophrenia in the population is about 1% and has remained relatively stable across time and among cultures. Although the DSM-IV lists various subtypes of schizophrenia (*paranoid, disorganized, catatonic, undifferentiated, residual*),

they can also be classified by *positive* and *negative* symptoms. The positive symptoms of schizophrenia involve excesses of behavior and include *delusions, hallucinations,* and *loosening of associations.* The negative symptoms of schizophrenia involve deficits in functioning and include *isolation, withdrawal,* and *apathy.* Schizophrenia has a strong biological component, and the positive symptoms often are dramatically reduced by antipsychotic medication. Unfortunately, the negative symptoms of schizophrenia tend to persist, which has led investigators to hypothesize that this form of schizophrenia is related to structural brain abnormalities. One recent hypothesis regarding the cause of schizophrenia is that it is related to a slow-acting *virus* that becomes evident in symptomatology when an individual reaches young adulthood.

Are Personality Disorders Truly Mental Disorders?

The *personality disorders* are a controversial category of disorders marked by inflexible and maladaptive ways of interacting with the world. While the DSM-IV lists three categories of personality disorders by general behavior (*odd/eccentric, dramatic/emotional/erratic, anxious/fearful*), there is considerable overlap among the traits in the individual disorders. This has led to a reduction in reliability of diagnosis. Two of the personality disorders that have received considerable research investigation are *borderline personality disorder* and *antisocial personality disorder.*

Borderline personality disorder is characterized by a poor sense of self, emotional instability, and impulsivity. These individuals can be very dramatic and exhibit self-mutilation or suicidal behaviors. Borderline personality disorder has been linked to low serotonin levels and a history of physical and/or sexual abuse. Individuals with antisocial personality disorder demonstrate little empathy for others or remorse for their self-gratifying behaviors. This disorder is seen frequently in prison populations and has been related to low levels of arousal, poor response to punishment, and deficits in frontal lobe functioning.

Should Childhood Disorders Be Considered a Unique Category?

The final category, *childhood disorders,* remains controversial, because children show varied rates of development. What is seen as abnormal at one stage may be normal at another. *Autism* is a severe childhood disorder characterized by deficits in social interaction, impaired communication, and restricted interests. It is hard to believe that not long ago this disorder was associated with poor parenting; whereas, today it is understood to have a largely biological cause. Genetic and neurochemical research appears to have tremendous promise in improving our understanding and treatment of autistic behaviors.

Attention-deficit/hyperactivity disorder (ADHD) has received considerable research and media attention in recent years. ADHD children are characterized by restlessness, inattention, and impulsivity. The unfortunate aspect of these symptoms is that they are associated with academic, social, and vocational underachievement. ADHD has been related to poor parenting and sociocultural factors; however, there also is a clear genetic component. Noted deficits in functioning in the frontolimbic system and caudate nucleus provide potential areas for future treatments.

FILL-IN-THE-BLANK QUESTIONS

1. _____ sickness or disorder of the mind

2. _____ probable outcome of a disorder

3. _____ factors that contribute to the development of a disorder

4. _____ based on the idea that the behavior of an individual must be considered within a social context, in particular the family

5. _____ views psychopathology as the result of the interaction between individuals and their cultures

6. _____ central principle of this approach is that abnormal behavior is learned

7. _____ perspective on mental disorders that focuses on how physiological factors, such as genetics, contribute to mental illness

8. _____ stipulates that a person is insane, and therefore not responsible for his actions, if he does not know right from wrong

9. _____ person is not responsible for criminal behavior if the behavior is the result of mental illness or mental defect

10. _____ whenever the state determines that people should be involuntarily committed to mental institutions

11. _____ characterized by excessive anxiety in the absence of true danger

12. _____ fear of a specific object or situation

13. _____ characterized by attacks of terror that are sudden and overwhelming

14. _____ particular acts that the OCD patient feels driven to perform over and over again

15. _____ fear of enclosed spaces

16. _____ category of disorders characterized by extreme emotions

17. _____ disorder characterized by severe negative moods and a lack of interest in normally pleasurable activities

18. _____ form of depression that is not severe enough to be diagnosed as major depression

19. _____ characterized by elevated mood, increased activity, diminished need for sleep, grandiose ideas, racing thoughts, and extreme distractibility

20. _____ less extreme than manic episodes, these are characterized by heightened creativity and productivity

21. _____ disorder in which people fluctuate between major depression and hypomania

22. _____ overgeneralizing based on single events, magnifying the seriousness of bad events, and personalizing bad events

23. _____ psychotic disorder characterized by alterations in thoughts, perceptions, or consciousness

24. _____ schizophrenic symptoms involving deficits in functioning such as apathy, lack of emotion, and slowed speech and movement

25. _____ false personal beliefs based on incorrect inferences about external reality

26. _____ false sensory perceptions that are experienced without an external source

27. _____ category of mental disorders marked by inflexible and maladaptive ways of interacting with the world

28. _____ personality disorder characterized by identity, affective, and impulse disturbances

29. _____ developmental disorder characterized by deficits in social interaction, impaired communication, and restricted interests

30. _____ disorder characterized by restless, inattentive, and impulsive behaviors

31. _____ autistic individuals who have an area of great ability

MULTIPLE-CHOICE QUESTIONS

1. Emil uses the most common text in the United States to diagnose Sybil. The book he is using is known as the _____.
   a. *Minnesota Multiphasic personality inventory* (MMPI)
   b. *Diagnostic and Statistical Manual of Mental Disorders* (DSM-IV)

c. *Mental Health Guide Book* (MHGB)

d. *International Classification of Diseases* (ICD-10)

2. When Sybil is being diagnosed, she is not given one label but is rated on factors, such as clinical syndromes, personality disorders, and psychosocial stressors. This is the case because the DSM-IV employs a _____ system to classify disorders.

   a. multivariate

   b. cross-cut

   c. multiaxial

   d. diathesis-stress

3. According to Freudian psychoanalytic theory, mental disorders are mostly due to _____ that date back to childhood.

   a. incorrect learning experiences

   b. unconscious conflicts

   c. blocked self-actualization strivings

   d. maladaptive cognitions

4. Kramer has a family history of psychotic behavior. However, he does not exhibit these symptoms until he goes through an extremely stressful period with his mother and girlfriend. This interaction of factors that causes Kramer's difficulties is representative of the _____ model of mental disorders

   a. diathesis-stress

   b. interactive

   c. synergistic

   d. cognitive-behavioral

5. The current definition of insanity states that a person is not responsible if, at the time of the crime, a mental illness or defect led to a lack of capacity to appreciate the criminality of the act or to an inability to conform to the requirements of the law. This is known as the _____ rule.

   a. American Law Institute

   b. Durham

   c. M'Naughten

   d. Hinckley

6. The issue of whether a defendant can understand the legal proceedings and can contribute to his or her own defense is known as _____.

   a. the insanity defense

   b. competency to stand trial

   c. civil commitment

   d. criminal commitment

7. Dr. Jones is in therapy with Brooke. She is so angry with her husband that she states she is going to kill him. She has bought a gun and indicates a specific time that she is going to commit the act. According to the *Tarasoff* case, Dr. Jones has a duty to _____.

   a. maintain confidentiality

   b. contact the police

   c. warn Brooke's husband

   d. consult with a colleague

8. Ever since Adam fell off the top bunk at camp when he was 12 years old, he has had a fear of heights. Because of this fear, he refuses to climb the Empire State Building, go out on his balcony, or ever sleep on the top bunk again. What type of disorder is he experiencing?

   a. specific phobia

   b. social phobia

   c. xenophobia

   d. agoraphobia

9. Theresa has been dreading her oral presentation in her public speaking class. As she rushes through her material, she suddenly begins to shake tremendously and becomes fearful of saying something silly to the class. Finally, it gets so bad she is unable to continue. Theresa is suffering from _____.

   a. social phobia

   b. mixed anxiety disorder

   c. agoraphobia

   d. simple phobia

10. Rebecca notices that her roommate, Tabitha, freaks out when a professor tells her that she needs to study a little more. Rebecca also notices that Tabitha is constantly worried about her relationship with her boyfriend, even though it is a wonderful, loving one. Because of this constant worry that is not linked to an identifiable source, Rebecca thinks Tabitha suffers from _____.

   a. phobic disorder

   b. panic disorder

   c. generalized anxiety disorder

   d. obsessive-compulsive disorder

11. Poor Amber can't seem to go anywhere and has become a prisoner of her own dorm room. She no longer shops at the mall or goes to the movies, and she is in constant fear of having a panic attack in front of others. Amber's intense fear of public places in which escape would be difficult is referred to as _____.

   a. agoraphobia

   b. xenophobia

   c. aichmophobia

   d. parthenophobia

12. When Monica leaves for work in the morning, she checks three times to see if her curling iron is off and then checks the coffee maker three times. Next, she checks the locks to the house three times before finally leaving. Monica is likely suffering from _____.

   a. obsessive-compulsive disorder

   b. repetition disorder

   c. somatoform disorder

   d. dissociative disorder

13. Which of the following choices can be considered an obsession related to obsessive-compulsive disorder?
    a. washing one's hands 15 times before leaving the bathroom after each use
    b. a baseball player banging his shoes in the dirt before hitting
    c. thinking about how you might have left your door unlocked before class
    d. cutting your food into even-numbered amounts before eating

14. Jack suffers from constant fears of contamination and washes his hands repetitively to calm his anxieties. The part of the basal ganglia that seems most associated with this behavior is the _____.
    a. substantia nigra
    b. caudate nucleus
    c. locus coeruleus
    d. mesolimbic system

15. Rita has been suffering from ever-increasing panic attacks. The brain area most associated with this is the _____.
    a. substantia nigra
    b. locus coeruleus
    c. somatosensory cortex
    d. hippocampus

16. One week, Katy was so happy to be a college student. She excitedly told her entire family how much fun she was having, and she decided that she was going to have as much fun as possible while in college. Now, 2 weeks later, Katy has trouble getting out of bed in the morning and is even thinking about dropping out of school. This drastic change in mood is characteristic of the disorder currently known as _____.
    a. bipolar disorder
    b. unipolar disorder
    c. manic-depression
    d. schizophrenia

17. Patty cycles through about 2 months of major depression, 2 months of relative normality, and 2 months of mania. Her specific DSM-IV diagnosis is _____.
    a. bipolar I disorder
    b. bipolar II disorder
    c. unipolar mood disorder
    d. cyclothymia

18. Elaine suffers from mild affective swings characteristic of a mood disorder. She experiences both hypomania and mild depression. Elaine would be diagnosed with _____.
    a. bipolar I disorder
    b. bipolar II disorder
    c. dysthymia
    d. cyclothymia

19. William lives in a city in the northern United States. He finds that he becomes depressed every winter when the days become shorter and there is little sunlight. William likely suffers from _____.
    a. unipolar disorder
    b. dysthymia
    c. seasonal affective disorder
    d. autumnal melancholia

20. Which of the following is NOT part of the Beck's cognitive triad of depression?
    a. learned helplessness
    b. negative thoughts about the self
    c. negative thoughts about the situation
    d. negative thoughts about the future

21. After studying for hours and still failing the first two exams in his anthropology class, Jay has given up studying for the class completely. He feels that he has no control whatsoever when it comes to this class, and he is bound to fail despite his level of studying. Jay's expectation of failure and the resulting apathy and depression are examples of _____.
    a. dysthymic cognitions
    b. self-perpetuating style
    c. melancholia
    d. learned helplessness

22. Matt was diagnosed as having paranoid schizophrenia. He has delusions of the world being taken over by giant lizards and hallucinations of insects crawling over him. Matt's schizophrenic behaviors are an example of which type of symptom?
    a. negative symptoms
    b. positive symptoms
    c. flattened affect
    d. mood disorders

23. Pete was sitting in his psychology class when he thought he saw an individual staring at him from the outside. He began to notice those around him acting odd and he felt he was being watched every place he went. He even checked the phones in his apartment because he believed they were tapped. Pete was having which type of delusion?
    a. persecution
    b. reference
    c. grandeur
    d. somatic

24. The stress of school has pushed Ginger over the edge into exhibiting some schizophrenic symptoms. When asked a question about the Scantron sheet during the test, she replies, "When a sperm and egg come together, they make a beautiful baby." This represents the category of symptoms known as _____.
    a. loosening of associations
    b. disturbance in thought content

c. perceptual disturbances

d. affective symptoms

25. Amy has been admitted to a prestigious graduate school on the East Coast. However, the housing situation at the school is so bad that Amy deteriorates into speaking in clang associations to her professors. Which of the following represents what she most likely said?

   a. How are *you* today? How are you *today*? How *are* you today?

   b. School, rule, fool, tool, drool, ghoul, jewel, *cool toadstool*!!

   c. Fred blue hammer Tar Heel Jordan basketball Tobacco Road!

   d. I am so tired of dregling for parsingian apartments!

26. April's personality has begun to closely resemble those of some of the most notorious murderers of the past few decades. She has become very manipulative and self-serving. She feels sorry for nothing and seems to lack of conscience. April suffers from the disorder currently known as _____ personality.

   a. psychopathic

   b. sociopathic

   c. antisocial

   d. narcissistic

27. Heather has shown symptoms of autism since she was a little girl. She now is exhibiting the speech symptom of echolalia. Which of the following represents what she would most likely say?

   a. How are *you* today? How are you *today*? How *are* you today?

   b. School, rule, fool, tool, drool, ghoul, jewel, *cool toadstool*!

   c. Fred hammer Spartans beach basketball operant conditioning!

   d. I am so tired of dregling for parsingian fish tales!

28. Mara was highly upset at not being named athlete of the week in the local college newspaper. This stress of this crushing blow caused her to relapse into catatonic schizophrenic behavior. Which of the following symptoms is Mara most likely to exhibit?

   a. she giggles hebephrenically and smears her feces on the wall of the lobby

   b. she believes that her coach has talked the newspaper editor into writing bad things about her in the paper

   c. she curls up in the corner by the candy machine and exhibits mutism

   d. she shows a lot of prominent schizophrenic symptoms that do not clearly fit any one pattern

29. Dr. Beck, a psychology professor, is beginning to display delusions of control. Which of the following symptoms is he most likely exhibiting?

   a. he thinks his students are plotting to steal his children because they are sick of their pictures in the lectures

   b. he believes that he will be named teacher of the year by the teaching division of the American Psychological Association

   c. he thinks the neurotransmitters in his brain are being influenced by a supercomputer housed in the administration building

   d. he believes, while watching her telephone commercials, that Jamie Lee Curtis is sending him coded messages that she wants to go on a date with him

30. Nancy was watching *Friends* on television, when she falsely believed that Joey (one of the actors) turned to her and said, "How you doin'?" She did not find it odd that a television actor was hitting on her from her TV, and they continued to flirt until the show was over. Nancy is suffering from delusions of _____.

   a. control

   b. reference

   c. specificity

   d. somatization

THOUGHT QUESTION

Although the syndrome of ADHD has been around for quite some time, its prevalence seems to have exploded in recent years. Speculate as to possible biological and cultural reasons for this increase.

ANSWER KEY

Fill-in-the-Blank Questions

1. psychopathology
2. diagnosis
3. etiology
4. family systems model
5. sociocultural model
6. cognitive-behavioral
7. biological
8. M'Naughten rule
9. Durham rule
10. civil commitment
11. anxiety disorders
12. phobia
13. panic disorder
14. compulsions
15. claustrophobia
16. mood disorders
17. major depression
18. dysthymia
19. manic episodes
20. hypomanic episodes
21. bipolar II disorder
22. errors in logic
23. schizophrenia
24. negative symptoms
25. delusions
26. hallucinations
27. personality disorder
28. borderline personality disorder
29. autism
30. attention-deficit/hyperactivity disorder
31. idiot savants

Multiple-Choice Questions

1. b The DSM-IV is the standard diagnostic text in the United States; it is now in the fourth edition.

2. c The DSM-IV employs a multiaxial system to classify disorders.

3. b According to Freudian psychoanalytic theory, mental disorders are due to mostly unconscious conflicts that date back to childhood.

4. a The diathesis-stress model of mental disorders proposes that disorders are caused by an underlying predisposition (diathesis) and stressful circumstances.

5. a The current definition of insanity is known as the American Law Institute rule.

6. b The issue of whether a defendant can understand the legal proceedings and can contribute to his or her own defense is known as competency to stand trial.

7. c According to the *Tarasoff* case, if a clinician believes a patient to be dangerous to someone else, the clinician has the obligation to warn that person.

8. a Specific phobias are fears of particular objects or situations such as heights (acrophobia).

9. a Social phobia is a fear of being negatively evaluated by others and includes fear of public speaking.

10. c People with generalized anxiety disorder are constantly anxious and worry incessantly about even minor matters.

11. a Agoraphobia is a fear of being in public situations in which escape is difficult or impossible.

12. a Obsessive-compulsive disorder involves frequent intrusive thoughts and compulsive actions.

13. c Obsessions are recurrent, intrusive, and unwanted thoughts, ideas, or images.

14. b The caudate nucleus, a region in the basal ganglia associated with suppressing impulses, has been implicated in OCD.

15. b Research suggest that panic disorder is part genetic and linked to abnormalities in the locus coeruleus.

16. a Those who are diagnosed with bipolar disorder have periods of major depression but also experience episodes of mania.

17. a Individuals experiencing episodes of major depression and mania are diagnosed with bipolar I disorder.

18. d Individuals with cyclothymia experience hypomania and mild depression.

19. c Seasonal affective disorder results in periods of depression corresponding to the shorter days of winter in the northern latitudes.

20. a Beck's cognitive triad of depression includes negative thoughts about the self, situation, and future; learned helplessness is not part of this.

21. d People suffering from learned helplessness come to expect that bad things will happen over which they will have little control.

22. b Positive symptoms of schizophrenia involve excesses of behavior (e.g., delusions, hallucinations).

23. a Delusions of persecution involve the belief that others are persecuting, spying on, or trying to harm oneself.

24. a Loosening of associations is a symptom of schizophrenia in which individuals shift between seemingly unrelated topics as they speak.

25. b Clang associations are a schizophrenic symptom involving the stringing together of words that rhyme but have no other apparent link.

26. c Antisocial personality disorder is marked by a lack of empathy and remorse.

27. a Echolalia is the repetition of words or phrases, sometimes including an imitation of the intonation and sometimes using a high-pitched monotone.

28. c Catatonic schizophrenia is characterized by extreme motor immobility, negativism, mutism, bizarre movements, and/or echolalia.

29. c Delusions of control are the belief that one's thoughts and behaviors are being controlled by external forces.

30. b Delusions of reference are the belief that objects, events, or other people have particular significance.

Thought Question

Answers will vary but, as with all disorders, greater awareness of it leads to improved diagnosis. In addition, students might consider the American cultural phenomenon of having both parents in the workforce. More students are being placed in structured day-care settings at an earlier age and are expected to follow rules and behave cooperatively with others. Similarly, class sizes in school have increased appreciably, so that two or three disruptive children represent a significant problem. Poor parenting has been related to ADHD, and students might relate this to the breakup of the traditional family and high divorce rates. Overall, the pace of life has quickened in society, and exposure to rapid information media (e.g., television v. books) may serve to reduce attention spans. Finally, students might speculate as to biological reasons that contribute to the underarousal of frontal lobes seen in ADHD. Undetected environmental toxins from an industrialized society are a possible culprit.

| Treating Disorders of Mind and Body

The final chapter of the book presents the findings from psychological science as they apply to psychotherapy. The placement of this chapter at the end of the text is appropriate as empirically based psychotherapy is an integration of the information learned in previous chapters. The authors present the basic principles of the major approaches to treatment and identify the common factors that enhance all treatments. Then they present research findings on the most successful treatments for anxiety, mood, schizophrenic, personality, and childhood disorders. In some cases, one approach to treatment has shown to be superior, while in others multiple approaches may be equally effective. For some disorders, the prognosis for improvement remains poor. Regardless of technique, social context and familial influences play a major role in therapeutic success. Effective psychotherapy is an ongoing process that combines the art of a caring therapist and the most recent findings from psychological science.

How Is Mental Illness Treated?

The first section of the chapter presents the principles of the major approaches to treatment. Historically, much of what was done in psychotherapy was based on the practitioner's theoretical orientation. One's views about the causes of psychological disorders heavily influenced one's approach and the techniques used.

Psychodynamic therapists employ *free association* and *dream analysis* to achieve *insight* about unconscious influences. Humanistic therapists use *reflective listening* as in *client-centered therapy* to facilitate greater self-understanding and personal growth. Behavioral therapists use specific techniques such as *social-skills training* and *systematic desensitization* to learn more adaptive behavior through the principles of operant and classical conditioning. Cognitive-behavioral therapy (CBT) incorporates these learning principles as well as addresses the faulty cognitions that lead to maladaptive behaviors and emotions.

Table 17.1 TREATMENT THEORIES

Approach to Treatment	Basic Principles of Treatment
Psychodynamic	uncover unconscious conflicts that give rise to maladaptive behaviors\
Humanistic	help people fulfill potential for growth through self-understanding
Behavioral	maladaptive behavior is unlearned through conditioning principles
Cognitive-behavioral	eliminate distorted thoughts that cause maladaptive behaviors
Group	use group for social skills, interpersonal learning, and social support
Systems	improve family interactions as issues arise in larger social context
Biological	directly treat abnormalities in neural and bodily processes

Practitioners from different theoretical approaches use the social support and interpersonal learning found in group therapy to address their clients' issues. The systems approach to psychotherapy considers that one's individual problems arise in a larger family context and that one must address how the family interacts to achieve a more durable result. Finally, biological therapies recognize that some psychological disorders result from abnormalities in neural and bodily processes. They attempt to change these processes, most commonly through the use of *psychotropic medications* such as *antianxiety drugs, antidepressants,* and *antipsychotics.*

It is noteworthy that numerous research studies have found these approaches to be effective. It is equally interesting that, overall, no one approach has been found to be clearly superior to the others. Part of this may be attributable to the fact that there are some *common factors* that contribute to the effectiveness of all approaches despite the specific techniques used. Common factors include a strong relationship between the therapist and client and the powerful emotional reaction of confession (i.e., *catharsis*).

What Are the Most Effective Treatments?

The next section presents research findings on what are the most effective treatments for anxiety, mood, and schizophrenic disorders. One of the major changes in psychological treatment in recent years has been the shift of therapists from an allegiance to one approach to the more eclectic use of multiple approaches, depending on the person and problem. For specific phobias, behavioral techniques based on exposure (e.g., *systematic desensitization*) are the treatment of choice. CBT and medication (e.g., *imipramine*) have been found to be useful in the treatment of panic disorder. For those who have panic disorder with agoraphobia, the combination of CBT and drugs is significantly better than either treatment alone. CBT and medication (e.g., *clomipramine*) have also been helpful in the treatment of obsessive-compulsive disorder (OCD). *Exposure* and *response prevention* are the critical components of the behavioral intervention for OCD.

There are multiple effective treatments for the mood disorders. For depression, several classes of medication have been found to be effective including *monoamine oxidase (MAO) inhibitors, tricyclics,* and *selective serotonin reuptake inhibitors* (SSRIs). The SSRIs, including Prozac, are used more frequently as they tend to result in fewer side effects. For depression, results from cognitive behavioral therapy and treatment with medication are equal, which gives clients a choice based on individual preference. CBT attacks the distorted cognitions that result in negative mood. Some recent studies suggest that combining CBT and antidepressants is more effective than either approach alone.

Phototherapy, exposure to high-intensity light, is effective in the treatment of seasonal affective disorder. For more severe treatment-resistant forms of depression, *electroconvulsive therapy* (ECT) has been a last resort. More recently, *transcranial magnetic stimulation* (TMS) has been proposed as an alternative to ECT and medication. Thus far, it appears that TMS is more effective for nonpsychotic depression, whereas ECT is more effective for psychotic depression. For individuals with bipolar disorder, the choice of treatment is clear—the drug *lithium* has far surpassed other approaches.

Psychotropic medications have been found to be the most effective treatment for schizophrenia. Traditional antipsychotics (e.g., *chlorpromazine, haloperidol*) work by blocking dopamine receptors. Unfortunately, they result in significant side effects (e.g., *tardive dyskinesia*) and change only the positive symptoms of schizophrenia. Newer antipsychotics (e.g., *clozapine*) address the positive and negative symptoms of schizophrenia. The efficacy of these drugs improves substantially when combined with family support, social- and self-care skills training, and cognitive interventions.

Can Personality Disorders Be Treated?

Since personality disorders are, by definition, chronic maladaptive ways of interacting with the world, they are extremely difficult to treat. Individuals with these disorders tend to see the environment rather than their own behaviors as the cause of their problems, thus they are unmotivated to change. Treatments for two well-researched personality disorders are presented.

Dialectical behavior therapy (DBT) has been the most successful treatment program to date for borderline personality disorder. In DBT, the therapist targets the client's most extreme and dysfunctional behaviors, explores past traumatic experiences that may be at the root of emotional problems, and facilitates the development of self-respect and independent problem solving. Despite many varied attempts, little has been found to help individuals with antisocial personality disorder. One can hope for a reduction in antisocial behaviors after age 40, perhaps due to a reduction in biological drives. It appears that efforts in this area are better spent in prevention and support for the individual's family.

How Should Childhood Disorders Be Treated?

The final section of the chapter looks at treatments for two of the childhood disorders. Although autism is considered a biological disorder, biological interventions have been largely ineffective. Autistic children seem to benefit the most from highly structured behavioral therapies based on principles of operant conditioning; however, the long-term prognosis for autism remains poor. More options are available for children with attention-deficit/hyperactivity disorder (ADHD). Pharmacological treatment (e.g., *methylphenidate*) is beneficial for many; however, its use has sparked much controversy. As with most medications, Ritalin is not a magic bullet that removes all problems. Its effect is significantly enhanced when children also receive some type of behavior modification. Recent research indicates that medication plus behavioral therapy is more effective in treating ADHD than either treatment approach alone.

FILL-IN-THE-BLANK QUESTIONS

1. _____ generic name given to formal psychological treatment

2. _____ treatments based on the medical approach to illness and disease

3. _____ treatment of mental disorders by the use of medications that affect brain or bodily functions

4. _____ psychoanalytic technique in which the therapist interprets the hidden meaning of dreams

5. _____ goal of some types of therapy; the personal understanding of one's psychological processes

6. _____ empathetic approach to therapy that encourages personal growth through greater self-understanding

7. _____ client-centered therapy approach for problem drinkers; success is attributed to the warmth shown the client

8. _____ principles of operant conditioning are used to reinforce desired behaviors and ignore or punish unwanted behaviors

9. _____ treatment designed to teach and reinforce appropriate interpersonal behavior

10. _____ treatment technique in which the therapist acts out the appropriate behavior and encourages the client to imitate it

11. _____ treatment in which patients are encouraged to express their emotions and explore interpersonal experiences

12. _____ behavioral therapy technique that involves repeated exposure to an anxiety-producing stimulus or situation

13. _____ therapy that strives to help patients recognize maladaptive thought patterns and replace them with ways of viewing the world that are more in tune with reality

14. _____ therapy pioneered by Albert Ellis in which therapists act as teachers who explain and demonstrate more adaptive ways of thinking and behaving

15. _____ incorporates techniques from behavioral therapy and cognitive therapy to correct faulty thinking and change maladaptive behaviors

16. _____ includes making critical comments about the patient, being hostile toward him or her, and being emotionally overinvolved

17. _____ drugs that affect mental processes

18. _____ class of psychotropic medications used for the treatment of anxiety

19. _____ class of drugs used to treat schizophrenia and other disorders that involve psychosis

20. _____ side effect of some traditional antipsychotics that produces involuntary movements of the lips, tongue, face, legs, or other parts of the body

21. _____ antipsychotic medication that acts on multiple neurotransmitter receptors and is beneficial in treating both the negative and positive symptoms of schizophrenia

22. _____ class of drugs that work to prevent seizures; periodically used to treat symptoms of mania

23. _____ list of situations in which fear is aroused, in ascending order; part of systematic desensitization therapy

24. _____ tricyclic antidepressant that prevents panic attacks

25. _____ drug of choice for treating obsessive-compulsive disorder

26. _____ treatment for seasonal affective disorder in which patients are exposed to a high-intensity light source for a period of time each day

27. _____ treatment for depression in which an electro-magnetic coil is placed on the scalp and transmits pulses of high-intensity magnetism

28. _____ psychosurgical procedure in which nerve-fiber pathways in the prefrontal cortex were severed

29. _____ most successful treatment to date for borderline personality disorder, it combines elements of the behavioral, cognitive, and psychodynamic approaches.

30. _____ central nervous system stimulant medication used to treat ADHD

MULTIPLE-CHOICE QUESTIONS

1. According to a recent study, there are approximately _____ approaches to psychotherapy.
   a. 5
   b. 50
   c. 100
   d. 400

2. While Joann is therapist shopping, she tries a clinical psychologist who describes herself as eclectic. This means that her therapist _____.
   a. uses a combination of cognitive and behavioral approaches
   b. does not use techniques from any of the major approaches
   c. tries mostly new experimental techniques that have been supported by empirical research
   d. uses a mix of techniques based on what she believes is best for the client's particular condition

3. Marika is a therapist who specializes in the techniques of psychoanalysis. What is her goal for psychotherapy sessions?
   a. uncover unconscious feelings and drives that give rise to maladaptive thoughts and behaviors
   b. relearn maladaptive behaviors that were acquired through improper learning
   c. facilitate personal growth and self-actualization through reflective listening and unconditional positive regard

d. identify problem areas that are amenable to psychopharmacology

4. Samantha has been feeling quite depressed lately and decides to go see a psychoanalyst. When she goes to her first session, she is told to say whatever comes to mind, no matter how crazy or embarrassing it may seem. This basic technique of psychoanalysis is known as _____.
   a. free association
   b. transference
   c. word association
   d. systematic desensitization

5. Shelby goes into her therapist's office and spills all her current troubles. At the end of her monologue, the therapist says, "It sounds like you have a lot going on right now. You are having problems with your parents, your boyfriend, and at school, and you are unsure how to proceed." This is an example of the client-centered therapy technique of _____.
   a. analysis of resistance
   b. confronting irrational beliefs
   c. unconditional positive regard
   d. reflective listening

6. Jerry is suffering from obsessions about germs and cleanliness and decides to seek out behavioral therapy. From his choice, it is obvious that Jerry believes his problem can be alleviated through _____.
   a. uncovering unconscious feelings and drives that give rise to maladaptive thoughts and behaviors
   b. unlearning maladaptive behaviors by the use of classical and operant conditioning
   c. facilitating personal growth and self-actualization through reflective listening and unconditional positive regard
   d. identifying problem areas that are amenable to psychopharmacology

7. Joey is horrified by the idea of being in public. His therapist teaches him to pair relaxation with being in public. At first, Joey thinks about public places and relaxes. Then he steps outside and relaxes. Then he steps off his porch and relaxes. This goes on until Joey is able to go to the mall and stay without panicking. This treatment technique is called _____.
   a. systematic desensitization
   b. flooding
   c. implosion
   d. cathartic submersion

8. Katie has been suffering from frequent panic attacks, so she goes to see a psychologist. The psychologist instructs her to hyperventilate, which causes her to panic. Then she teaches her to respond calmly to her panicked feelings. Soon, Katie is able to calm herself when she feels the onset of panic. What type of therapy is the psychologist using to treat Katie?

a. aversion therapy
b. cognitive therapy
c. psychoanalytic therapy
d. client-centered therapy

9. Curly, Moe, Larry, and Shemp are in treatment to reduce their aggressive behaviors. The group setting provides an opportunity for members to improve their social skills, support one another, and learn from each others' experiences. The generic term for this treatment approach is _____.
   a. interpersonal therapy
   b. transpersonal therapy
   c. group therapy
   d. supportive therapy

10. Carly and Gus are in therapy with the Whitaker family. They notice that as one child begins to improve her behaviors, the other child becomes more disruptive. When both children are better, the mother and father begin to fight. Carly and Gus are trying to get the entire family to communicate and behave better. They are taking a _____ approach to psychotherapy.
    a. dynamic
    b. supportive
    c. systems
    d. integrative

11. Benzodiazepines, such as Valium, increase the activity of γ-aminobutyric acid (GABA), and are used in the treatment of _____.
    a. depression
    b. mood disorders
    c. psychotic disorders
    d. anxiety

12. Christine's semester has been going downhill steadily. She is behind on all her course assignments and is having difficulty concentrating. Her physician decides to put her on antidepressants. Which of the following classes of medications is NOT a choice for her?
    a. MAO inhibitors
    b. tricyclics
    c. neuroleptics
    d. SSRIs

13. Carla has been very depressed lately. Her boyfriend just broke up with her, and she is failing two of her classes. Her psychiatrist put her on antidepressants. Now Carla feels a lot better about herself and is starting to pull up her grades. How do these pills work to improve Carla's mood?
    a. increase the supply of melatonin and diethylamide
    b. increase her metabolism
    c. increase the supply of norepinephrine, serotonin, or dopamine
    d. increase the supply of GABA and endorphins

14. Donny is a client at a day-treatment facility for schizophrenics. When he takes his traditional antipsychotic

medication (specifically chlorpromazine), his hallucinations are greatly reduced. This drug acts by _____.
a. blocking serotonin
b. releasing serotonin
c. blocking dopamine
d. releasing dopamine

15. Most of the time Eileen is laughing, but she also has periods of wild mood swings that range from mania to depression. As she is diagnosed with bipolar disorder, which of the following medications is she most likely taking?
a. Prozac
b. Librium
c. Tofranil
d. lithium

16. Kevin is worried about whether he will be wasting his money by seeking out psychotherapy. Connie tells him that a recent study on psychotherapy by *Consumer Reports* found all of the following EXCEPT _____.
a. cognitive therapy was found to be superior to behavioral therapy as well as psychoanalysis
b. the majority of respondents felt that intervention had helped them
c. those who sought help from mental health professionals reported more positive results than those who consulted with a family doctor
d. the longer the length of therapy, the greater was the reduction of psychiatric symptoms

17. Dr. Freud is counseling a woman who has difficulty trusting men. She thinks they are all out to get her and will use her and toss her aside if she gives them the chance. Her therapist encourages her to open up to him and talk freely about her past experiences with men, including her father. What is Dr. Freud hoping to achieve by advising his patient to open up?
a. eclecticism
b. conditional positive regard
c. reciprocal determinism
d. catharsis

18. Manuel is afraid of heights. As he lives in a small town, it is not easy to find a tall building to expose him to his fears. His therapist uses a computer to simulate for Manuel the experience of standing on the edge of a really tall building. His therapist has effectively created an exposure technique through the use of _____.
a. virtual environments
b. cybercasting
c. split reality
d. in vivo environments

19. Which of the following is the most effective treatment for panic disorder with agoraphobia?
a. structured supportive therapy
b. cognitive-behavioral therapy (CBT)

c. medication (e.g., imipramine)
d. CBT and medication

20. Steve decides to pursue behavioral therapy to treat his obsessive-compulsive disorder. From reading up on empirically validated treatments, Steve knows that the two most important components of behavioral therapy for OCD are _____.
a. relaxation and confrontation
b. contingency and reinforcement
c. insight and action
d. exposure and response prevention

21. For which of the following disorders is electroconvulsive therapy (ECT) most effective?
a. depression
b. schizophrenia
c. dissociative identity disorder
d. obsessive-compulsive disorder

22. TMS seems to be more effective for _____ depression, whereas ECT seems to be more effective for _____ depression.
a. dysthymic; bipolar
b. unipolar; bipolar
c. nonpsychotic; psychotic
d. manic; unipolar

23. Which of the following statements is TRUE regarding the prognosis for schizophrenia?
a. those diagnosed with schizophrenia later in life tend to have a poorer prognosis than those who experience their first symptoms during childhood or adolescence
b. men tend to have a better prognosis than women
c. schizophrenia in developing countries is often not as severe as in developed countries
d. supportive family networks tend to interfere with improvement in schizophrenic individuals

24. Which of the following is NOT one of the stages of dialectical behavior therapy?
a. therapist targets the client's most extreme and dysfunctional behaviors
b. therapist confronts the client's manipulations
c. therapist helps the client explore past traumatic experiences that may be at the root of emotional problems
d. therapist helps the patient develop self-respect and independent problem solving

25. Keith is a 30-year-old male who is in prison for embezzlement. He has a lengthy criminal history and is diagnosed with antisocial personality disorder. The prognosis for Keith's improvement is _____.
a. poor
b. fair
c. guarded
d. good

26. Which of the following therapies is most effective for children with autism?
    a. supportive therapies
    b. structured therapies
    c. play therapy
    d. unstructured therapies

27. The long-term prognosis for children with autism is _____.
    a. poor
    b. fair
    c. guarded
    d. good

28. Which of the following therapies is most effective in the treatment of attention-deficit/hyperactivity disorder?
    a. play therapy
    b. stimulant medication (e.g., Ritalin)
    c. behavior modification
    d. stimulant medication plus behavioral therapy

29. According to the surgeon general, what percentage of Americans have some form of diagnosable mental illness in a given year?
    a. 1%
    b. 5%
    c. 10%
    d. 20%

30. Sandi is interested in becoming a clinical psychologist. She is looking into graduate schools and notices that some offer a Ph.D. and some offer a Psy.D. What is the difference between these two clinical psychology degrees?
    a. both degrees have training in psychotherapy; however, the Ph.D. degree has more training in psychological research
    b. the Ph.D. offers training in prescribing medication; the Psy.D. offers more traditional psychotherapy training
    c. the Ph.D. has more of an environmental focus; the Psy.D. has more of a medical/biological focus
    d. although the degrees have a different history, they are virtually identical in everyday practice

31. Jerry, George, Elaine, and Kramer are seeing a psychologist in group therapy during their stay in prison. What are their chances of receiving medication from him to deal with their mental health issues?
    a. none—psychiatrists are the only mental health professionals allowed to prescribe medication
    b. none—nurses and medical social workers are the only mental health professionals allowed to prescribe medication
    c. slim—only New Mexico has passed legislation to allow clinical psychologists to prescribe medication, provided they receive appropriate training

    d. fair—recently graduated psychologists in all 50 states have completed special training programs and are allowed to prescribe medication

32. Kevin is having some psychological problems, but he is very picky about the qualifications of his therapist. He looks in the yellow pages under the term *psychiatrists*. From our knowledge of therapist training we can tell him that _____.
    a. we know nothing about these therapists' qualifications
    b. we know that these therapists have at least a master's degree in a mental health field
    c. we know that these therapists have a medical degree and a supervised residency
    d. we know that these therapists have a graduate degree and a one-year internship in a mental health setting

THOUGHT QUESTION

How would you know if you needed to seek professional psychological help? If you did, what type of mental health practitioner would you choose? Why? What type of therapy approach would you prefer?

ANSWER KEY

Fill-in-the-Blank Questions

1. psychotherapy
2. biological therapies
3. psychopharmacology
4. dream analysis
5. insight
6. client-centered therapy
7. motivational interviewing
8. behavior modification
9. social-skills training
10. modeling
11. interpersonal therapy
12. exposure
13. cognitive restructuring
14. rational-emotive therapy
15. cognitive-behavioral therapy
16. negative expressed emotion
17. psychotropic medications
18. antianxiety drugs
19. antipsychotics
20. tardive dyskinesia
21. clozapine
22. anticonvulsants
23. fear hierarchy
24. imipramine
25. clomipramine
26. phototherapy
27. transcranial magnetic stimulation
28. lobotomy
29. dialectical behavior therapy
30. methylphenidate

Multiple-Choice Questions

1. d According to a study by Kazdin, there are over 400 approaches to psychotherapy.

2. d Today, many practitioners use an eclectic mix of techniques based on what they believe is best for the client's particular condition.

3. a Psychoanalytic treatment is based on uncovering unconscious feelings and drives that give rise to maladaptive thoughts and behaviors.

4. a Free association is the psychoanalytic technique in which the patient says whatever comes to mind.

5. d Reflective listening is when the therapist repeats the client's concerns to help the person clarify his or her feelings.

6. b The basic premise of behavioral therapy is that behavior is learned and, therefore, can be unlearned using the principles of classical and operant conditioning.

7. a Systematic desensitization is an exposure technique that pairs the anxiety-producing stimulus with relaxation techniques.

8. b Cognitive therapy is based on the theory that modifying maladaptive thought patterns via specific treatment strategies should eliminate the maladaptive behaviors and emotions.

9. c Group therapy provides an opportunity for members to improve their social skills and to learn from each others' experiences.

10. c According to a systems approach, an individual is part of a larger context and any change in individual behavior will affect the entire family system.

11. d Benzodiazepines, such as Valium, increase the activity of GABA, and are used in the treatment of anxiety.

12. c Neuroleptics are antipsychotic medications.

13. c Antidepressants work by increasing the supply of norepinephrine, serotonin, or dopamine.

14. c Traditional antipsychotics bind to dopamine receptors without activating them, which blocks the effects of dopamine.

15. d Lithium is the most effective treatment for bipolar disorder, although the neural mechanisms of how it works are currently unknown.

16. a The *Consumer Reports* study found that no specific type of therapy yielded more positive results than any other. The other statements are true.

17. d Freud incorporated the term *catharsis* into his approach to refer to the powerful emotional reactions and subsequent relief that would come from opening up and talking about unconscious material.

18. a One way to expose people to their fears without putting them in danger is to use virtual environments, sometimes called virtual reality.

19. d For those who have panic disorder with agoraphobia, the combination of CBT and drugs is significantly better than either treatment alone.

20. d The two most important components of behavioral therapy for OCD are exposure and response prevention.

21. a Electroconvulsive therapy is most effective for treatment of depression.

22. c TMS seems to be more effective for nonpsychotic depression, whereas ECT seems to be more effective for psychotic depression.

23. c Schizophrenia in developing countries is often not as severe as in developed countries; the other statements are false.

24. b Dialectical behavior therapy involves the therapist targeting the client's most extreme and dysfunctional behaviors, helping the client explore past traumatic experiences, and helping the patient develop self-respect and independent problem solving; having the therapist confronts the client's manipulations is not one of the stages.

25. a The prognosis for improvement in antisocial personality disorder is poor.

26. b Because generalization of skills must be explicitly taught, structured therapies are more effective for autistic children than unstructured interventions, such as play therapy.

27. a Although there are a few reports of remarkable recovery, the long-term prognosis for autistic children is poor.

28. d Recent research has shown that medication plus behavioral therapy is more effective than either approach alone.

29. d According to the surgeon general, 20% of Americans have some form of diagnosable mental illness in a given year.

30. a Both degrees have training in psychotherapy; however, the Ph.D. degree has more training in psychological research.

31. c Their chances are slim; only New Mexico has passed legislation to allow clinical psychologists

to prescribe medication, provided they receive appropriate training.

32. c Psychiatrists have a medical degree and a supervised residency.

Thought Question

Answers will vary. In terms of seeking therapy, students should consider issues of personal discomfort as well as impairments in relationships, school, and work. When seeking a therapist, one will have to consider issues of fees as well as preferred approach. For example, psychiatrists will have more of a biological emphasis whereas psychologists will use more of an environmental approach. Personality issues will factor into one's preferred approach. Some individuals will prefer the directness of behavioral and cognitive approaches, while others will prefer the exploratory nature of psychoanalytic and humanistic approaches. Finally, some students may simply prefer the most effective, empirically validated treatment for their specific problem.